FREUD
AND
MODERN
PSYCHOLOGY

VOLUME 1: THE EMOTIONAL BASIS
OF MENTAL ILLNESS

EMOTIONS, PERSONALITY, AND PSYCHOTHERAPY

Series Editors:
Carroll E. Izard, *University of Delaware, Newark, Delaware*
and
Jerome L. Singer *Yale University, New Haven, Connecticut*

A Continuation Order Plan is available for this series. A continuation order will bring delivery
of each new volume immediately upon publication. Volumes are billed only upon actual ship-
ment. For further information please contact the publisher.

FREUD
AND
MODERN PSYCHOLOGY

VOLUME 1: THE EMOTIONAL BASIS
OF MENTAL ILLNESS

HELEN BLOCK LEWIS

Yale University
New Haven, Connecticut

PLENUM PRESS · NEW YORK AND LONDON

Library of Congress Cataloging in Publication Data

Lewis, Helen B
 The emotional basis of mental illness.

 (Her Freud and modern psychology; v. 1)
 (Emotions, personality, and psychotherapy)
  Bibliography: p.
  Includes index.
  1. Psychology, Pathological. 2. Emotions. 3. Interpersonal relations. 4. Freud, Sigmund,
 1856-1939. 5. Psychoanalysis. I. Title. II. Series.
 RC454.L48   616.89′001′9   80-20937
 ISBN 0-306-40525-3

© 1981 Plenum Press, New York
A Division of Plenum Publishing Corporation
227 West 17th Street, New York, N.Y. 10011

Printed in the United States of America

This book is dedicated to my grandchildren
EMMA LEWIS BERNDT
DAVID ASHER DANGERFIELD LEWIS

Preface

The tension between Freud's clinical discoveries about the power of human emotions and the theoretical framework in which he embedded these discoveries has been most eloquently detailed by Freud himself. His agonizing reappraisal, in 1926, of the libido theory of anxiety is just one example. But, as is usually the case, theoretical difficulties point to gaps in existing knowledge. At the time when Freud made his fundamental discovery that hysterical symptoms (and dreams) were understandable as reflections of forbidden ("strangulated") affect, anthropology was essentially nonexistent as a science. The cultural nature of human beings (our species' unique adaptation to life) could only be adumbrated by Freud (for example, in the myth of *Totem and Taboo*). As a consequence, the primacy of human attachment emotions in the acculturation process could not be postulated as a theoretical base. What Freud adopted as his base of theorizing was the most forward-looking materialist concept of his time: the Darwinian concept of individual instincts as the driving force in life. Freud assumed that the vicissitudes of instincts determine the fate of "ideas" in consciousness. Freud's theoretical base thus impelled him to speculate about the origin and fate of ideas instead of about the origin and fate of human emotional connectedness.

This book is a small step along the road which should ultimately bring Freud's discoveries into a modern theoretical framework in psychology. I actually began this journey of revisiting Freud's works some years ago when I first undertook a phenomenological study of shame and guilt (Lewis, 1971). Shame and guilt are two "instinct" inhibitors that are also themselves "instinctive" and transcultural. My way into that study was much facilitated by the research on field dependence in which I had participated for many years. Field dependence is a cognitive style that catches the *self* not only in its characteristic relationship to its surround but also to its own value system. The *self* is another construct that was stimulated by Freud's work, although Freud, unfortunately, did not make much use of it. While the role of the self is different in shame and guilt, both states are universal modes of maintaining threatened affectional bonds. That the two sexes differ in their use of the two affective-cognitive states was the theme of my book, *Psychic War in Men and Women* (Lewis, 1976).

A theoretical stance that sees emotional connectedness as the essential ingredient of humanity is itself largely a product of Freud's influence. The task of freeing his discoveries from the metapsychology he so painstakingly erected around his observations has been implicit in the work of many revisionists since Freud, as well as in the work of such contemporary psychoanalytic critics as Lacan (1968) and Schafer (1978). Many have felt, and I concur, that accomplishing this task should improve techniques of psychoanalytic psychotherapy insofar as these have been hampered by Freud's metapsychology. For example, conceptualizing symptoms as products of by-passed shame creates a very different therapeutic task than conceptualizing them as products of a "narcissistic" or "borderline" personality. As the reader will see, my own view of the enterprise centers on the need for psychology to build a theory of human emotions combining both the individual arousal and the communicative aspects of emotional life which Freud so brilliantly described.

It is a pleasure to acknowledge the assistance of many people who have helped in this work. The first outline of the work was developed in a course of undergraduate lectures at Yale, and the questions and comments of my students were an invaluable stimulus to my own thought. Dr. Zenia Fliegel has read all and Drs. Joel Allison, Sandra Buechler, Stanley Rachman, and Jerome L. Singer have read parts of the manuscript of Volume 1, and offered useful advice. Professor Carroll Izard has been a most helpful and encouraging editor. My thanks are due to the Behavioral Science Publications Fund of the Yale Department of Psychology for financial assistance in the preparation of the manuscript. Most of all, my husband, Naphtali Lewis, has, as always, been my most reliable support.

May, 1980

Contents

Introduction

This book asks the question: What has become of Freud's major discoveries and hypotheses in the light of nearly a century of subsequent research? Freud's impact on twentieth-century thinking is literally immeasurable. It ranges from the flowering of the modern psychological novel to anthropologists' hypotheses about child-rearing practices as predictors of the severity of initiation rites. Why, then, a book that seeks to assess the immeasurable outcome of Freud's work?

The answer lies in a paradox. On the one hand, the influence of psychoanalysis on present-day psychiatry is waning. Fifteen years ago, in one leading medical school that I know, the majority of residents in psychiatry were also in psychoanalytic training, or planning to get it. Today scarcely five percent intend to become psychoanalysts. On the other hand, some Freudian interpretations of behavior are so taken for granted in everyday life that they are no longer recognized as Freud's. When feminists, for example, criticize Freud for being a sexist, they are making use of a Freudian concept. Sexism refers to an unconscious bias. In order to defend his male ego, Freud believed certain fantasies about the inferiority of women. Or, to take another example, when we say someone is "uptight" or "tightass" we are using a slang expression for Freud's description of the anal character. This paradox — that Freud's discoveries about mental illness and its treatment are falling into disuse while his corollary discoveries about normal behavior have become household wisdom — invites inquiry.

Freud's first discovery was that mental illness can result from guilt or shame over sexual longings. What this discovery implied is that emotions and, by implication, the social life of human beings are powerful enough to banish reason. This latter notion had been a part of folk wisdom and has

1

been expressed in literature since ancient times. Sophocles' *Oedipus Rex* and Shakespeare's *Hamlet* spring to mind as familiar examples. Freud, however, was the first person to trace sequences from forbidden sexual longings to their clearly recognizable translations as neurotic symptoms. Freud's scientific work thus joined folk wisdom to become part of the twentieth-century *Zeitgeist*.

Although the power of emotional forces had always been respected by folk wisdom, the scientific study of emotions was neglected in Freud's time and continues to be neglected at the present. This neglect has resulted in a hostile, not to say scornful, attitude toward the scientific validity of Freud's ideas. The fate of his work has thus varied enormously: among lay people it has had a revolutionary impact on cultural values; among experimental psychologists and other "hard-headed" scientists Freud's work is often dismissed as fanciful. Freud's own attitudes toward the emotions were partly governed by his own scientific training and were consequently ambivalent (to use a Freudian term). And to a certain extent Freud's defensive efforts to keep his discoveries scientific, as he understood the canons of science, actually hindered progress which could have been made in psychoanalysis as a therapy.

Freud himself described his discoveries on two levels, a clinical level and a theoretical level. On the clinical level, which means speaking in ordinary descriptive language, he directly implicated the emotions — rage, terror, shame, guilt, sexual longings — in the formation of neurotic symptoms. Specifically, he uncovered a kind of "psychic alchemy" by which forbidden sexual longings are transformed into such symptoms as a bodily pain, a terrifying obsession, a phobia, or a profound depression. By studying his own dreams, Freud came to realize that the same transformation system at work in neurosis is at work in each of us in our nightly hallucinations. To this transformation system he gave the name "primary process," meaning to imply that unfulfilled (sexual) longings begin to operate in earliest childhood even before they can be expressed in language. "Primary process" is the special, ancient language of emotional experience. It operates also in sophisticated metaphors. From the study of the similarity between dreams and neurotic symptoms he concluded that each of us has a ready potential for the formation of neurotic symptoms; in other words, that the boundary between normalcy and neuroticism is slim. Especially since he was able to discern echoes of his own childhood experiences in his dreams, he deduced that forbidden sexual longings occurred all during the course of development from childhood on, and persisted in their childhood form. From this he concluded that emotions are "indestructible." All these discoveries clearly had implications for the understanding both of mental illness and of normal human behavior.

Still on the clinical level, Freud also discovered that encouraging his patients' "free associations" by an explicitly accepting atmosphere — "talking out" to a listener who explicitly and implicitly tried to banish guilt or shame — was a more effective therapy than hypnosis, electrical massage, hydrotherapy, or rest cures, the only therapies in the armamentarium of psychiatry at the time. This last discovery implied more clearly to Freud's students (Adler, Horney, and Fromm) than to Freud that the social connectedness of human beings is central to their well-being (or their mental illness).

Difficulties in translation, reflecting difficulties in understanding terminology, show clearly how difficult it was for Freud to deal with the affects theoretically. For example, Freud (1894) spoke of the fact that his patients encountered "unverträglich," that is "incompatible," ideas (p. 51), but in subsequent publications, according to the editors of the Standard Edition (footnote 4), the term "unverträglich" was misprinted as "unerträglich," which means unbearable or intolerable. It is not totally clear, however, that this was indeed a misprint, since "unbearable" appears in several places, including the carefully edited Collected Papers. Freud could easily have alternated between the more cognitive and the more affective aspects of states of shame and guilt in describing his patients' emotional conflicts or dilemmas. In his theorizing Freud wrote as if a "quota of affect" and a "sum of excitations" were interchangeable terms, by which he sometimes means "affect" and sometimes the more emotionally neutral "excitation." Freud writes that "in mental functions something is to be distinguished — a quota of affect or sum of excitations which possesses the characteristics of quantity (although we have no means of measuring it), which is capable of increase, diminution, displacement and discharge, and which is spread over the memory-traces of ideas somewhat as an electric charge is spread over the surface of a body" (p. 60). This is, indeed, a clear description of affect "covering" the surface of experience as if it were an electric charge, which then becomes a simile or metaphor for affect. But a quota of affect is a real experience in nature, more directly observable than electric charges, and with powers to move people's behavior which can also be directly observed. Affects can thus be the foundations for a psychological system, as Tomkins (1963) and Izard (1971) have since demonstrated.

In dealing with "quota of affect" Freud, as just noted, found it necessary to use a less affective synonym, "sum of excitations." It was to render Freud's meaning in this connection that James Strachey originally proposed in 1922 that the invented word "cathexis" be used (footnote, p. 63). Strachey derived the word from the Greek, meaning "to occupy." Strachey further says that Freud was unhappy with this term on the ground that it was artificial, although Freud may have become reconciled to it in the end. It may be a fruitless speculation, but one cannot help wondering (always with hindsight) how differently psychoanalysis might have developed if affects had been permitted their own powers of prediction.

On the theoretical level, speaking out of his background as an experimental neurologist, Freud formulated a system of behavior based not on emotions or social connectedness, but on the existence of unknown or unconscious forces of energy — instincts — seeking the pleasure of discharge (after the manner of nerve impulses) but blocked by counter-forces (also unknown). These theoretically formulated forces Freud at first called "ego instincts" vs. "sexual instincts"; later he labeled them "Eros" vs. "Death Instinct." These unknown hypothetical energies were represented in consciousness as "ideas." Ideas, however, do not only represent consciousness but also unconscious forces. On the theoretical level, the conflict between feelings was described as a conflict between forces, resulting in "compromise" energy-formations. These compromises underlie the ideas in dream symbols, neurotic symptoms, and societal taboos. The fact that Freud felt constrained to introduce this theoretical level as a level above the direct clinical study of emotions was itself an expression of his adherence to the scientific canons developed during the Enlightenment. The fate of Freud's work both within his own thinking and in the world of knowledge has been largely determined by the tension between his clinical work and the established scientific canons.

These canons require a brief description if we are to understand their relation to Freud's work. The first canon of scientific thinking is its secularization. The Enlightenment was first of all an abandonment of medieval theology, and the establishment of a materialist basis for the universe. Materialist forces replaced a divine set of spiritual forces. From the Renaissance on, the secularization of knowledge had occurred in stages, with philosophy forming the bridge between theology and science. It had proceeded at an uneven rate, depending upon the growth of knowledge. In the fields of physics and chemistry there had been remarkable successes. Newton had made it possible, by means of a few fundamental laws of immense scope, to determine at least in principle the properties and behavior of every single particle of every material body in the universe. How natural, therefore, that the application of mathematical techniques and language to the measurable properties of what the senses revealed should become the true method of discovery in all science. In the field of psychology, in contrast, knowledge was still highly speculative at the time of the Enlightenment, holding only the promise that the mathematical and mechanical laws Newton used so well in physics were equally applicable to human behavior. Psychology was hardly considered a science at all until well into this century. A brief anecdote from my own life illustrates this point. My first appointment in psychology in

1934, in an urban college, was to a department of philosophy, psychology, and anthropology! I was even assigned to teach a course in anthropology, an experience from which I fortunately never recovered.

In the psychology of perception, which is the study of how we get in touch with the universe, the promise of mathematics has seemed realizable. So, for example, at the time Freud was working, the nineteenth-century psychologist-philosopher Fechner had worked out a mathematical formula governing the relation between physical stimulus and sensory response. The psychology of emotional behavior and of human social interaction, however, was only just being rescued from the domain of religion. Questions of guilt and shame, of ethical behavior, because they involve a person's values, were clearly of a different order from questions about how we perceive color, motion, or distance. They were questions that reflected a person's relationship to God. Yet despite this difference, the realization of the promise contained in the efficacy of Newtonian laws required that these questions also be treated in the same way as questions of perception.

So, for example, Isaiah Berlin (1956) tells us that Locke, one of the most influential Enlightenment philosophers, treated the mind as if it were a box containing mental equivalents of Newtonian particles. These mental particles were called "ideas"; they were distinct and separate entities, and "simple," that is, possessing no parts into which they could be split, but combining and compounding themselves into complex forms for the higher mental functions. Thought, according to Locke, was a kind of inner eye comparable to the eye which receives external stimulation. Freud, in the tradition of Locke, also considered that "ideas" were the appropriate basic units of scientific theorizing about human behavior. "Ideas," for Freud, were the mental representatives of physical energy, whether its source was inside or outside the organism. Because his basic unit of theorizing was "ideas" rather than emotions or feelings, Freud was immediately involved in having to demonstrate that "ideas," or units of consciousness, were also representative of unconscious forces, an enterprise which carried with it all the difficulties attached to conceptualizing unknowns. On the other hand, to base his thinking on the value-laden quality of emotions seemed to Freud, as to other scientists, to be inviting only disturbances in the orderly process of logical deduction or induction.

The second canon of scientific thinking is that facts cannot be ascertained unless there are logical safeguards which guarantee their truth. Observations must be made under controlled conditions to eliminate artifacts or extraneous variables; constructs must be operationally defined so that their referents are identifiable and visible; and hypotheses must be testable, that is, confirmable or disconfirmable, not accepted *a priori*.

These were the canons by which Freud abided; it was, in fact, in an effort to make his observations more congruent with such a rational system that he formulated theories about "ideas" rather than about the emotions and dyadic social interactions he was observing. Still, he was well aware of the split between observation and theory, and of the dangers of theorizing. In his obituary of Charcot (1893) he writes:

> On one occasion, a small group of us, all students from abroad, brought up on German academic psychology, were trying his patience with doubts about his clinical innovations. "But that can't be true," one of us objected, "it contradicts the Young–Helmholtz theory." He did not reply "so much the worse for the theory," "the clinical facts come first," or words to that effect, but he did say something which made a great impression on us: *"La théorie, c'est bon, ma ça n'empêche d'existe"* (Theory is good but it doesn't prevent things from existing) (p. 13).

It is fascinating to speculate on what might have been the course of intellectual history if Freud had chosen either emotions or the social nature of human beings as his theoretical base. One hoped-for outcome of this book is that it will at least initiate a better integration of Freud's findings with information that has since become available about the emotions and about the social nature of human beings.

Ricoeur (1970), for example, has interpreted Freudian theory from the standpoint of its connection to the theory of language. His approach derives from the fact that Freud's discoveries were made in dialogue with patients. The unit of observation is not "ideas" but "signifiers" or symbolic transactions between persons. Freud, says Ricoeur, developed the "semantics of desire." This is a felicitous term for primary-process transformations. Lacan (1968) has also pursued within psychoanalytic theory the notion that what psychoanalysis should rightfully study is the "language of the self," since this language symbolically reflects basic human social relationships.

Ricoeur's study of Freudian theory leads him into a reinterpretation of the philosophy of religion. He accepts Freud's critique of religion as the expression of a desire for consolation, and for closeness to the hated father; at the same time, he rejects Freud's "scientism" in conceptualizing reality without incorporating into it the "love of Creation." Ricoeur's assumption, like Freud's, is that the fanciful and mythological (two pejorative descriptions often given to Freud's work) may often represent emotional truths. At the time Freud was writing, however, emancipated thinking had been only too recently freed from the bondage of absolutes to be comfortable with anything but a logical as contrasted with an emotional reality.

Freud developed his theoretical formulations without the benefit of information from the social sciences, which hardly existed in his time, and without the benefit of information from biochemistry and biophysics, which were also much later developments. So, for example, Freud wrote of a "special chemism" of sexual longings and behavior at a time when the existence of hormones was entirely unknown. Likewise, knowledge of the physiology and functioning of the autonomic nervous system in emotional life was still in the future. Walter B. Cannon's famous book, *The Wisdom of the Body*, was not published until 1932. Cannon (1942) was able to demonstrate that legendary cases of "voodoo death" could actually be authenticated: prolonged, unrelieved terror can produce a chain of physiological events which culminate in death. In Freud's day, the later developments in the biochemistry of mood were also entirely unknown.

Today's advances in biochemistry are sometimes cited as evidence that psychoanalysis and other "talking cures" in psychiatry will soon be replaced by a sophisticated drug therapy. What this prediction overlooks is that the chemical compounds are aimed precisely at regulating emotional states, and that a really clear understanding of these states is itself necessary in order for the drugs to hit their targets. So, for example, a recent review of the field of behavioral neurochemistry in *Science* (Barchas et al., 1978) focuses on the relation between the "neuroregulators" and emotional states and drives. The review points out that the emotional states need as "careful delineation and articulation as do neurochemical events" (p. 967). For example, the difference between schizophrenia, which involves the "stress of social interaction," and depression, which is a "stress reaction to social loss," points to the existence of very different patterns of neuroregulators. The tremendous advances in biochemistry over the past twenty years thus suggest that Freud was on even safer ground than he knew when he pinpointed emotional distress in mental illness. Freud was uncertain enough, however, to be more comfortable with a neurological rather than a humanistic theoretical model of mental illness.

Two major scientists of the nineteenth century, Marx and Darwin, were important influences leading Freud both to his discoveries and to his formulations of them. The implications of Marx's and Darwin's thinking for psychology could only be glimpsed by Freud, however, and there was little direct observation to support the perspectives they brought to psychology. Let us look first at Darwin's influence on Freud.

Darwin's evolutionary theory had only recently been incorporated into scientific thought. Darwin's theory implied that human beings share with other animals the fact of an adaptive relationship to their environment. Human beings, along with other species, have instincts which facilitate their adaptation to their surroundings and thus contribute to the preservation of their species. In such a theoretical formulation human beings lose their unique relationship to God and replace it by an adaptive interaction with their ecology. It is for this reason that Darwin's theory is still regarded by many people as heresy.

Freud's choice of the sexual instinct as his focus of study was based in part on its adaptive function as well as on his clinical experience. From Darwin's work Freud understood that the sexual instinct is unique in that it has to do not only with an individual's personal development, but with the preservation of the species. No one ever dies for lack of sex, but the species would (Freud, 1914). As I read this statement, more than 60 years after it was written, I can interpret it to mean that the sexual instinct is a uniquely social instinct. This formulation of the sexual instinct as a uniquely social one can in fact have several levels of meaning. It can have the meaning which Freud gave it, or it can be put in a more modern idiom: The sex drive is the only drive which involves (although it does not always literally require) union with another individual for its consummation. Freud's concentration on it turned out to be even more productive than he foresaw. It led to the very useful concept that psychosocial and psychosexual development are interrelated. They are both governed by primary process, which means that social development is also based on indestructible longings. Human personality somehow incorporates and "transforms" significant beloved figures into the self. Lévi-Strauss (1968), commenting on the fact that in every society human beings have names, makes a similar point when he says that "every individual's personality [is] his own totem: it is the signifier of his signified being" (p. 214).

From Darwin Freud also took the idea that human behavior develops in natural stages or sequences. But this was a notion that had not yet led to any direct studies of animal behavior or of the actual course of human development from infancy to adulthood. These studies, particularly those by the Harlows (1962) and Bowlby (1969), have produced strong evidence for the tremendous power of the early "affectional systems" in which people develop. Modern studies have brought forward clear evidence that the human infant at birth is, as one psychologist puts it, "social by biological origin" (Rheingold, 1969, p. 581). This clearly stated, fundamental axiom is only adumbrated in Freud's identification of the sexual instinct as one of the mainsprings of human behavior, a choice which had already been made possible by the Darwinian notion of "instinctive" human adaptiveness.

It is interesting that Freud makes little explicit reference to Darwin in his writings (Bowlby, 1973). In fact he was so little an explicit Darwinian that he believed in the inheritance of acquired characteristics. He accepted Lamarck's view of evolution as more congruent with psychoanalytic theory. It seemed likely to Freud that a human being's intense emotional needs could modify the structure of his organism in so profound a way that these modifications would be transmitted to the offspring. This was the basis on which he theorized, in *Totem and Taboo* (1913a), that the guilt over the original parricide committed by the primordial band of males was transmitted to future generations. These notions of the transmission of primal guilt were put forward long before the discoveries that precluded the inheritance of acquired characteristics: the chromosomes, genes, DNA, and RNA.

At a time when the study we call anthropology had only just begun, Freud had the insight that human beings are somehow acculturated "by nature." But because there was no field work available to support such a view, he had to express this insight in what Lévi-Strauss (1968) calls a "culture-myth": the legend of *Totem and Taboo*. It should be noted in passing that according to Abram Kardiner (one of his students), Freud himself regarded *Totem and Taboo* as a parable (Kardiner, 1977).

Marx's theory of the class struggle contained two important implications for psychology, both of which figured in Freud's thinking. The first is the concept that the relation between the individual and an oppressive society governs the behavior of both the oppressors and the oppressed. Marx described the alienation of the worker who sells his labor; he wrote of the "icy waters of egotistical calculation" that pervade human relationships in a class society. By implication, a classless society, free of oppression, would foster the development of loving rather than aggressive human behavior. A second concept, more explicitly developed by Marx, is that the class struggle breeds ideologies congruent with the embattled positions of the contestants. These ideologies provide moral and ethical justification for behavior that is actually driven by class necessities. Marx analyzed the role of social institutions such as the church, the law, and marriage as ideological superstructures maintaining the interests of the exploiting class.

Freud had little confidence that the optimistic predictions about human behavior contained in Marx's thinking would be fulfilled. What Freud did with the Marxist concept of ideology was to transpose it, complete with warring forces, to a scene of operations within the person. From the larger canvas of institutional ideologies it was an easy step to the concept of personal ideologies which function in the interest of sexual and aggressive wishes and are often in conflict. We now take for granted that everyone has a personal ideology. We have become suspicious of the most self-evident ideas about truth and right, wanting to know what interests these ideas serve. It is not that we do not get caught by charismatic ideas. But we have mechanisms that Freud gave us for examining the emotional basis of concepts which may seem, on the surface, far-removed from their base in personal interests. We routinely ask whose axe is being ground; and the notion that people grind axes, if not originally a Freudian idea, is one to which his work gave much substance. It has been the basis, in fact, for clarifying possibilities of bias in scientific thinking: Observers in psychology and other sciences must often make themselves "blind" to what hypothesis is being tested by their observations lest their egotistical self-interest incline them to "see" what fits their preconceived notions.

It follows from the concepts of institutional and of personal ideology that concepts of absolute truth and absolute morality must be examined cross-culturally, to see how truths and values vary with differing social conditions. Nowadays we have systematic ways of looking at such questions cross-culturally because we have a developed science of anthropology. Freud did not. What he had for the comparative study of other peoples was accounts of "strange customs," or comparative studies of sexual behavior as collected in Frazer's *Golden Bough* or in Havelock Ellis's work. Anthropology, in the sense of systematic observation made on the basis of field work among nonliterate people, was then a science only just beginning. Franz Boas, the "father" of modern anthropology, published *The Mind of Primitive Man* in 1912, almost a generation after Breuer and Freud's *Studies in Hysteria* (1893–1895).

What is now much more clearly evident than it could have been to Freud is that everywhere anthropologists have looked they have found human beings organized into a society ruled by cultural laws governing the interaction of its members from birth to death. In this respect, human beings are unique on earth. Some anthropologists, for example, La Barre (1954), have suggested that this human cultural order is our species' form of adaptive relationship to nature. Lévi-Strauss (1976) puts it this way: "Mankind [is] inconceivable outside society" (p. 514). This is a concept very similar to the psychologists' concept that infants are social by biological origin. We human beings have evolved from fur-bearing to culture-bearing animals as our species' unique means of survival. And although the actual content of cultural laws varies from culture to culture, all are systems of moral law which each of us imbibes with our mother's milk (Edel and Edel, 1968).

This centrality of moral law in human functioning is illustrated in the ethical dilemmas that anthropologists themselves face, since the values by which they judge other societies are the products of their own acculturation. In a beautiful little essay entitled *A Little Glass of Rum* (referring to the drink offered condemned criminals about to be guillotined), Lévi-Strauss (1976) suggests that anthropologists often choose their vocation out of scorn and hostility for the evil in their own society. In a very Freudian interpretation he suggests, moreover, that Western Europe is unique in producing anthropologists precisely because it is a prey to strong feelings of remorse: the anthropologist is the "symbol of atonement" (p. 510). Thus, when Freud focused on his patients' ethical dilemmas as the origin of their illness, he was adumbrating what anthropologists can now confirm — that moral law is immanent in human society and thus in "human nature." But Freud himself was operating out of a more individualistic view of human nature, a view that was still aimed at rescuing psychology from theology.

When Freud discovered the emotional basis of mental illness he had neither a viable theory of human emotions nor a science of anthropology on which to base a concept of human cultural nature. It is only recently, for example, that a cross-cultural study (Rosenblatt, Walsh, and Jackson, 1976), using the Murdock Human Relations Area Files, has demonstrated the universality of grief during bereavement. In *Mourning and Melancholia* (1917) Freud took for granted that grief is a normal process but he was also puzzled about it. He wondered why it should be so "extraordinarily painful." It was remarkable, he thought, that "this painful unpleasure is taken as a matter of course by us" (p. 245). Specifically, Freud was puzzled by the "economics" of grief. In Freud's theoretical system, "economics" was based on the tendency of the organism to throw off stimulation as quickly as possible. Why then decathecting, which reduces stimulation, should be so painful, and why each memory should first be hypercathected and then decathected was surely puzzling in terms of such a theoretical system of economics. As we shall see in Chapter 6, in a modern theoretical system, based on the primacy of human social life, grief is a biosocially "given" affect inevitably consequent on lost affectional bonds.

Modern academic psychology is still backward when it comes to the amount of attention it devotes to the emotions. It is also dominated by the assumption that affects are secondary to cognition in human life, although this fundamental assumption is now being called into question by experimenters in the academic mainstream (for example, Zajonc, 1980). Zajonc assembles considerable evidence that "feeling is first" (Zajonc quotes e. e. cummings) rather than always postcognitive, as contemporary academic psychology still believes. As we shall see in Chapter 3, Freud wrestled with just this problem in revising his theory of anxiety. By 1926 he abandoned his libido theory of anxiety in favor of an essentially cognitive model of anxiety. This was because it seemed to him that on a theoretical level affect must be postcognitive, however primary it appeared to be clinically.

In his thinking about obsessional neurosis Freud was similarly hindered by the absence of a viable theory of human emotions and sociability. In analyzing the Wolf-Man, for example (as we shall see in Chapter 4), Freud encountered what is really an amazing phenomenon in the world of affects, namely the affect of indifference. He was so irritated by it that when he encountered it again in his brief analysis of a young homosexual woman (Freud, 1920b), he called it "Russian tactics." "Once when I expounded to her a specially important part of the [psychoanalytic] theory, one touching her nearly, she replied in an inimitable tone, 'How very interesting,' as though she were a *grande dame* being taken over a museum and glancing through her lorgnon at objects to which she was completely indifferent" (p. 163). Partly in response to the Wolf-Man's affect of indifference, Freud set a terminal date for the analysis, a move he later regarded as a technical error. He referred to this in his later warnings to therapists to beware of the temptation to short cures.

The affect of indifference, on the face of it, is a contradiction in terms. It is in this respect on a par with "unconscious ideas" in the logical puzzle it appears to represent. Freud struggled patiently to clear up the contradiction between an idea and unconsciousness of it. The affect of indifference, in contrast, was never subjected to a similar analysis. As we think about it it forces us to realize that an emotion can be conceptualized in two categories: the category of individual arousal, and the category of communication to others. An emotion can be conceptualized as occurring simultaneously in what Hartvig Dahl (1979) would call the Me category (arousal) and in what Dahl would call the It category (communication to others). In a failure to be impressed by the other's wisdom, we do not necessarily feel overtly scornful or hostile, but simply not aroused. In that state (zero affect in the Me category), we are simultaneously communicating a bundle of hostile and derogatory affects (high value in the It category) — depending, of course, on the emotional state of the recipient.

My understanding of the affect of indifference is that it bypasses shame. It succeeds in warding off feelings of humiliation in the self and it can succeed in evoking them in the other. As I have shown in a recent paper (Lewis, 1980a) some cases of so-called "narcissistic personality" are actually cases in which bypassed shame has not been identified either in the patient-therapist relationship or in life. There is a considerable difference between a theoretical formulation that conceptualizes a case as narcissistically regressed and a formulation that conceptualizes the consequences of bypassed shame. The latter problem is easier to overcome.

The circumstances of Freud's personal life also created pressures which determined the schism between his clinical and his theoretical formulations. In the exposition of this, the final point of my introduction, I shall use Freud's methods to understand Freud's ideology — the emotional basis of some of his ideas. I shall draw heavily on the official biography of Freud by Ernest Jones (1954), on an unofficial biography by Helen Puner (1947), and on an illuminating account of Freud's intellectual history by Mannoni (1971).

Freud, a Jew trained in the Talmud in a Hebrew school, found his revolutionary stance toward the culture in which he was reared in the materialist basis of nature. Freud's profound belief was in atheism. One way open to a very intelligent, nonreligious Jew in an upwardly mobile merchant family was to study medicine at the University. Freud chose medicine not because he so loved the idea of being a healer, but because by studying medicine he could pursue science. He averred to the end of his life that he had no talent for being a physician; he saw his own greatest gifts as lying in his abilities as a researcher, a theorizer, an observer of phenomena rather than as a healer. Medical school was a way of becoming a professor in academia. Freud's first chosen subject was not psychiatry, but neurology. He apprenticed himself to Brücke, an outstanding neurologist of the day, and had Freud not been a Jew he might indeed have become, like his mentor, a famous neurologist.

It is not often remembered that between 1877 and 1897 Freud had some twenty publications in neurology. It is, of course, better known that Freud was very close to being able to claim credit for the discovery of the anesthetic properties of cocaine. And it is touching to remember his story of his pride at the fact that his own father was one of the early recipients of the benefits of this discovery when he needed eye surgery. In fact, Freud was so pleased with the new knowledge of the psychological effects of cocaine that in the early days of his psychiatric practice he prescribed it for his patients, without any inkling of the possibility that the drug might be addictive. His description of the "roses" that come to the cheeks of the depressed women for whom he prescribed cocaine amuses us today. Freud's reputation as a psychiatrist was not enhanced when it developed that some patients had indeed become addicted.

But the promising career of the productive neurologist was doomed because Freud was a Jew. No possibility existed for him to obtain a professorship; and a man could not marry and support a family on the salary of a research worker. So Freud reluctantly switched careers, and chose psychiatry, in which one could make a living in private practice. When he went to Paris to study psychiatry with Charcot, the most forward-looking psychiatrist of the day, he brought with him — to show Charcot — the silver-staining technique he had developed for preparing slides. Charcot was not interested!

It is important to realize that when Freud entered private practice as a psychiatrist it was without the kind of extensive training he had acquired as a neurologist. That he had no strong background in psychiatry was actually no loss, since so very little was known about mental illness beyond the classification of symptoms. What is important is that Freud entered clinical psychiatry with a keen sense of inadequate training, and remained for many years preoccupied with whether his clinical work was good. So, for instance, his famous dream about the injection of the patient Irma is about whether or not he had overlooked some serious disease. In *The Psychopathology of Everyday Life* (1901) there is a most moving footnote. Freud is analyzing how he came to forget the name of a patient. As he was preparing his bills, he came upon the initial M — and simply could not remember the name, although the case was a very recent one. It turned out that the case was that of a fourteen-year-old girl brought by her parents for hysterical symptoms, which Freud cured. The parents then took the youngster out of treatment — a fact which Freud seems to have resented. And then it developed that although she had indeed had a set of hysterical symptoms — and Freud is very emphatic about this — she also developed incurable cancer of the "abdominal glands" and died. No wonder Freud couldn't remember the family's name.

The contrast between Freud's established skills and competence as a neurologist and the uncertainties which must have accompanied his clinical practice as a psychiatrist is really very strong. One consequence can, I think, be seen in Freud's intellectual productions. He writes clinical accounts of his experiences with his patients which are eye-openers of insight into how emotional conflicts are translated into symptoms. But he is apologetic about the fact that his clinical accounts sound like short stories — they surely do not sound like treatises in neurophysiology. He writes a *Project for a Scientific Psychology* (in 1895, published only posthumously in 1950), in which he forces himself to set out the neurological foundations for behavior; and he bravely discards it because he realizes that it is psychology, not neurology that he wants to pursue. But when it comes to theorizing about his findings — to the formulation of a theoretical framework in which to put his observations — he still falls back upon the concepts with which he is most familiar: the neurophysiological concepts of energy, or stimulation, developing and then discharging. In thinking about the most fundamental motivation in human behavior, Freud chooses as his theoretical foundation the tendency of energy to discharge. People's behavior is governed by the need to get rid of stimulation: at the bottom there is a *Death Instinct.*

This narrow theoretical framework was hardly able to encompass the wealth of insight which Freud brought to his descriptions of his patients' dilemmas. Yet when Freud's disciples began to think things out in their own clinical and theoretical terms, they found Freud all too often terribly dogmatic. So first Adler, then Jung, then Horney joined the list of brilliant students with whom the master parted company on the bitterest terms. One cannot help observing that the uncertainties inherent in his late choice of psychiatry, in his lack of conventional training, and in the tremendous innovation which he was making when he insisted on the emotional basis of mental illness — that all of these combined to push Freud into clinging to a mechanistic theoretical system like the systems he was familiar with in neurology, as well as into personal dogmatism. It was Freud who taught us (in this instance by example as well as precept) that when people are uncomfortable with uncertainty they tend to become dogmatic.

* * *

The chapters that follow will show in detail how the tension between Freud's clinical work and his theoretical formulations impeded psychoanalysis in the pursuit of its most important scientific discovery: the power of human emotional connectedness. The chapters in Volume 1, on the emotional basis of mental illness, will consider each of the important diagnostic categories separately. A first chapter, on Freud's interpretation of a case of demon-possession in the seventeenth century, illustrates the secularization of guilt. Next, we shall see how Freud's first observations on hysteria focused on "strangulated affects." As he turned to phobias, obsessional neurosis, depression, and paranoia, he probed more and more deeply into early childhood. His attention turned also from sexual longing to the humiliated fury which is evoked by unrequited love. Humiliated fury was also conceptualized as an "instinct of aggression." In each chapter we shall examine alternative modes of therapy that have been offered in opposition to psychoanalysis. These alternatives are mainly better ways of altering feeling states. The final chapter in Volume 1 will assess psychoanalysis as a therapy today.

CHAPTER 1

The Secularization of Guilt
Reinterpreting Christoph Haizmann's Story

In 1923 Freud published the "case history" of Christoph Haizmann, a painter living in the seventeenth century who had become possessed of the Devil and then been granted a miraculous cure through prayer to the Virgin Mary. This paper of Freud's, though brief, is nevertheless full of the clinical detail that has been so informative in psychiatry. The case account also illustrates very clearly the difference between Freud's clinical descriptions and his theoretical formulations. Let us spend a few moments with Christoph Haizmann's story, since it contains so many of Freud's insights as well as so many of the psychological problems that remain today.

Freud's account is based on a manuscript found some two hundred years after the miraculous events at Mariazell, an important pilgrimage shrine in Austria. The manuscript had aroused considerable interest for its similarity to the Faust legend. It contained two sections. One, written in Latin, was the church fathers' account of Christoph Haizmann's miraculous cure by the appearance to him of the Virgin Mary, who forced the Devil to give back the contract Christoph had signed. The second section, written in German, was Haizmann's own diary, illustrated by nine of his paintings depicting scenes with the Devil.

Freud used this fascinating case account as an example of how psychoanalytic concepts could now interpret as neurosis what the Church had thought of as demon-possession. Freud's interpretation of Haizmann's account of his experiences with the Devil is a masterpiece of insight into the Devil as a primary-process transformation of Haizmann's conflicted attitudes toward his own father. It illustrates dramatically how the secularization of thought has transposed the problem of Devil-possession into a problem of neurosis-possession. It emphasizes that emotions are the "psychical powers" so potent that they can issue in hallucinations and seizures. Thus, Freud (1923b) writes: "The demonological theory of those dark times has won in the end against all the somatic views of the period of 'exact' science . . . . In our eyes the demons are bad and reprehensible wishes, derivatives of instinctual impulses that have been repudiated and repressed" (p. 72). As we can see, however, in the preceding sentence, "bad and reprehensible wishes" are not conceptualized only as emotions, but as derivatives of instincts.

The church fathers' account tells us that Christoph was brought to Mariazell on September 5, 1677, after having suffered frightful convulsions on August 29 while in church in the nearby town of Pottenbrunn, where he lived. When these convulsions recurred, he was examined by the Prefect of his district, who asked him if he had been trafficking with the Evil Spirit. Upon this, the man admitted that nine years before, while in a state of despondency about his art and doubtful whether he could support himself, he had yielded to the Devil, who had tempted him nine times. Christoph had given his bond in writing to belong to the Devil body and soul after a period of nine years. The period was due to expire on the coming September 24th. Christoph was thus in imminent danger of losing his immortal soul to eternal damnation.

After he had undergone a period of penance and prayer at Mariazell, at midnight on September 8 in the sacred Chapel of the Nativity of the Virgin, the Devil appeared to him in the form of a winged dragon and gave him back the pact, which was written in blood. Haizmann later painted this appearance of the Devil. The church fathers do not themselves confirm that they saw a vision of the Devil. They state only that at midnight Christoph tore himself away from the priests who were holding him in his agony of remorse, rushed into the corner of the Chapel where he saw the apparition, and returned with the paper in his hand.

The miracle was great and the victory of the Holy Mother over Satan without question, but unfortunately the cure was not a lasting one. After a short time, the painter left Mariazell in the best of health and went to Vienna, where he lived with a married sister. On October 11, however, he experienced fresh attacks — severe "absences" and paralysis, as well as convulsive seizures. In St. Stephen's Church in Vienna (again in church, where good triumphs over evil) he saw a handsome woman who attracted him. The

Devil then appeared to him and offered to make him a king surrounded by humble courtiers. This time, however, it was not only the Devil who tormented him but the sacred figures of the Virgin and of Christ himself. In opposition to the Devil, the Blessed Virgin and Christ insisted that Christoph renounce all worldly pleasures and enter a life of service to God. In his diary Christoph refers indiscriminately to both the Virgin and the Devil as tormenting visions.

Christoph returned to Mariazell and confessed to the church fathers that he had concealed from them a still earlier pact with the Devil. Freud interprets this confession of an earlier pact as a fabrication by Christoph to explain to the fathers (and perhaps to himself) why the Virgin's intervention had not continued to be effective. In any case, this time, once more, the fathers and the Holy Virgin helped Christoph to win release from the pact by prayer. Christoph then entered a monastery as Brother Chrysostomus. There were several other times during his subsequent life in the Order when Christoph was repeatedly tempted by the Devil, especially, writes the Superior of his monastery, when Christoph had had too much wine. But for the rest, his life was uneventful. He died "peacefully and of good comfort" in the year 1700.

Consulting Christoph's own descriptions of the specifics of the Devil's temptations appended to each of his paintings, Freud discovered which of the temptations it was that had captured Christoph. By Christoph's own account he had on eight separate occasions resisted the Devil's temptations to introduce him to the magical arts, to give him money, and to give him entertainment of a sexual kind (although this one he accepted for three days). It was only on the ninth occasion that he signed a bond with the Devil in order to be freed from the depression from which he was suffering. (A present-day patient might well remark wryly that making a relatively long-term contract for psychotherapy in order to be freed from depression feels a bit like signing away one's soul.) Christoph's father had just died, leaving him in a state of melancholy in which he was unable to paint. The Devil then approached him, asked him why he was so downcast and promised to "help him in every way and to give him support" (p. 81). So, says Freud, Christoph trafficked with the Devil from an "excellent motive, as anyone will agree who can have an understanding of the torments" of depression and inability to work (p. 81).

The exact wording of the contracts Christoph signed with the Devil forms the basis of one of Freud's typically brilliant analyses of "primary-process transformation" under the press of forbidden wishes. Freud points out that the bonds contain no *undertaking* actually given by the Devil but instead a *demand* made by him on Christoph. This demand is that Christoph "become his bounden son," a demand to which Christoph subscribes. The pact can therefore be paraphrased to read that the Devil undertakes to replace the painter's lost father for nine years. The bond is thus a bond of love. A man who has fallen into melancholy on the death of his father must have been very fond of him, writes Freud, so it is very strange that such a man should have hit on the idea of taking the Devil as a father substitute. What must be involved, therefore, is a transformed expression of the conflict between the man's love of his father and his hatred of him: a conflict between "affectionate" and "hostile" impulses. The painter's bond with the Devil is a neurotic fantasy expressing both sides of the painter's feelings.

Freud adduces evidence for this interpretation in the details of Haizmann's paintings of the Devil. The first appearance of the Devil is as an ordinary old man — an "honest elderly citizen with a brown beard, dressed in a red cloak and leaning on a stick" (p. 85). At this first appearance, the Devil could be anyone's father. Later on his appearance grows more and more terrifying — more mythological. He is equipped with horns, eagle's claws, and bat's wings, finally appearing in the Chapel as a winged dragon. Another line of interpretation of the presence of forbidden wishes comes from the frequent appearance of the number nine in Haizmann's account. Nine is the number associated with pregnancy, and from its frequent appearance Freud deduces that the painter may have had a wish to take his mother's place in his father's love — a wish expressed in the form of a pregnancy fantasy. This detail of interpretation assumes greater likelihood when it is put together with the fact that the Devil is depicted as having two pendulous breasts and a large penis ending in a snake. The contradiction between accepting the Devil as a father substitute and then depicting him as a feminine man points to the conflict between Christoph's love and hatred of his father, and its transformed expression in the details of a double-sexed monster.

The Devil with two pendulous breasts and a large penis ending in a snake is also a caricature of a father figure. Scorn and contempt, those particularly gratifying forms of hatred, are expressed by caricatures. This is a theme that Freud developed not only in *The Psychopathology of Everyday Life* (1901) but in his book on *Jokes and Their Relation to the Unconscious* (1905b).

Freud does not interpret it, but the fact that Christoph's second bout of symptoms came with the Blessed Virgin and Christ as his torturers may be understood, once again, as a reflection of the ambivalent attitudes Christoph must have had toward the Church figures on whom he had become dependent in his illness. This is a dilemma that often occurs in modern psychotherapy: the helping one is loved for the relief obtained and hated for the dependency that has developed. This conflict is often expressed in a renewal of symptoms at a time when therapy is scheduled to terminate. In any event, Christoph solved it by forsaking the world and joining the religious life of the Fathers.

Freud's study of Haizmann's case made the fundamental step of converting demon-possession into neurosis, but many questions about neurosis still
remain to be solved. In this paper Freud asserts the basic importance of
"psychical powers" and describes the emotions of affections and hostility to
which he refers by this term. He also traces the transformation of emotional
conflict into the metaphors that express and disguise it. But the actual process by which the emotions work to transform themselves into symptoms is
still an unsolved question. One reason for this is that the tendency to turn attention away from emotional experience itself to "higher" theoretical formulations of them, such as "psychical powers" or "instincts," is still very
much a part of the present-day scientific atmosphere.

For example, although Christoph at the time of his illness was in a state
of acute guilt for something he had done nine years before, Freud never explicitly identifies the emotional state as guilt. In one sense, it doesn't need to
be said, it is so self-evident from the fact that Christoph felt he needed to
pray for forgiveness. It is also self-evident that when forgiveness was attained and Christoph mercifully absolved of his guilt, he was (at least temporarily) cured.

The observation that neurotic symptoms are somehow the product of
undischarged guilt is a major tenet of psychiatry today. Popular psychology
and psychiatry, today's folk wisdom, contain many variants on this theme.
When I Say No, I Feel Guilty is the title of a popular book that exhorts you
not to do that any more so you won't be neurotic. Another recent book is entitled *Your Erroneous Zones*, a cute way of suggesting a substitute for Freud's
concept of erogenous zones. The author's message in that book is the same as
all the rest of popular advice: don't feel guilty; don't put yourself down! It is
also still true, however, that some schools of psychiatry pay little direct attention to the emotional basis of mental illness, concentrating rather on the
chemical or physiological basis of behavior, including the emotions. What
both approaches to the problem of the role of the emotions in mental illness
have in common is that they are both still seeking the answer to the question:
How exactly does it work? How does it happen that an acute state of guilt
issues in a terrifying obsession of doom? Is there some chemical released that
alters thinking? If so, which comes first, the state of guilt or the release of the
chemical?

For the most part, when you or I are in a state of guilt — having done
something wrong — we figure out something to do that makes amends for
our transgression. Or, if we cannot make amends, we resign ourselves to
having been guilty and resolve not to commit the transgression again. Thus
we get rid of the guilt: As Freud would say, using the language of
physiology, we discharge it. But how does it come about that sometimes, instead of being able to discharge it, we fall into some kind of neurotic or
psychotic state? In Haizmann's case, one answer is apparent, although again

Haizmann's state of helplessness is so self-evident that Freud never explicitly names it. Since Haizmann himself had signed a contract with the Devil, a most powerful supernatural force, he (Christoph) was, in his own belief system, powerless to obtain his own release without the intervention of the angels of mercy sent by the Virgin Mary. From this example we extrapolate that the combination of guilt and helplessness to extricate oneself — i.e., feeling trapped — will somehow create neurotic or psychotic symptoms. We also perceive that one set of factors may lie in some individual predisposition to take fright and feel trapped.

Expanding on the latter set of factors, Freud proposed the hypothesis that the existence of unresolved childhood fixations rendered some adults more likely to take fright and feel trapped than others. And in answer to the question why some children should be more prone to suffer fixations, Freud postulated a combination of unknown constitutional factors and special difficulties in the parents' attitudes, resulting in a neurotic interaction between the child and its parents. In any case, the "explanation" for the individual's illness remained admittedly hypothetical, and easily perverted into a form of circular reasoning in which the result is presupposed by the hypothetical cause. However justly Freud has been accused of being dogmatic toward his followers, he never pretended that he had the answer to the question: How does it happen that one particular individual rather than another falls prey to mental illness? What he did insist on was that the pursuit of childhood sexual fixations in the patient's life history was the only method of treatment that should be called "psychoanalysis," and was the method most likely ultimately to provide the answer.

As for the first set of factors in Haizmann's case, his belief in the existence of the Devil was unquestioned. It was an established truth of Christoph's time, a part of his objective reality. The crime he had committed in trafficking with the Devil was also "real." Thousands of people had been burned for it in preceding centuries and many were still being burned for it in Christoph's time. Norman Cohn, in his illuminating book, *Europe's Inner Demons* (1975), has traced some of the social forces that combined to produce the great witch-hunts of the fifteenth, sixteeth and seventeeth centuries. Cohn tells us that belief in witches trafficking with the Devil was not just an outgrowth of ignorant peasant superstition. It was, in fact, an obsessive fantasy of learned monks, priests, and bishops. It was a belief sometimes cynically used by the rich and powerful for their own ends. Cohn also offers a psychoanalytic interpretation of the collective fantasies in which the Devil exercises his power as the products of "unconscious resentment against Christianity as too strict a religion" (p. 262), especially with respect to sex.

If someone in our own time tells us that he has trafficked with the Devil and is shortly to lose his immortal soul for it, we automatically diagnose him as schizophrenic, since his beliefs are so clearly out of step with those of our secular time. Christoph's belief was validated by the consensus in his time. His terror was real and required the fact of prayer to accomplish his release from a contract which to him and his contemporaries was real. Freud's substitution of the term neurosis rather than psychosis of demon-possession is a reflection of this circumstance of Christoph's relation to his world. The symptoms of mental illness are thus not unvarying but are relative to existing social norms. In fact, in recent times psychiatrists such as Laing and Szasz have gone so far as to term mental illness a social myth by means of which some persons are oppressed by the prevailing powers. In any case, one reason why the church fathers may have been as successful in Christoph's case as they were is that he and they took his beliefs at face value and behaved in a way that both parties — therapist and patient — believed appropriate. In our own time, therapists also strive to enter into and empathize with their patients' belief systems, in a technique originally developed by Freud. So even when a "schizophrenic" tells us that he has trafficked with the Devil, therapists say, in response, "Tell me more about your experience," rather than, "I just don't believe you; that's impossible." That is, of course, a tacit recognition that some emotional conflict is being expressed by the patient's belief system.

Christoph's symptoms vanished when his guilt was relieved. They came back again when he fell into a state of guilt again (this time over the presumed earlier contract with the Devil). By implication, when guilt is relieved, symptoms cease. This observation contained in the Haizmann case is an empirical one that can be confirmed today.

But transference improvement leads at once to theoretical difficulties. Especially when hard-headed scientists contemplate this kind of happening, it all seems too simple. It is also very difficult to believe that something as objectively trivial as mere feelings can make a person go crazy. Something more substantial must be involved — some chemical released or some energy dammed up.

The "scientific" prejudice against feeling states as the basis for mental illness is not as strong today as it was in Freud's day, but it is still very much with us. It makes great difficulty for studies of treatment in which we compare the effects of psychotherapy with the effects of no treatment or of chemical treatment in "blind," controlled conditions. Suppose in doing such a study one assigns one group of prospective patients to psychotherapy and a matched group at random to a two-month waiting list. And suppose, as has happened, a particular study shows that the people on the waiting list had the same rate of improvement as those who had two months of treatment. One would be bound to say that the control group was no worse off than the treatment group — which would make it appear that psychotherapy is no more effective than no therapy. But what could have happened, of course, is that some of the people on the waiting list patched up their quarrels, went back to their wives, or in other ways solved a guilty dilemma; or that they were helped by the knowledge that help would be forthcoming in two months. This means only that the process of cure in psychotherapy may be no different than it is in ordinary life. It is a special characteristic of mental illness that it can arise out of emotional upset and vanish with emotional relief. Affects have this quality of incidence and subsidence.

An anecdote from my personal experience illustrates this point. I started my professional life as an academic psychologist. I had been doing research and teaching for about eight years after receiving my doctorate when, for a variety of reasons, I decided I wanted to become a therapist. I chose to train as a psychoanalyst because in the 1940's this seemed the best way to acquire the necessary skill. I undertook a personal analysis, and I also sought to get some clinical experience. I had had no formal training as a psychiatrist, but I talked the soft-hearted clinic chief in the psychiatry department of a large urban hospital into letting me do psychotherapy under supervision (and, of course, without pay). Thus I found myself in something of the same dilemma I have described for Freud, which may be why I have some empathy for it. I was not sure I was quite qualified since I had come from another field of work.

I still remember very vividly my first session as a psychotherapist. I did not know it at the time, but I was suffering from acute guilt stemming from the fact that I did not feel qualified — actually, a combination of guilt and shame. I have no recollection of what I said to the patient. I believe I said very little if only because I was so anxious. However, it was her first session also, and as she was very busy telling me her troubles, I doubt that she noticed mine. But at the next session she arrived, all smiles, and said, "Oh, doctor, I'm feeling so much better." A transference improvement had occurred — a real phenomenon having nothing to do with my skill but with my presence, that is, with the fact of an emotional relationship which she formed out of her need. I was another person — a doctor with some presumed skill — with whom she was now connected, and who offered her sympathy and hope. This was a lesson about the power of the emotions that I have never forgotten.

The finding that psychotherapy and faith healing are both powerful agents of change evokes scorn only in a "scientific" atmosphere that denigrates the emotions as changeable as opposed to immutable "hard" data. Cures or improvement are easy to dismiss as being without substance, especially where insufficient attention has been paid to the direct study of how emotional change comes about.

The fact that the process of cure or symptom relief may be the same in psychotherapy as it is in ordinary living does not mean that *nothing* happens in either psychotherapy or in ordinary living, or that the process of relief has no substance. But lest the reader form the impression that all controlled studies of psychotherapy find it no more useful than no treatment, I hasten to correct any such notion. On the whole, psychotherapy has been found to be more effective than no treatment or chemical treatment alone. And among the most significant factors leading to a favorable outcome of psychotherapy are the empathy and warmth of the therapist.

My own experiences as a psychoanalyst led me into undertaking a phenomenological study of the emotional states of shame and guilt (Lewis, 1971). I was motivated in part by a growing conviction that something in the patient–therapist relationship itself was hindering progress and the hunch that this something was the patient's unacknowledged or bypassed shame. Surprisingly enough, although Freud had from the first spoken of forbidden wishes and soon hypothesized the existence of a forbidding agency, which he named the superego, my study of the actual experiences of shame and guilt was the first of its kind. With hindsight, it is self-evident that such a study should have been undertaken long before. In any case, with the help of tape-recorded transcripts of psychotherapy sessions, I was able to trace sequences from unanalyzed shame and guilt into "primary-process" transformation as neurotic symptoms.

Although shame and guilt are often evoked simultaneously by some transgressions, they often occur independently and in different life circumstances. In these instances it is clear that shame and guilt are very different emotional states. In guilt, the *thing* done or undone is the focus of awareness; in shame, it is the *self* which is focal in experience. Guilt thus has an objective quality: it is about something and requires one to do something to make amends. As a result, there is an affinity between guilty and the driven feeling which underlies obsessive and compulsive symptoms. Shame, in contrast, comes down on the *self* in the form of depression or paralyzing disability.

Recognizing that one is in a state of guilt is frequently difficult because one becomes absorbed in the very activity that seeks to make amends. So, for example, we say that we are bothered about something, that we are worried and we can't shake it — "bugged" is our slang term for feeling obsessed. Without being explicitly aware of it, we are in a state of guilt. What we are aware of is thought or cognitive content that will not let us relax. A very little introspection (usually when we are more rather than less relaxed) can make it readily apparent that the affective state we have been in is really guilt.

Christoph Haizmann was in a state of guilt for something he had done nine years earlier that was coming back to terrify him with its just retribution. And as we observed earlier, his state of guilt was so taken for granted that Freud never explicitly mentioned it. Christoph's experience was that he had to *do* something to get the contract back, and yet was powerless to do it, powerless to discharge his guilt, without the Virgin's intervention. And after she had intervened and had saved him, she came back to "bug" him again with an insistence that he become a monk. So in Haizmann's case one can discern a familiar pattern: something amiss in the patient–therapist relationship occasions a relapse. My guess is that for Christoph it was unacknowledged shame that he who had once defied it by traffic with the Devil now needed the Church's help.

As we shall see when we come to Freud's earliest cases of hysteria in women, they had not *done* anything to occasion a state of guilt. They were, however, hideously ashamed of themselves for their forbidden sexual longings. This hint in Freud's work of a sex difference in proneness to depression and hysteria versus obsessional neurosis and paranoia is confirmed by present-day statistics. Women are indeed two to three times more prone to depression and to hysteria than men; men are more prone to obsessional neurosis and paranoia than women, although not by so big a ratio (Lewis 1976).

Once I had undertaken my study of shame and guilt, I discovered that my focus on my patients' actual experiences of these emotions itself resulted in a considerable improvement in my therapeutic efficiency. For one thing, my relentless pursuit of patients' unacknowledged or bypassed shame because of their position as patients made them more aware of their good reasons for hating me and less likely to transform this affect into additional or recurring symptoms. Christoph Haizmann's experience of recovery when his guilt was relieved and relapse over the shame of his helplessness is a pattern I am able to confirm in my own experience as a therapist.

My experience also forced me to recognize that Freud had confounded questions about the technique of therapy with questions about the origin of neurosis. Freud's discoveries about the transformation of emotional conflict into symptoms led him to probe deeper and deeper into his patients' childhood, when earlier versions of conflicts had presumably occurred. On the one hand, he was making important discoveries; on the other hand, it appeared to him that if his patients did not improve it was because the childhood experiences had not been completely reconstructed. This is a form of illogical reasoning which it is easy to fall into, especially when one is trying to do therapy and research at the same time. There is, however, no reason why the technique of repairing something should be the same as the technique of discovering its etiology. One uses a microscope to determine whether or not there is a bacillus, but prescribes an antibiotic, not a microscope, to destroy the bacillus if there is one.

Probing more and more deeply into childhood also avoids the hatred that is evoked in patients by the patient–therapist relationship. In the pursuit of childhood experiences, patient and therapist are more likely to be in friendly cooperation. Moreover, if the childhood fixation can be recovered and resolved, there is somehow more substance to the proceedings than if the present emotional states are considered on their own. In any event, there is no theoretical reason why patients' becoming acquainted with the "primary-process" transformations that occur in the wake of evoked states of shame and guilt should not be sufficiently helpful to them to warrant the end of treatment.

At the end of his career, Freud was rather more pessimistic than optimistic about the effectivenss of psychonalysis as a therapy. And the defenses he used to explain its lack of effectiveness were accepted by his followers. In *Analysis Terminable and Interminable* (1937), written at the end of his life, Freud spoke in reasonable tones of the attempts to shorten psychoanalytic treatment as "based on the strongest considerations of reason and expediency." But he quickly added that endeavors to shorten treatment would likely contain also some "trace of the impatient contempt with which medical science of an earlier day regarded the neuroses as being uncalled-for consequences of invisible injuries. If it had now become necessary to attend to them they should at least be disposed of as quickly as possible" (p. 216). Later on in the same paper, he remarked that in the early days of his practice he was indeed hopeful of a reasonably quick result, but in more recent years had been involved in training analyses, which aim at a thoroughgoing investigation of the potential therapist's personality. This aspect of the psychoanalytic training of prospective therapists — that it does not aim only at therapy but also at a thoroughgoing understanding and improvement of the therapist's personality — has also contributed to a devaluation within psychoanalysis of therapeutic results. One consequence has been that the extent of early childhood reconstruction is equated with the success of the procedure, regardless of therapeutic outcome.

Freud's concentration in his later years on theory also functioned as a kind of abandonment of psychoanalysis as a mode of therapy. At the same time, the procedure became rigidified into so-called "classical" psychoanalysis — the patient talking from the couch at least four times a week to a benignly neutral analyst for at least two to three years. The aim of the lengthy process was a thoroughgoing personality change and a resolution of all childhood fixations. So, for example, a "classical" analyst (Eissler, 1963) reported the case of a patient who had terminated analysis at her own request after four years. The patient regarded herself as improved since her symptoms bothered her less. But because the analysis had not penetrated deeply enough into her past, the analyst considered it a failure.

Ironically enough, as its efficacy grew more doubtful, classical psychoanalysis was increasingly elevated into the highest form of treatment in a developing hierarchy of therapeutic methods. (This is a mechanism of defense that Freud described as "splitting" or "denial.") Brief psychotherapy, in which the patient's ego is "supported" rather than confronted with "insights" about the self, was assigned an inferior place in this hierarchy. That hierarchy is now being discarded, but while it was in vogue it seriously impeded the development of psychoanalysis as an effective therapy.

Freud's view of the effectiveness of psychoanalysis was pessimistic, however, on theoretical grounds. "Let us start from the assumption," he wrote (Freud, 1937), "that what analysis achieves for neurotics is nothing other than what normal people bring about for themselves without its help. Everyday experience, however, teaches us that in a normal person a solution of an instinctual conflict only holds good for a particular strength of instinct . . . . Irrefutable proof of this statement is supplied by our nightly dreams. . ." (pp. 225–226). Instincts, Freud is saying, are too powerful for us to suppose that we can develop an effective instrument against them. His theoretical formulation of the powerful force as an instinct rather than as an emotional state thus clearly justifies his pessimism. And, to a certain extent, this view of Freud's has become a self-fulfilling prophecy.

Freud's account of the Haizmann case illustrates also his dogmatism toward his students. The paper on Haizmann was written when Freud was in mid-career. He was already internationally famous, his triumphant trip to America more than a decade behind him. Yet even in this relatively obscure paper he is furious with Adler (who had broken with him more than a decade before). Adler had suggested that people's need for power was another kind of "forbidden wish," on a par with sexual longings as a potential source of "primary-process" transformations. Freud's treatment of Adler on this point is fierce: Adler's idea that longing for power is as central as sexual longings is the result of Adler's own unanalyzed sexual longings! Such statements hardly engender an atmosphere conducive to fresh observations.

I happen to believe that Freud's insistence on the sexual side of things was inspired as well as dogmatic. It was inspired because he was on the track of the social nature of human beings without fully realizing it himself. My own focus on the affects of shame and guilt is also a focus on the most social of human feelings, which I have come to understand as a means by which we keep ourselves connected to beloved figures in our lives (Lewis, 1980b).

Some of the efforts made within the psychoanalytic movement to correct Freud's most apparent theoretical errors, such as Hartmann's (1950, 1951) formulation of the existence of an "autonomous ego" (that is, an ego not governed by affects), actually led psychoanalysis further and further away from the study of human affective life into a more respectable "ego-psychology." This version of psychoanalysis focused heavily on stages of development conceptualized as a progression from the chaos of infant emotional life to the logic of adult "reality testing." The aim of ego-psychology was to integrate psychoanalysis with general psychology. The unfortunate effect, however, of this attempt was that it made neurosis and psychosis even more shameful states than they had ever been. Neurosis now represented some kind of a "failure" of ego development rather than a conflict of passions.

Some hint of this kind of attitude is already apparent in Freud's remarks on Haizmann. Speculating on what aspects of Haizmann's personality may have made him susceptible to mental illness, Freud (1923b) wrote: "Perhaps he . . . was one of those types of people who are known as 'eternal sucklings' — who cannot tear themselves away from their blissful situation at the mother's breast, and who, throughout all their lives, persist in a demand to be nourished by someone else" (p. 104).

This concept of neurotics and psychotics as people with failed ego development has also offered psychoanalysis a convenient rationalization for therapeutic difficulties (Lewis, 1980a). The patients who do not improve must have had too primitive or demanding an ego, that is, they must have been too "narcissistic" to begin with. This kind of circular reasoning persists today even though many patients in psychoanalysis are clearly able to operate at quite high levels of productivity except for their neurotic troubles.

CHAPTER 2

Hysteria

The Problem of Forbidden
Sexual Longings

It is sometimes a source of ironic (sexist) gratification to me to think that the very first scientific insight into the emotional basis of mental illness was derived from the sufferings of hysterical women. Members of the "second sex" in middle-class Vienna, living with a set of values that fostered a benign degradation of womanhood, transformed their forbidden rage into forbidden sexual longings and thence into incapacitating neurotic symptoms. Somehow the message of their sexual longings first penetrated the awareness of two physicians, Breuer and Freud, both of whom, especially sensitized by being Jewish, were personal adherents of a humanistic tradition and both of whom were men. The very circumstance of their being men involved them in embarrassing questions of how to respond appropriately to the women's longings (a problem unfortunately still current in twentieth-century psychiatry). It was a long and difficult route that Freud followed from these first observations into the broader concept that neurosis contains an implied critique of the social order. And it was the women's hysterical symptoms — neuralgias, anaesthesias, contracted limbs, epileptiform seizures, chronic vomiting, anorexia, disturbances of vision — that were the first alert. These symptoms directly affect the body and clearly betray their origin in strong feelings. Women's bodies are the species' "means of reproduction"; women

31

are both valued and devalued for this reason. Women are socialized into a culture in which they are taught to be expressive of tender feelings; and women were both valued and devalued for their expressiveness. It is hardly surprising, therefore, that the first glimpse of the critique that our social order needs to be more loving came from the emotional turmoil of women.

Freud's profound immersion in the spirit of the Enlightenment was evidenced by his choice of Charcot as his teacher. Along with Charcot, Freud assumed that the symptoms of hysteria must be governed by scientific laws. Freud's description of the discredit in which hysteria was held before Charcot is itself illuminating. He wrote: "It was held that in hysteria anything was possible, and no credit was to be given to a hysteric about anything. The first thing that Charcot did was to restore its dignity to the topic. Little by little, people gave up the scornful smile with which the patient was certain of being met. She was no longer necessarily a malingerer" (Freud, 1893, p. 19).

Specifically, moreover, Freud described the puzzle presented by hysteria as follows:

> If I find someone in a state which bears all the signs of painful affect — weeping, screaming and raging — the conclusion seems probable that a mental process is going on in him of which these physical phenomena are the appropriate expression. A healthy person, if he were asked, would be in a position to say what impression it was that was troubling him; but the hysteric would answer that he did not know. . . . How is it that a hysterical patient is overcome by an affect about whose cause he knows nothing? (p. 20)

The details of the history of any great discovery are fascinating in their own right, and they are of special interest when they involve a collaboration. Although the collaborators themselves have put rivalry behind them to create a joint communication, historians cannot help speculating about the relative importance of the two contributors. In the case of Breuer and Freud the story is additionally complicated by the fact that the issues they raised in their joint publication are still unresolved. Freud went on to pursue his own concepts and to develop a theoretical system for the first as well as the later discoveries. It has become the conventional wisdom to adopt Freud's retrospective view (expressed more than half a century later in a letter to Zweig) that Breuer "held the key in his hand" but failed to see how to use it. In fact, however, the meaning of Breuer and Freud's discovery of the sexual basis of hysteria is still far from clear. Freud's theoretical formulations (in contrast to his clinical descriptions) have not necessarily advanced our understanding of hysteria, and his statements about the theoretical disagreements between himself and Breuer reflect the fact that many problems in hysteria (and in psychoanalysis) are still wide open today.

For example, the use of hypnosis as an adjunct to the process of emotional catharsis was gradually abandoned by Freud and later expressly excluded by him from psychoanalytic technique. In fact, although Breuer and Freud specifically implicated a "hypnoid state" as a condition for symptom formation, Freud later tended to play down the importance of that state. The term "hypnoid state" had too much of a cognitive connotation, implying something like Janet's "psychic insufficiency." Yet it is a commonplace observation that in instances of extreme affect — for example, in acute shame or in states of inexpressible rage — the experience resembles a special state of restricted awareness. We phrase it by saying, "I was beside myself."

The notion that hypnosis has a benign influence in assisting relaxation has never died, however, even though Freud banned it. Within the psychoanalytic movement itself, Brenman and Gill (1947) reported good results using hypnosis as an adjunctive stimulus to the free-association process. Similarly, stimulating hypnagogic states has very much facilitated therapeutic progress (Kubie, 1943). A combination of white noise and a visual "Ganzfeld" has shown facilitative effects in stimulating the flow of hypnagogic primary-process ideation (Bertini, Lewis, and Witkin, 1964).

But it has been left to the behaviorists to revive the adjunctive use of hypnosis in administering the relaxation part of behavioral programs for symptom removal. It is significant, moreover, that labeling a relaxation procedure as hypnosis yields better results than the identical relaxation procedure unlabeled (Lazarus, 1973). Hypnosis is indeed some kind of powerful affective connection between two people.

An entire issue of the *Journal of Abnormal Psychology* (October 1979) was recently devoted to the subject of hypnosis and psychopathology. One of the important contributions in this issue is that of Sackeim, Nordlie, and Gur (1979), in which they put forward a model of hysterical and hypnotic blindness. Comparing the behavior of hypnotically induced and actual cases of hysterical blindness, the authors make use of a model of visual information processing which is compatible with current cognitive theories. Ordinarily when an iconic representation of information occurs it is followed by extraction and transformation of that information. In the hysterically blind the perceptual representations are blocked from awareness, and "under some motivational circumstances the information that is extracted from the representations may be subject to a denial operation that results in incorrect identifications of visual stimuli" (p. 479). Experiments using hypnosis confirm this concept of "blocking" plus motivationally determined "denial." Sackeim et al. thus posit a "critical dissociation between awareness and nonawareness . . . akin to psychoanalytic perspectives" (p. 487). People can, indeed, respond to perceptions of which they are unaware. It was this puzzling phenomenon, still mysterious today, that first alerted Freud to the basis of hysterical symptoms in affects whose causes and consequences the patient does not know. In the absence of a viable theory of human emotions, however, Freud's theoretical explanations focused on the fate of "ideas" (consciousness) rather than on the fate of emotional attachments.

STUDIES ON HYSTERIA

Let us spend a few moments with the history of Breuer and Freud's *Studies on Hysteria*, which bears a publication date of 1893–1895. This double date reflects the fact that they first published a preliminary communication about hysteria in 1893, and subsequently, at Freud's urging, a set of case accounts and a theoretical statement in 1895.

Josef Breuer, fourteen years older than Freud, was a well-established physician in Vienna, with an excellent practice and a high reputation. Like Freud, he had also been a student of Brücke in neurology and had, in fact, made an important contribution to the physiology of breathing. The path from research in physiology to private practice of medicine was the same path Freud followed some years later. Breuer was Freud's friend and his mentor in the days of Freud's obscurity. He lent Freud money, referred patients when Freud began to practice medicine, and was in many ways a most important intellectual influence (Roazen, 1974).

Between 1880 and 1882, more than ten years before their joint publication, Breuer treated a woman patient, Anna O., who was suffering from a variety of severe hysterical symptoms. His treatment involved following her daily moods carefully and, when she fell into her worst affective state, putting her under hypnosis and instructing her to tell him what was troubling her. This use of hypnosis was radically different from anything that had ever been tried before. The French, who had been experimenting with hypnosis since the days when Mesmer tried it on Marie Antoinette, used it to suggest symptoms away. This was the technique that Charcot was teaching in Paris. Breuer also suggested to Anna O. that her symptoms should disappear, but what caught his attention was that, under hypnosis, the patient relived terrible memories of her beloved father's lingering death and that when *she* had talked herself out the symptoms abated.

Breuer told Freud about his experiences with Anna O. in 1882, when Freud was just qualifying as a physician. Freud at the time was still mainly interested in the anatomy of the nervous system. As he tells it in his autobiography (Freud, 1925), Breuer's account made only a slight impression on him and dropped from his mind. When Freud went to Paris to study with Charcot he told Charcot about Breuer's use of hypnosis to encourage patients to talk, but Charcot was not interested. It was not until Freud had returned to Vienna and had begun his practice that, around 1887, under the press of clinical necessity, he tried Breuer's idea and found it enormously useful. He then persuaded Breuer to prepare a joint publication which should include Breuer's case of Anna O., Freud's cases in which he also emphasized emotional catharsis, and a theoretical statement about how catharsis or abreaction of feelings might be supposed to work to effect symptom relief. Freud had to persuade Breuer to agree to this publication. He was much more in need of making a career than Breuer, whose career was very well established.

Freud was particularly eager that the concept of emotional catharsis or abreaction, which connected mental illness to patients' emotional life, should be recognized as different from Charcot's teaching. Charcot, and his pupil, Janet, understood the phenomena of hysteria as involving some kind of "psychic insufficiency," an inability on the patients' part to keep their consciousness intact. In this conception, the patients were thought to be suffering more from cognitive dysfunction than from emotional distress. Freud knew that a publication was expected from Janet in 1893 and he was also eager to forestall his rival. (A few years later, in 1898, he wrote to Fliess: "I picked up a recent book of Janet's on hysteria and *idées fixes* with beating heart and laid it down again with my pulse returned to normal. He has no suspicion of the clue" (Freud, 1954, p. 247).)

In his autobiography, Freud speaks as if he had been the first to use hypnosis to induce catharsis instead of (in the conventional manner) to suggest symptom disappearance. Actually it was Breuer who was the first to do so. Freud himself, moreover, made quite a bit of use of conventional hypnosis. In fact, in 1892 he published a fascinating account of how he hypnotized a young mother who was unable to nurse her first baby. He describes the young woman as a healthy personality who had fallen into a hysterical state just whenever she had to nurse the baby (an *"hysterique d'occasion,"* as Charcot would have said). When Freud was brought in to see her (by Breuer, who made the referral), her abdomen was distended, she was vomiting, unable either to eat or to retain food, and flushed with fury at herself for her inability to nurse. Freud used hypnosis to suggest to her that she would be able to nurse, and after a few days and a few repetitions of hypnotic suggestion she was perfectly able to do so. With the advent of her second child, a similar set of events occurred, and still a third repetition with the third baby. In the intervals between deliveries, however, the patient was perfectly well.

Freud ascribes her inability to nurse to an anxiety that she would be unable to live up to expectations. He also picks up the patient's shame on needing treatment. "'I felt ashamed,' the woman said to me [explaining her hostility to him], 'that a thing like hypnosis should be successful where I myself, with all my will-power, was helpless'" (Freud, 1892, p. 120). Freud does not elaborate on the possibility that shame at her failure might have increased her initial anxiety. He describes the patient as being beset by "antithetical ideas" or a "counter-will" which "put itself into effect by an innervation of her body" because she was either excited or exhausted by her first delivery. This counter-will is responsible also for the "hysterical deliria" which in the Middle Ages took the form of "violent blasphemies and inhibited erotic thoughts" (p. 126). In this comment, Freud was thus expressing the idea that mental illness is the product of moral struggles over forbidden wishes. In this rich clinical account, however, Freud was making use of straight hypnotic suggestion rather than catharsis, even though he later claimed to have used catharsis "from the first."

In addition to the issue of catharsis versus conventional use of hypnosis the two authors of *Studies on Hysteria* were also dealing with the issue of the sexual etiology of neurosis. Breuer had told Freud of Anna O.'s inhibited sexual fantasies. But what Freud did not know then, because Breuer had not yet told him, was that Breuer had terminated his treatment of Anna O. because she had made a sexual advance to him. As Freud later tells the story, Anna O. had said, while having an (hysterical) attack of abdominal cramps, "Dr. Breuer's child is coming," thus revealing her childbirth fantasies and her sexual longings for Breuer. Why Breuer should have been so frightened by this advance can only be the subject of speculation, but the mores of nineteenth-century Vienna before the development of psychoanalysis made his position difficult. Freud later interpreted Breuer's reluctance to publish *Studies on Hysteria* as the product of guilt over the case of Anna O.

The full story of these events, however, will never be known. Freud's version of it is that he reconstructed the facts after the publication of *Studies on Hysteria*, taxed Breuer with the reconstruction, and obtained an admission from him. But the circumstances of this story are still very puzzling. In his case account in *Studies on Hysteria*, Breuer makes no mention at all of these events. He describes his case as having a successful termination. In direct contrast, Freud is said by Strachey (the editor of the definitive edition of Freud's works) to have pointed his finger to the text (p. 40) and told of a hiatus in the case account. According to Freud's letters, Breuer had abandoned Anna O. to a colleague on account of her sexual advance, and in consequence she had been rehospitalized for several months before regaining her sanity. Thus, the question whether Breuer's treatment was successful or not cannot be answered. That Breuer's treatment was not totally destructive to her is attested by the fact that Anna O., whose real name was Bertha Pappenheim, went on to have a distinguished career as a pioneer social worker and feminist (Pollock, 1973).

It may also have been that Breuer was reluctant to continue working with Freud because he found it difficult to accept the sexual etiology of hysteria on intellectual as well as personal grounds. In a letter to Fliess, dated

1895, a few months after their joint publication, Freud (1954) describes the following scene: "Not long ago Breuer made a big speech to the physician's society about me, putting himself forward as a convert to the belief in sexual etiology. When I thanked him privately for this he spoiled my pleasure by saying: 'But all the same I *don't* believe it.' Can you make head or tail of that? I cannot" (p. 134).

It is impossible from this account to know just what aspect of the sexual etiology of hysteria Breuer did not believe. Freud himself believed for a time that hysterical women patients had been seduced in childhood by their fathers or brothers. So, for example, in a letter to Fliess in 1897 (Freud, 1954, pp. 195–196) Freud describes a patient who "confirms" his "theory of paternal aetiology." "It has nothing to do with my brother," said the patient. "So it was your father, then," replied Freud. "Then it came out that when she was between eight and twelve her allegedly otherwise admirable and high-principled father used regularly to take her into bed with him and to practice external ejaculation (to make wet) with her. Even at the time she felt anxiety . . . Quod erat demonstrandum."

But some months later, again in a letter to Fliess (p. 215), Freud acknowledges that he was mistaken in believing his women patients' stories of sexual seduction in childhood. He had discovered that their accounts were sometimes (although not always) fantasies which, given the nature of primary-process transformations, had the same emotional status in their lives as reality. It should be noted, at this point, that Freud did not suppose that all accounts of father–daughter incest were untrue, but he "could not imagine that perverted acts against children were so general" (p. 216). As we shall see later in this chapter, we now know that the incidence of father–daughter incest is much greater than had previously been supposed (Herman and Hirschman, 1977) and that the psychological effects on the daughters are still as severe as they were in Freud's time. In any case, Breuer's reluctance to go along with Freud on the issue of sexual etiology of neurosis may not have been so completely puzzling as Freud made it out to be in his letter to Fliess. It may have been a disagreement over the issue of actual paternal seduction.

Or, as another possible source of disagreement, Breuer may have been unwilling to accept sexual etiology as the *only* cause of neurotic symptoms. This is just the issue over which Freud broke with his students, Adler and Jung, even though Freud himself was later to disavow a belief in sexual etiology as the *only* cause. Breuer himself is emphatic in naming sex as *a* source of hysterical symptoms. Speaking in general theoretical terms about the "instincts" which cause increases in excitation which in turn cannot be discharged, Breuer emphasized (Breuer and Freud, 1893–1895, p. 200) the importance of the "sexual instinct as the most powerful source of persisting increases of excitation (and consequently of neurosis)." But he does not say that it is the only source.

Freud's interpretation of Breuer's reluctance to continue working with him was that Breuer lacked the moral courage to face the opprobrium that was the consequence of stressing sex in nineteenth-century Vienna. In his autobiography, Freud writes, sadly, that his pursuit of psychoanalysis cost him Breuer's friendship. But one wonders whether Freud's personal vulnerability was not already in evidence in the trouble with Breuer that surrounded this first, seminal publication.

In summary, then, the two authors were dealing with three important issues in *Studies on Hysteria*. First, Breuer's "accidental" discovery that hypnosis is better used to evoke an emotional catharsis than for suggesting symptoms away; second, the corollary discovery that hysteria is based on emotional turmoil rather than on "psychic insufficiency"; and third, that a specific emotion, sexual longing, is a particularly powerful and frequent cause of neurotic symptoms. The difficulties and disagreements that the two authors had over these points were the symptoms of unsolved problems in understanding complicated psychological events, as well as of their personal vulnerabilities. In the preface to the second edition of *Studies on Hysteria*, in 1908, Freud emphasized how far psychoanalysis had gone beyond the "simple" catharsis that he and Breuer had espoused. But whether patients can benefit from hypnosis as an aid to catharsis, or from the more general personality reorganization that classical psychoanalysis now recommends, is still a wide-open question today.

Let us turn now to the text of *Studies on Hysteria* to see how cases sounded in 1895, and where we stand today.

In a forthright opening paragraph of their preliminary communication Breuer and Freud tell us that hysterical illness is based on memories of unpleasant emotional events. It is instructive to note that their very next point addresses itself to the issue of whether the hysterical symptoms are "idiopathic" (a formal way of saying that the symptoms are without cause) or clearly connected in meaning to the content of the emotional stress. (The idea that the sense of hysterical symptoms is unimportant or at least irrelevant to treatment is still with us today in the "hard-nosed" thinking of some therapists who employ hypnotic suggestion or behavior modification.)

Breuer and Freud give some examples of instances in which the connection between symptoms and emotional events is easy to comprehend. A "painful emotion" arises during a meal, is "suppressed at the time," and then produces "nausea and vomiting which persist for months in the form of hysterical vomiting" (p. 4). "A girl [Anna O.] watching beside a sick-bed in a torment of anxiety, fell into a twilight state and had a terrifying hallucination [a snake crawling toward her] while her right arm, which was hanging over the back of her chair, went to sleep; from this developed a paresis of the same arm, accompanied by contracture and anaesthesia" (p. 4). "A highly intelligent man was present while his brother had an ankylosed hip-joint extended under an anaesthetic. At the instant at which the joint gave way with a crack, he felt a violent pain in his own hip-joint which persisted for nearly a year" (p. 5).

In these instances, the mechanism Breuer and Freud are invoking to explain the connection between event and symptoms is something like the formation of a conditioned response that is learned or fixed with a single trial. Such instances of one-trial conditioning have indeed been demonstrated by experimental psychologists. They can occur especially when there is powerful emotion (which activates the autonomic nervous system), and when the conditioned response is itself a part of the emotional experience. If, for example, you fall off a bicycle, the fright you experience is congruent with the danger of falling. It can occur the next time you mount a bicycle even though you are now not falling. Behavior-modification techniques of therapy current today make use of the concept of conditioning or deconditioning the patient into a more comfortable response to the originally distressing situation. Hypnotic suggestion has the same purpose, although it uses different methods.

The examples cited by Breuer and Freud all involve an emotional experience that rests upon an emotional connection between the patient and some other important person. A man experiences an empathetic pain at the moment he hears his brother's joint crack; a woman is in a state of anxiety at someone's sickbed; a girl suppresses a painful emotion during a meal, either out of love or fear of someone else who is presumably present, but in either case not without resentment at the someone in whose interest the emotion is suppressed. As we can see, it is easy to think of emotion as an internal arousal (which it is), and also to think of it as a connection to someone else (which it also is). This difference in viewpoint can become a difference in theorizing about emotions.

In their first statement about the therapy of hysteria, Breuer and Freud tell us that to their "great surprise *each individual hysterical symptom immediately and permanently disappeared when we had succeeded in bringing clearly to light the memory of the event by which it was provoked and in arousing its accompanying affect and when the patient had described that event in the greatest possible detail and had put the affect into words. Recollection without affect almost invariably produces no result*" (p. 6) (Breuer and Freud's italics).

In this statement, two therapeutic factors are named: the recall of the forgotten memory of the unpleasant event and the release of the accompanying affect. It is clear that the recall of the forgotten memory is not sufficient and it is definitely not an end in itself. Recall of memories is merely a means to the release of affect. Hypnosis, moreover, is merely a technique by which memories are jogged; the hypnotic state for some reason is one in which unpleasant memories are more readily recovered. This is a very different attitudinal framework from the one psychoanalysis developed later: namely, that only full recall of childhood memories constitutes a successful analysis, and that the "best" therapeutic technique is one which aims at childhood reconstruction. Conventional psychoanalytic wisdom has it that psychoanalysis has proceeded "beyond catharsis," but without any demonstrable evidence that catharsis was an inferior technique. Needless to say, many present-day non-psychoanalytic therapies aim directly at catharsis, again without clear-cut evidence that catharsis alone will do the trick.

Breuer and Freud do not at first address themselves to the question of why release of affect is therapeutic, but rather to the question of why their patients' memories of unpleasant events did not fade away after the manner of most memories. The explanation they give clearly rests on the assumption that affects must "discharge"; they become attached to memories when they are not discharged. Although Breuer and Freud use the terminology of physiology, the examples they give are all drawn from the subtleties of interpersonal relations. Affects remain charged when the appropriate emotional relationship to someone cannot be made to prevail. "An injury that has been repaid," they write, "even if only in words, is recollected differently from one that has had to be accepted. Language recognizes this distinction, too, in its mental and physical consequences; it very characteristically describes an injury that has been suffered in silence as 'a mortification' [*Kränkung*, literally, making ill]" (p. 8). Mortification and its appropriate repayment, revenge upon or humiliation of the other one, can be carried out in exquisite ways, all of which depend on the fact that our emotional connectedness makes us very vulnerable to emotional hurt. Breuer and Freud go on to cite frequent circumstances in which appropriate reactions are excluded, and all of them involve interpersonal considerations. So, for example, they cite the trauma of the loss of a loved person, or something the patient "wished to forget," by implication something either guilt- or shame-connected. They cite, as another condition of unavailable discharge, the possibility that the patient was already so overwrought by terror or other paralyzing emotion as to be in a "hypnoid state." They are aware that this kind of situation may be one in which the neurotic state has already been formed.

Breuer and Freud end their preliminary communication with a summary of why their procedure is therapeutic. "It brings to an end the operative force of the idea which was not abreacted in the first instance, by allowing its strangulated affect to find a way out through speech; and it subjects it to associative correction by introducing it into normal consciousness (under light hypnosis) or by removing it through the physician's suggestion" (p. 17). The two authors are very cautious about the usefulness of their procedure — they do not claim to cure hysteria or to prevent the recurrence of "hypnoid states." But they claim that their "radical" treatment is superior in efficacy to "direct suggestion as it is practiced today by psychotherapists" (p. 17). These words, written in 1892, have a most familiar ring in the world of psychotherapy today, although the shoe is now on the other foot. "Radical" treatments, more like direct suggestion, and supposedly more effective than psychotherapy or psychoanalysis, are now being proposed.

Let us look next at Breuer and Freud's case accounts. The one reference to a man who experienced an empathetic pain on hearing his brother's hip joint crack is not further developed, and thus all the case histories are of women. Four of the five women whose cases are presented — Anna O., Emmy von N., Elisabeth von R., and Lucy, the governess — are well educated, have middle-class values, and are dissatisfied with the lot of women. The case of Dora, published by Freud in 1905, also fits this pattern. Dora, who was planning to go to the University was also a middle-class young woman, extremely intelligent, with strong ethical values, and dissatisfied with the socially inferior lot of women.

The one exception in the group is Katharina, an ignorant country servant girl, who was being sexually molested by her father. An interesting sidelight occurs in connection with Katharina. In the case account, which is written by Freud, he disguises the story by saying that she was being molested by her uncle. Only many years later did he amend the account with an apology for the falsification he deemed necessary at the time. But such was the horror of father–daughter incest that the case account seemed to call for this attempt at softening the reality. The liberalization of opinion since Freud's time (partly as a result of his work) has made it possible to call into question whether incest is so awful a crime. In thinking about this ethical issue, feminists (Herman and Hirschman, 1977) point to the exploitation of the young and helpless woman by the more powerful man as the personal crime, while the noted anthropologist Yehudi Cohen (1978), a liberal male, wonders whether the horror of incest is not some outmoded remnant of primitive times. This is the same issue that Freud sidestepped in the case of Dora, as we shall see later on in this chapter.

Let us consider first the story of Anna O. Breuer describes her as "markedly intelligent, with an astonishingly quick grasp of things and penetrating intuition. She possessed a powerful intellect which would have been capable of digesting solid mental pabulum and which stood in need of it — though without receiving it after she left school" (p. 21). "This girl," Breuer continues, "who was bubbling over with intellectual vitality, led an extreme-

ly monotonous existence in her puritanically-minded family. She embellish-
ed her life in a manner which probably influenced her decisively in the direction of her illness, by indulging in systematic daydreaming, which she
described as her 'private theater'" (p. 22).

In this description Breuer is depicting not only the familiar emptiness of
puritanical middle-class life, especially for women who have no vocation,
but he points to a "solution" — daydreaming — which makes life tolerable
without open protest. The gentle erotization of forbidden rage (forbidden
because the target of it is loved as well as hated) makes sweet daytime fantasies especially compelling. The daydreamer, however, is juggling a public
and a private life, fearing the shame of exposure. The complete explication of
the many levels of existence which find their outlet in pleasurable fantasies
and particularly in their specifically sexual quality was to await Freud's later
work on "primary-process transformation." What Breuer was describing in
Anna's case was the "double life" of which she was ashamed and which made
her vulnerable to "hypnoid states" and thence to hysterical symptoms.

In July of 1880, Anna's passionately loved father fell ill (as it turned out,
terminally) with a lung abscess. During the first months of his illness Anna
devoted herself to nursing him, and was accustomed to taking the night shift
to relieve her mother. During the nursing, her own health deteriorated — she
had been eating little, sleeping less, and finally became so physically weak
that in December she took to her bed, unable to nurse her father any longer.
She remained bedridden until April 1, when her father died. For two days
after his death, Anna was better. But after the funeral she became suicidal to
the point where Breuer insisted on her being hospitalized.

During her illness, which Breuer quickly diagnosed as psychological
rather than physical in origin, she suffered all manner of hysterical symptoms: pains in her legs, contracture of her arm, a convergent squint of her
eyes, and, worst of all, hallucinatory states in which she was "naughty —
that is to say she was abusive, used to throw cushions at people, tore buttons
off her bedclothes and linen with those of her fingers she could move, and so
on" (p. 24). During these "absences," as Breuer called them following the terminology of Charcot, she would have hallucinatory experiences, for example, seeing her hair as snakes, at the same time telling herself not to be so silly, that it was only hair. She complained of "having two selves, a real one
and an evil one" (p. 24).

As we saw earlier, Breuer made the discovery that if he put her under
hypnosis during these "absences" or bad states, she recalled very vividly
scenes connected with her father's illness in which each of her particular current symptoms was embedded. Breuer relates that he for the first time caught
on to the connection between her emotional state and her symptoms when he
observed that she had been "very much offended" by something and had

determined not to speak of it. (He does not say what the something was.) When he had guessed this and obliged her to speak of it, her completely mute condition which had been in progress for two weeks cleared up completely (p. 25). He observed, further, that on days when she really was able to talk things out she was better, and on other days, when she was unable to do so, she was worse.

Breuer also makes the observation, which is an interesting indication of the patient–therapist relationship, that his system would work for two days and then on the third day his ministrations would not be effective. She would be "nasty" to him. This is really the first observation of the negative transference. As Breuer puts it, following Anna O.'s own view of things, when she was normal she was her "good self"; crazy was the "bad self." This is, unfortunately, still a mode of description that prevails in psychiatry today, whether in the sophisticated language of psychoanalysis, which describes the patient as too "narcissistic" or too "regressed," or in the grosser language of behavior modification, which suggests that patients be "rewarded" for noncrazy, that is, "good" behavior. With hindsight, it seems self-evident that Anna was nasty to Breuer out of unacknowledged shame at being a patient. But, as in the case of Christoph Haizmann, or in Freud's case of the nursing mother whom he hypnotized, affects of shame and guilt were noticed by Breuer and Freud but they attributed the patients' behavior to more "scientific" causes, such as strong instincts.

Freud's case of Emmy von N., the next one reported, is of particular interest because in it Freud discovered that memories of traumatic events can continue to be operative over many years. Frau Emmy was a widowed housewife, about forty years old, and the mother of two adolescent daughters. She was the thirteenth of fourteen children brought up with great severity and strictness. When she was twenty-three she met and married an extremely gifted and able man who had made a high position for himself as an industrialist, but was much older than she was. After a short marriage he died of a stroke and she was left with the task of bringing up two small daughters. To this task she attributed her own illness. The girls were sixteen and fourteen years old, often ailing and suffering from nervous troubles, when Freud was called in. Since her husband's death fourteen years earlier she had been suffering with nervous complaints, and traveling from one doctor and sanitarium to another in the hope of relief. Freud's first prescription in the case was that she separate from her two daughters (who were in the care of their governess) and enter a nursing home where he could see her every day. "This she agreed to without raising the slightest objection" (p. 50). (Clearly, Freud caught on quickly to the probability that she needed relief from her guilt over resenting her children.)

When Freud first saw Frau Emmy, he says that "she still looked young and had finely-cut features, full of character" (p. 48). She was obviously very depressed and agitated, keeping her fingers tightly clasped, and there were "convulsive, tic-like movements of her face and neck. . . . Furthermore she frequently interrupted her remarks by producing a curious 'clacking' sound which defies imitation" (p. 49). Every two or three minutes she would interrupt her perfectly coherent conversation to exclaim, "Keep still — don't say anything!" or "Don't touch me!" apparently without even noticing that she had interrupted her own train of thought.

Frau Emmy herself attributed her illness to the "troubles" of raising two children. The specifics of her story suggest that these troubles were compounded by a number of especially difficult life circumstances. Her husband's death was particularly traumatic for her; he had collapsed and died just a few days after the birth of her second child. This child was then seized with a serious illness which lasted for six months, during which she herself had been in bed with a high fever. "And there now followed in chronological order her grievances against this child which she threw out rapidly with an angry look on her face, in the way one would speak of someone who had become a nuisance" (p. 60). It became clear (while she was under hypnosis) that she had "hated this child for three years because she always told herself that she might have been able to nurse her husband back to health if she had not been in bed on account of the child." This child was still another source of guilt: She had always been fonder of her elder child than of this younger one — although no one would have "guessed it from my behavior. I did everything that was necessary" (p. 64). In addition to this chronic source of guilt, Frau Emmy had had to contend with the humiliated fury evoked by being the object of calumny by her husband's relatives, who were sure that she had married him for his money, and went so far as to spread the rumor that she had poisoned him. They had gotten a libelous journalist to print articles in the newspapers and then sent her the newspaper clippings. This had been the origin of her hatred of all strangers.

Frau Emmy's life in her family of origin was also the source of many traumatic events; for example, being witness while a cousin (who was "queer in the head") had all his teeth pulled out in one sitting. This was a recollection that was connected with her often repeated phrase "Don't touch me!" Her older brother had become a morphine addict. She had nursed this sick brother through his fearful attacks, during which he often seized hold of her. This memory connected to the memory of a time when her (hated) younger daughter, in a delirium, had also seized hold of her. Again this recollection was expressed in her phrase "Don't touch me!" At fifteen she had come home and found her mother lying on the floor, felled by a stroke; at nineteen she had come home to find her mother dead, with a distorted face. These were, as it happened, the very events that were repeated in the circumstances of her husband's death from a stroke.

Freud was also able to help her unravel the memories that gave rise to the "clacking" sound that so often interrupted her speech. This particular symptom had first occurred during a severe fright. She was driving with the children through a forest when a severe thunderstorm broke. A tree just in front of the horses was struck by lightning and one of the horses shied. She had the thought: "You must keep still now, or your screaming will frighten the horses even more and the coachman won't be able to hold them in at all." At that moment she uttered the "clacking" sound. It is as if the very severity of her demand upon herself were countered by an involuntary motor inner-vation which produced just the opposite result, bringing the patient into a state of helplessness.

Freud remarks about how "morally oversensitive" Frau Emmy was, and how profound was her "tendency to self-depreciation." He tells us that he brought this characteristic of hers to her attention with the hope of modify-ing the severity of her self-reproaches. "But," he continues, somewhat wryly, "she did not take in my lesson, I fancy, any more than would an ascetic medieval monk, who sees the finger of God or a temptation of the Devil in every trivial event of his life, and who is incapable of picturing the world even for a brief moment or in its smallest corner as being without reference to himself" (pp. 65–66).

Freud had a very high opinion of Frau Emmy's character. For example, he attributed her refusal to remarry to a wish to protect the fortune of her two children, which would have been injured by a new marriage, and to her sensible fear of fortune hunters.

> The moral seriousness with which she viewed her duties, her intelligence and energy, which were no less than a man's, and her high degree of education and love of truth impressed both of us [Breuer and himself] greatly; while her benevolent care for the welfare of her dependents, her humility of mind and the refinement of her manners revealed her true qualities as a lady. To describe such a woman as a "degenerate" would be to distort the meaning of that word out of all recognition (p. 103–104).

This early attitude of respect for the hysterical patient is quite unlike the pe-jorative attitudes which then prevailed, and which once again surround hysteria today.

But the outcome of Freud's treatment of Frau Emmy was a disappoint-ment. She fell ill again when her elder (favorite) daughter began to oppose her. In a footnote to the case, written in 1924, Freud tells that other doctors had had his experience of helping her, only to discover that she was ill again and in the hands of still other doctors. The favorite elder daughter, moreover, subsequently worte to Freud in an effort to have the mother declared mentally incompetent, describing her as a cruel and ruthless tyrant who refused to help her children financially. (This daughter had obtained a doctor's degree and was married.) In his footnote, Freud acknowledges that he had paid insufficient attention to the immediate emotional situation surrounding Frau Emmy's illness when he was treating her: there was someone who had then wanted to marry her, but this would have meant that her two daughters, not herself, would have been the principal beneficiaries of their father's fortune.

If, as appears from this remark, Frau Emmy did not remarry because she would lose her husband's fortune to the children, her motives may not have been so high-minded as Freud had thought. One can speculate that the cause of her continuing illness was her guilt over her own "selfishness" in wanting to hold on to her husband's money — a topic too shameful, therefore, to be discussed with Freud. One also realizes that the fact that a widow's inherited fortune would be hers only as long as she did not remarry was an instance of the social inferiority of women, out of which background Frau Emmy's conflict arose. As for Freud, his disappointment in the fact that his treatment did not hold is clearly apparent in the less admiring and somewhat vexatious tone of his 1924 footnote.

The case of the governess, Miss Lucy R., is an important one in that it is an instance of a cure that seemed to hold, and an instance of the complete resolution of the feelings that were involved. Unlike the case of Emmy von N., in which Freud did not explore the patient's most immediate emotional difficulty, Lucy's feelings were rather quickly discovered and they ceased to be a source of distress. Lucy was a young Englishwoman, employed in the home of a managing director of a factory. Very simply, she was in love with her employer, and hoped to marry him. Her symptoms of depression, and of a chronic rhinitis and some hallucinatory experiences in which she thought she smelled cigar smoke, were readily traced by Freud to the complicated feelings she was experiencing about her employer. By the time of Lucy's case Freud had grown tired of the repetitious formulas that are needed for inducing hypnosis. Moreover, he had had, ever since Breuer's case of Anna O., clear indications that hypnosis itself was nothing more than a means to catharsis. So in Lucy's case, when he discovered that she did not fall into anything like a hypnotic state, he gave up hypnosis and substituted the pressure of his hand on her forehead. As he puts it, the important thing is that the patients "learn to relax their critical faculty" (p. 111).

The dialogue between Freud and Lucy on the subject of her feelings about her employer is worth reading, since it reflects the difficulty people have (both the listener and the speaker) in dealing with feelings of shame. After thinking over what Lucy had told him about her feelings for the children she was supervising (their dead mother had been a distant relation), and the feelings she had that the house servants were treating her without their usual respect,

> I was bold enough to inform my patient of [this] interpretation: "I cannot think that these are all the reasons for your feelings about the children. I believe that really you are in love with your employer, the Director, though perhaps without being aware of it yourself, and that you have a secret hope of taking their mother's place in actual fact. And then we must remember the sensitiveness you now feel toward the servants, after having lived with them peacefully for years. You're afraid of their having some inkling of your hopes and making fun of you." She answered in her usual laconic fashion: "Yes, I think that's true." — "But if you loved your employer, why didn't you tell me?" — "I didn't know, or rather I didn't want to know. I wanted to drive it out of my head and not think of it again; and I believe latterly I have succeeded." — "Why was it that you were unwilling to admit this inclination? Were you ashamed of loving a man?" "Oh, no, I'm not unreasonably prudish. We're not responsible for our feelings, anyhow. It was distressing to me only because he is my employer and I am in his service and live in his house. I don't feel the same complete independence towards him that I could towards anyone else. And then I am only a poor girl and he is such a rich man of good family. People would laugh at me if they had any idea of it" (p. 117).

What is so striking about this dialogue is the way in which Lucy denies that she is ashamed of her unrequited love since it is not reasonable to be ashamed. But in spite of her good sense her imagery is all of someone "put down" and the subject of ridicule. There is humiliated fury in the loss of her feelings of independence and in the imagery of people laughing at her. Freud, for his part, appears very naive in asking her why she didn't just tell him she was in love with her employer, as though that kind of admission could be made without embarrassment. Neither the patient nor Freud is really willing to take her feelings of shame seriously. And yet those feelings are clearly creating an upheaval in her life.

Lucy's cigar-smell symptoms did not disappear after this dialogue, nor did her mood seem much improved. Continuing his inquiry into the details of her experience, Freud discovered that her sensitivity to smell had its origin in a very painful scene with her employer. The Director had some weeks before talked to her quite intimately about the children's future, and it was on this occasion that she first realized she loved him. But some weeks later, without any real provocation that she could understand he scolded Lucy severely, in the most humiliating way, for permitting a friend of the family to kiss the children on the mouth. This, he said, was a grievous dereliction of duty, and if it ever happened again he would dismiss her. Thus abruptly had her hopes about him been dashed. And it was this scene of her humiliated, throttled fury that had become accidentally connected to the smell of cigar smoke.

A few days after this clarification, Lucy appeared in excellent spirits. So much so, that Freud for a moment thought that her employer had become her fiancé. "But no, nothing had changed. 'It's just that you don't know me . . . I'm always cheerful as a rule.' — Are you still in love with your employer?' — 'Yes, I certainly am, but that makes no difference'" (p. 121). Freud then examined her nose and found it no longer sensitive to pain. Her sense of smell was fairly well restored. This recovery occurred over a nine-week period, and when Freud accidentally met her some four months later she told him that her recovery had been maintained. Not only had Lucy's longings for her employer been talked out, but her feelings of shame had been confronted and overcome without being called shame.

In the case of Elisabeth von R., Freud abandoned hypnosis entirely in favor of the method of free association. Elisabeth's symptoms were pains in her legs and inability to walk. She was the youngest of three daughters in a prestigious Hungarian family. Her mother was troubled with an eye affliction and with nervous complaints. Her father, in contrast, was a vigorous and lively man to whom Elisabeth was much drawn, as he was to her because of her vivaciousness. He used to say of her that she "took the place of a son" (p. 140). He also used to say that she would have trouble getting a man because of her "cheekiness" and "cocksureness," and also her ambition to be a musician which made her "greatly discontented with being a girl" (*Ibid.*).

Elisabeth's beloved father fell seriously ill when she was in her late teens and she nursed him tenderly until his death. (Breuer and Freud remark on how many cases of hysteria have involved patients who had nursed loved ones.) Both Elisabeth's sisters married, creating a loss in her family; in the case of the elder sister, the loss was the greater since this sister's husband was unfriendly. The second sister's marriage was to a more agreeable man, but unfortunately this sister became sick during her second pregnancy and died in childbirth. It was at the precise moment when she heard the news of her sister's death that Elisabeth had the thought, which flashed like lightning through her mind, "Now he is free again. I can be his wife!" (p. 156). And at that instant, the pains in her legs began. The hysterical symptoms thus occurred in the context of a sexual attraction "whose acceptance was resisted by her whole moral being" (p. 157).

As in the case of Lucy, Freud seems here to have been peculiarly insensitive to the exquisitely painful and humiliating nature of unrequited love. The phenomenology of this acutely painful shame state — all the more painful because the person in it rejects it intellectually as "silly" or inappropriate — was taken for granted rather than analyzed by Freud. So, for example, he not only interpreted her love for her brother-in-law to Elisabeth, but he discussed it with Elisabeth's mother, obtaining from the latter information about the brother-in-law with which he sought to persuade Elisabeth that the match was not suitable. After the treatment was terminated, on the whole with much relief of Elisabeth's symptoms, her mother raised the subject with her of the brother-in-law, at which point, understandably, Elisabeth flew into a rage at Freud for betraying her personal secret. Simultaneously the pains returned. The episode is often cited, along with others, as an indication of Freud's early blindness to the "transference" and to "countertransference" feelings on the therapist's part. It is an instance of the blindness of inexperience, certainly, but one reason for it was his tendency to turn away from the specifics of an emotional experience into formulations about instincts and discharge mechanisms. And, inevitably, it was also difficult for a sensible, rational man like Freud to take seriously the humiliations of women. His own attitudes contained built-in sexist prejudices which made these humiliations seem as absurd or "exaggerated" as they felt to the patients themselves. This point is most clearly illustrated in the case of Dora, to which we shall shortly turn.

One other important observation emerged in Elisabeth's case. This was the existence of "symbolic" representations in the details of hysterical symptoms. In previous cases, Breuer and Freud had discerned only "accidental" connections between a symptom and the emotional state of the patient at the time it arose. Lucy had been humiliated by her employer (for letting someone kiss the children on the mouth), and this humiliation was connected to cigar smoking, of which her employer happened to be fond. In the case of Elisabeth, the pains in her legs were not accidentally conditioned responses which happened to occur in some traumatic scene, but a way of making it impossible that she should ever be *able* to marry her brother-in-law. The pains in Elisabeth's legs were "a somatic expression for her lack of an independent position and her inability to make any alteration in her circumstances" (p. 176), and the symptoms thus served as a "defense" against forbidden resentment and forbidden longings. These symptoms formed by using the language of these strong feelings as a bridge between the feeling and its somatic innervation. "I cannot stand it" became literally a feeling of being unable to stand.

Similar "symbolic" connections are described in the case of Frau Caecilie M., who, having had the thought that insult feels like "a slap in the face," actually developed a facial neuralgia. An everyday phrase for being slighted or insulted is "stabbed to the heart." Freud speculates that this figure of speech would not have evolved unless there were, in fact, some precordial sensations at the moment of an insult.

> What could be more probable than that the figure of speech "swallowing something," which we use in talking of an insult to which no rejoinder has been made, did in fact originate in the innervatory sensations which arise in the pharynx when we refrain from speaking and prevent ourselves from reacting to the insult? All these sensations and innervations belong to the field of the *Expres-*

sion of the Emotions, which as Darwin (1872) taught us consists of actions which originally had a meaning and a purpose (p. 181).

Whether or not this adaptive function is served by innervations in the pharynx when we swallow an insult, strong emotions of humiliated, throt-tled fury are being described. These are worth describing in their own right and in their own language, and not only because of their hypothetical in-stinctive basis.

The clearest instance of the neglect of a patient's actual emotional state because of a theoretical attachment to "instinctual forces" is to be found in the case of Dora. Freud published this case in 1905, after he had worked out the details of primary-process transformations of strangulated affect in dreams. The case also seemed to Freud to be a clear example of symptoms arising out of throttled sexual longing, an emotional state which he could base upon the sexual instinct. But as one reads this case today, one can see how much of the patient's actual emotional situation Freud missed com-prehending. One can also see how his sexist bias joined with his scientism to blind him to the unbearable, covert aggression that was being directed against his patient from the "loving" and beloved parental figures. Freud's sharp clinical acumen made it possible for him to describe (from his own male point of view) the sexual situation Dora was in, but he could not quite empathize with Dora's oppressed situation as an intelligent adolescent girl in a patriarchal family.

Let us first briefly review the outline of Dora's case history (Freud, 1905c). A young girl of eighteen tells her father that Herr K., a close friend of the family, has made sexual advances to her. It is a terrible accusation. Dora's father says he does not believe her. Herr K. and Frau K. are Dora's parents' closest friends; Dora had often visited the K.s, loved them both, and had cared for their children. Dora is so enraged by her father's refusal to believe her that she falls unconscious after they have had an argument about it. She has also become so depressed that the next day she leaves a suicide note. Dora had been suffering from a variety of mysterious physical ailments for at least two years previously. She sometimes couldn't eat; sometimes she lost her voice; sometimes she had terrible headaches − in short, a case of hysterical conversion. Her suicide threat pushed Dora's father into con-sulting Freud about his nervous daughter, the father's purpose being to have Freud help Dora get over her neurotic nonsense.

Freud's first task in this case was to ascertain the truth of the situation, and to refuse to collude with Dora's father in a denial of it. The introduction to the case consists of Freud's account of the father's shrewdness in bringing Dora to Freud for help. Freud is not reproachful of the father for lying to Dora; he rather understands that the father was "one of those men who know how to evade a dilemma by falsifying their judgment upon one of the alternatives" (p. 34). In fact, Freud is eager to show Dora that *she* had neurotic reasons for insisting on the truth — namely, that she herself is a dissembler.

Dora's actual situation was this: Her father was having an affair with Frau K. Because of this affair, it was convenient for Dora's father to look away from the sexual advances Herr K. might have made to Dora. Herr K. had denied Dora's story. Dora's father was only too eager not to stir up Herr K.'s anger, since that might make K. fuss about his wife. So, Dora's father sided with Herr K. and Dora correctly suspected that she was being disbelieved by her father in the interest of her father's affair with Frau K. Dora was thus in the midst of a dreadful game that the supposedly loving adults around her were playing, a game Freud briefly acknowledges was calculated to drive anyone crazy and then turns aside from confronting.

Here, then, was the emotional dilemma in which Dora's father had placed her: He knew that Herr K. had in fact made an advance to her, but he insisted on calling her story a fantasy! She knew that her father knew that he was unwilling to reproach Herr K. because he (her father) was having an affair with Frau K., and yet he wanted Dora to collude with him in pretending that nothing was happening. For Dora to know, as she did, that her father's refusal to believe her was dishonest was a double personal betrayal. And, in addition, to compound the betrayal, Frau K., whom Dora also loved, sided against her. She told the parents that Dora had an overexcited imagination, and betrayed the fact that she and Dora read books about sex together. Thus, Frau K. was also willing to sacrifice Dora in the interest of her own safety. Everyone was lying except Dora, who couldn't get her beloved father to say he believed her, although she knew he did!

Freud's focus in this complicated interpersonal story was not on Dora's humiliated fury at personal betrayal, but on her guilt over forbidden sexual excitement. He specifies the traumatic event which precipitated hysterical symptoms as the sexual advance Herr K. made to Dora, but he considers her reaction of disgust as neurotic. What Dora ought to have felt (had she not already been neurotic) was sexual excitement and gratification at Herr K.'s advances; that would have been the normal expression of her sexual instinct!

In the case account Freud reports some very brilliant analytic work, in which he makes use of Dora's dreams to try to persuade her that she did indeed welcome, if not solicit, Herr K.'s advances; that she was unconsciously in love with him; that K. was a surrogate for her own father, with whom she was also unconsciously in love and whose sexual advances she also wanted. In this assumption that she ought automatically to have responded with pleasure to K.'s advances, Freud reveals his sexism: A woman should be glad to respond to the sexual advances of a man; if she does not, it is because of her unresolved Oedipus complex — in Dora's case, because of her unresolved unconscious longing for her father.

Along with his sexist attitude, however, Freud had what were, for the time, very enlightened views about sex. In the case account he calls attention to this issue. For example, he admonishes any narrow-minded individual who would think it wrong to talk about sex with a young woman. He defends calling the parts of the anatomy by their correct names. He excoriates people who might read this case history for prurient reasons. He stoutly defends the correctness of his talking about fellatio with Dora.

Freud was also dimly aware of Dora's benignly degraded position as a young woman in Vienna's middle-class society. His very choice of the pseudonym, Dora, which he describes in *The Psychopathology of Everyday Life* (p. 241), reflects his sympathy with the downtrodden. Dora was the name by which Freud's sister's housemaid was known, even though that was not her real name. But the housemaid had the misfortune to have the same name as her mistress, Rosa, and was therefore arbitrarily assigned a new name by the mistress. Freud speaks with pity of the poor creature who is so dependent she cannot even have her own name. So his conscious attitude was one of sympathy for Dora's situation and enlightenment about the sexual passions in which she was involved, but he was unable to take seriously her feelings of personal betrayal, or to take seriously the attack on her innocence which Herr K.'s first advance to his fourteen-year-old "daughter-figure" represented.

My use of the word "innocence" may suggest to some readers some remnant of Victorian prudishness. Is there such a thing as "innocence" in a sexually enlightened age? If sex is nothing "dirty," why should it be contrasted with innocence? The point, I think, is not that sex is dirty, but that when it is introduced to a person in the context of the difference between generations — when, in other words, it is not between consenting adults with equally free options — it is exploitative and in that sense a profound violation of the younger (weaker) party's rights. Dora was not aware of her sexual longings toward her father presumably because the incest taboo had already done its work. Freud himself had already explicated in *Three Essays on Sexuality* (1905a) how, in a *normally* developing person, the childhood wish to copulate with the parent of the opposite sex is transformed into a variety of innocent substitute forms. When a "father-substitute" breaks the incest taboo he is violating the younger person's trust, and in so doing he is violating her rights. Nowhere does Freud make explicit that in this sense Dora was profoundly injured by both her father and Herr K.

The attitude with which Freud received Dora's rage at Herr K. and her father is similar in some respects to the attitude with which women's stories of rape are often still received today. Women are thought to be "hysterical" over rape because (unconsciously) it is what they really wanted. And their accusations are received with a built-in disbelief which is both more comfortable for their male listeners and more in keeping with an "enlightened" view of sex.

In 1977, a (male) judge in Madison, Wisconsin, went so far as to free a young man convicted of rape on the grounds that the woman must have asked for it. In this case, public indignation in an enlightened university town forced the recall of the judge. But the sexist notion that women unconsciously ask for rape has actually been fostered by psychoanalytic enlightenment toward sex.

Some of my readers may ask at this point: Was Dora not neurotic to have responded to Herr K.'s sexual advance by suffering for two years with nervous cough, headache, gastric pains, and finally a despair so profound that when her father said he disbelieved her she considered taking her life? The answer is that of course Dora was neurotic — not, however, because she responded to Herr K.'s advances with disgust, but because she was unable herself to recognize the validity of her hatred and contempt for Herr K. and her father. Had she been able, for instance, to say to Herr K. on the spot something like, "Dirty old man — go choose someone your own age" or, "Don't forget the incest barrier," she might not have fallen ill. If, in other words, the extent of the covert aggression which was being directed against her could have been instantaneously apparent to her and she could have responded with some cool retaliation for the insult she had been offered, she might not have developed neurotic symptoms. In this formulation, it will be remembered, I am following Breuer and Freud's own dictum that "an injury suffered in silence" is a "mortification" (Kränkung, which means making ill). But if Freud, with all his sympathy for her, was unable to zero in on the extent to which she was a victim, how much less able was she to feel justified in hating the very people to whom she was most attached?

That somewhere she felt uncertain that she was justified was clear from the desperation with which she was trying to get her father to admit he believed her (that is, to side with her, since she knew he did believe her). What must have been torturing Dora is that she was not certain she was justified in her hatred. This is precisely the dilemma one is in when one is coping with the humiliated fury of being personally betrayed (rather than with clearly justified righteous indignation at some "objective" transgression). After all, the injury in personal betrayal is "only" to the "self."

It is clear that Freud felt sure she was not justified. So, for example, he tells us:

> When she was feeling embittered she used to be overcome by the idea that she had been handed over to Herr K. as the price of his tolerating the relations between her father and his wife; and her rage at her father for making such use of her was visi-

ble behind her affection for him. At other times, she was quite well aware that she had been guilty of exaggeration in talking like this. The two men had, of course, never made a formal agreement in which she was the object of barter; her father in particular would have been horrified at any such suggestion. But he was one of those men who knew how to evade a dilemma by falsifying their judgment (p. 34).

Since it was only a subjective reaction, Dora's mortification at being betrayed was an "exaggeration"; it had not the status of a proper reaction to a breach of "formal contract." Thus Freud, with all his enormous sensitivity to people's emotional situations, was unable to grasp the essential nature of Dora's emotional dilemma, and to help her to understand both the inevitability and the correctness of her emotional responses. Dora therefore remained guilty and ashamed for "exaggerating"; she remained ashamed of her humiliated fury as well as guilty for it. This "solution" was all the more inviting because it could leave her with the belief that her father "really" did love her, that she was *not* the victim of any betrayal because he loved Frau K. more.

Dora left treatment suddenly, in what Freud called an "unmistakable act of revenge" against him. What Freud could not comprehend was what he had done to deserve it. What he had been doing in the treatment was some brilliant analysis of the way her dreams could be interpreted to show her unconscious sexual longing for her father and for Herr K. Freud was also able to interpret Dora's unconscious homosexual longing for Frau K. The vagina as "jewel-box," "fire" as a reference to sexual excitement, early masturbation and bed-wetting episodes, were all interpretable in her dreams as "primary-process transformations" of sexual longing. What Freud did not perceive was that his line of interpretation was bound to evoke enormous shame in her (especially if it were true that she still loved Herr K. instead of despising him), and enormous fury at Freud in his blind insistence on dealing with only this part of her feelings. Dora's father, Herr K., Frau K., and now even Freud, were all implicitly demanding that Dora be more "loving" than Dora could possibly be. Dora must have left treatment with the conviction that nowhere could she find the vindication that was her due.

When Felix Deutsch (1957), a pupil of Freud's, was called into psychiatric consultation about Dora some twenty-five years later, he found her occupied with the same theme that had made her so distraught when she was Freud's patient — the theme of personal betrayal. But now the betrayal was at the hands of her husband, whom she believed unfaithful, and by her son, about whom she complained that he did not love her enough. Deutsch's response to these complaints was similar to Freud's: Deutsch could not take them very seriously. He observed, moreover, that Dora "play-acted" a good deal, that, among other things, she was snobbishly proud of having been a patient of Freud's. Deutsch was rather scornful of her behavior, and quotes an informant as calling Dora "a repulsive hysteric." It is clear that she irritated him, as her shame-based retaliatory behavior had "mystified" Freud.

Dora's case thus neatly illustrates, as do all Freud's early cases of hysteria, that symptoms form under the press of strangulated affect. But the question of which affects is still very much in dispute. Freud insisted to Dora (and to his colleagues) that the unbearable affect in her case was the pleasurable excitement at being kissed by Herr K. This excitement had made her so guilty that it was repressed (strangulated, unbearable), and therefore transformed into a variety of symbolically expressive symptoms. So, for example, she wanted to kiss Herr K.'s penis, but she developed instead a loss of voice and a nervous cough. My reading of the case, with the hindsight developed out of my experiences as a psychoanalyst, is that the unbearable affect for Dora was the shame of personal betrayal. Freud used a theoretical formulation about shame and guilt to the effect that they are "instinct" inhibitors. I have focused on the fact that shame and guilt are emotional experiences. They are emotional experiences which do inhibit other emotions (such as joy, or rage), but they are experiences in their own right, and most important, they involve the person in tension or agitation about the self in its relation to others.

The transformations which Freud traced from strangulated affect into symptoms are particularly clear if one follows them as they arise in states of shame and guilt. But we are no further advanced than he was when it comes to a full explanation of such transformation. The recognition that hysterical symptoms have an emotional base does not need to be "sold" in psychiatry today, as it did at the turn of the century. But beyond this elementary recognition, the specification of which emotional states generate symptoms, and the transformation process by which the symptoms are generated, are no closer to an agreed-on solution now than they were in Freud's day.

As an example of the present state of affairs, here is a quotation from an authoritative review of hysteria (Abse, 1974) in the 1974 edition of the *American Handbook of Psychiatry*. A case of hysteria in a young woman is described, clinically, in the following terms:

> The fits occurred about 6:30 P.M. every evening when she was listening to the radio. The attacks commenced following the dissolution of a love affair. A young man regularly appeared at the house at this time and had listened with her. The fit was preceded by a painful sensation on the right side of her body. Here she formerly experienced a pleasurable sensation, for her boyfriend had sat closely at her side.

This case account could have been written by Breuer and Freud, and carries us no further along than we were nearly a century ago.

Women's proneness to hysterical symptoms still highlights, as it did in the nineteenth century, how sexist attitudes infuse psychoanalytic theory and practice. An important part of Freud's theory, for example, is that different psychiatric illnesses represent different fixation points in sexual development. The earlier the level of fixation, the more severe the illness. It was clear early that hysterical illness had a strong "phallic" sexual component in it. On this basis, therefore, hysteria represented a later level of sexual development than obsessional neurosis, which is clearly "anal" in its imagery. But somehow, the statement that women's more frequent mental illness is at a later or higher developmental level than men's is not emphasized in psychoanalytic literature. In fact, revision within psychoanalytic theory of hysteria has emphasized its "oral," dependent, primitive quality (Marmor, 1953).

Another instance of the sexism that has come with psychoanalytic theory of hysteria is contained in the official nomenclature of the American Psychiatric Association's *Diagnostic and Statistical Manual of Mental Disorders, Third Edition* (1980) (usually abbreviated DSM-III). The term "histrionic personality disorder" now replaces the category that used to be called "hysterical personality." The essential features of this newly described histrionic disorder are "overly dramatic, reactive, and intensely expressed behavior and characteristic disturbance in interpersonal relationships. Individuals with this disorder are . . . prone to exaggeration [shades of Dora!] and act out a role such as 'victim' or 'princess' without being aware of it. . . . Such individuals are typically attractive and seductive. They attempt to control the opposite sex or enter into a dependent relationship. Flights into romantic fantasy are common . . ." (p. 314). The Manual goes on to say that "histrionic personality disorder" is "diagnosed far more frequently in females than in males" (p. 314).

The Manual's description of histrionic behavior of women is still embedded in Breuer and Freud's (1893-1895) accurate account of their hysterical patients' "private theater" of fantasy reflecting forbidden sexual longings. But the "interpretation" of such behavior is now still accompanied by a pejorative attitude toward people who are prone to such intense (shameful) longings. The authors of the DSM-III (1980) section on personality disorders are all men. Their polite language does not quite conceal their scornful attitude toward women's behavior when it is "seductive." Not all male authorities, of course, are so prejudiced. One of them (Abse, 1974) has called attention to the fact that the term "hysterical" is often used as a "defamatory colloquialism."

An attitude of scorn for hysterical defenses coincides with a deprecatory attitude toward the gender of the persons who still more frequently suffer from hysteria: women. In spite of the fact that careful studies show no actual relationship between hysterical symptoms and the so-called histrionic personality, the stereotype persists. One study (Easser and Lesser, 1965) of hysterical patients in psychoanalysis, for example, failed to show the "provocative, seductive, exhibitionistic" behavior which is supposed to characterize hysterical women. But the myth of Eve's wickedness dies hard.

One apparent change in the picture of hysteria today, as contrasted with a century ago, is in the class of women who suffer from it. As we saw earlier, the proportion of middle-class women in Breuer and Freud's roster of cases was large. This finding has been widely generalized, without any evidence, into a belief that hysteria was an illness of (self-indulgent) bourgeois women. No one ever inquired whether lower-class Viennese women also had the same frequency of hysterical symptoms as middle-class women. A careful study by Pauline Bart (1968) of the prevalence of hysteria in California discovered it to be the illness of the poor, rural, relatively uneducated women, rather than of their more affluent sisters. Some years previously, Hollingshead and Redlich (1958), noted epidemiologists of mental illness, had observed that hysteria occurs more often among the lowest social class (in both sexes). They observed, further, that the poor expect to be treated by doctors who prescribe "pills and needles." Following up on Hollingshead and Redlich's observations, Bart studied women between the ages of 40 and 59 who were admitted to the *neurological* service of UCLA Neuropsychiatric Institute, and who emerged with a psychiatric diagnosis, usually hysteria. These women tended to come from poor, rural areas where, as Bart puts it, they did not have available a sophisticated psychiatric "vocabulary of discomfort." They experienced themselves as *physically* ill — *their* expression of psychic distress. A comparable group of women who entered psychiatric services, that is, who volunteered that they were *psychiatric* patients, were of higher social status and better educated.

Bart's findings remind us that, in modern times, sexual enlightenment is more widespread, partly as a result of Freud's work. This may be one reason why an educated middle-class woman today might be more accepting of her own sexual longings than, say, Emmy von N. or Elisabeth von R. And it may be one reason why hysteria is more prevalent among lower-class women today. But the conflict that so often besets women — that, like Dora, they are ashamed of themselves if they are in a humiliated fury at someone they love, and ashamed of themselves if they are *not* furious, that is, if they are still in love — that inner conflict has not vanished from the twentieth-century scene.

In contrast, one productive consequence of Freud's idea that strangulated affect can somehow drive people into "crazy" body-symptoms is that it has helped to bring into existence the whole field of psychosomatic medicine. At the time when Freud first made his discovery about strangulated affect the existence of hormones was totally unknown. With the discovery by physiologists during the early twentieth century of the functions of the autonomic nervous system and the hormonal systems under its control, an actual linkage between powerful affects and body dysfunction became clear. So, for example, Walter B. Cannon (1932), the noted physiologist, described how in fear or rage (and he might well have included shame) the sympathetic branch of the autonomic nervous system is activated, with the result that the organism is geared for adaptive response. Constriction of the blood vessels, emptying of the stomach, rise of blood pressure, release of sugar into the blood stream, all rev up the organism for fight or flight. Cannon has a very interesting footnote about these physiological changes. He writes, "If these results of emotion are not worked off by action they could have a pathological effect." This is very like Freud's idea that unexpressed emotion leads to mental illness. The coming together of Freud's idea and the later work of the physiologists brought together the "psyche" and the "soma" in psychosomatic medicine.

It was Franz Alexander (1950) who brought together Cannon's concepts and psychoanalytic thinking in a classic formulation of the etiology of psychosomatic illness. He wrote: "Whenever the expression of competitive, aggressive, and hostile attitudes is inhibited in voluntary behavior, the sympathetic adrenal system is in sustained excitation, which persists because the consummation of fight or flight reaction takes place in the field of coordinated voluntary behavior" (p. 66). In this formulation the emphasis is on anger (or aggression) rather than on the inhibitory agency which must be some form of shame or guilt or both.

Alexander (1950) also had the idea that some people who exhibit a great need to be active in important and demanding jobs are really in the grip of an unconscious need to be passive which their high level of activity only masks. The more they defend themselves against their passivity by activity, the more tension they create within their bodies and the more prone they become to the pathological effects of tension, so that their gut literally erodes and they fall ill of peptic ulcer. Alexander suggested, further, that people with colitis are overtly passive and demanding people, always expecting other people to do things for them, in contrast to the overactive peptic-ulcer people.

Specific angry affects have been found to be inhibited in different psychogenic illnesses. For example, duodenal ulcer was found to be associated with patients' feeling deprived of what is due and wanting to get even, while patients with hives seemed to feel that they were taking a beating and were helpless to do anything about it (Grace and Graham, 1952; Graham, Stern, and Winokur, 1958). These are, in my vocabulary, distinctions between guilt at wanting revenge and an attitude of shame or humiliated fury at being helpless. Both are strong affects, but they are likely to be experienced differently within the self.

There is still no firm evidence of *causal* connections between duodenal ulcer/colitis and activity/passivity. Disorders of the gut, however, soon became a subject of experimental inquiry, particularly with animals as subjects. Similarly, psychic factors in the production of circulatory disturbance, such as heart disease and stroke, and respiratory disturbance, such as asthma, were soon actively studied experimentally. The very recent work on the relation between Type A personality and proneness to coronary heart disease is but one example of the many ongoing studies in psychosomatic medicine.

It is significant, also, that the record of psychoanalytic treatment in long-term psychosomatic illness tends to be rather favorable. As we shall see in Chapter 7, long-standing cases of ulcer, ulcerative colitis, and other psychogenic illnesses were greatly benefited by a course of analysis (Fisher and Greenberg, 1977).

Instead of considering all the areas of psychosomatics, I shall review the work on the role of stress in gastric ulcer as an illustration of how psychosomatic research has developed out of Freud's ideas. This choice of ulcer formation as subject for discussion is partly based on the existence of an excellent review of the work by Weiss (1977) in a recent volume on experimental psychopathology.

The hypothesis that prolonged tension can produce gastric damage has been amply confirmed. Much of the work of confirmation has been done on animals — rats, cats, and monkeys — which can be subjected to a variety of experimentally induced stresses that it is not possible ethically to inflict on human beings. These studies are designed to elucidate just which stresses do induce gastric lesions. The implications for human functioning are, of course, the main point of the studies, although no animal studies can reproduce the exquisitely refined cruelties that a few well-chosen words spoken by a human being can inflict on someone attached to him or her. But it is interesting and instructive to see how far these studies have been able to analyze the situations that animals confront, and to see that the affective troubles of "lower" species can be very similar to our own.

One of the earliest of these experimental studies was a series of investigations beginning in 1956 and carried out by a team consisting of Sawrey, Weisz, and Conger and their various collaborators. Psychoanalytic theorists often spoke of passivity as the equivalent of "orality" — referring metaphorically to the passive bliss of suckling at the mother's breast. One resultant of conflict over "oral" passivity could be that it would produce gastric hypersecretion, which would ultimately cause an ulcer. The experimental setup to test this notion involved placing rats in a "conflict" situation between hunger and an electric shock. Animals lived in a box with food at one end and a water tube at the other. Between the food and the water were sections of the box wired for electric shock. The animals could remain safely in a center section of the box, but if they attempted to get either food or water they would receive a shock. The animals lived in this condition for 47 out of every 48 hours over a period of 30 days. A comparison group of "control" animals was simply deprived of food and water for the same intervals as the experimental "conflict" condition. As predicted, gastric lesions were found in the experimental animals, but not in the control animals.

However, since the control animals had had no electric shock, and it might be argued that the electric shock alone was responsible for the lesions, a series of experiments was needed to tease out the relative importance of such factors as shock and degree of hunger and thirst, in short, to demonstrate conclusively that it was the *conflict* between needs that produced the ulcer. Weiss (1977) has recently been able to design such a series of studies, from which he concluded that the "conflict condition was one of the most ulcerogenic." Ironically, the conflict situation Weiss designed involves an analogue of human personal betrayal. Weiss first exposed rats to a situation in which the animal was required to respond by turning a wheel to *avoid* a shock. After 24 hours, the conditions were "slightly altered" so that responses which formerly avoided a shock now *resulted* in a brief shock to the tail. A "matched" control received the same number of shocks as the experimental animal, but was not subjected to the conflict between a response which had at first proved useful and then turned out to be noxious. The animals which had been "betrayed" developed gastric damage, while the animals that had simply been shocked did not.

A number of other experimental analogues to human suffering have been designed for study in the animal laboratory, among them a set of studies that caricature some aspects of the human condition. Hans Selye's notion, for instance, that "immobility" produces stress has been experimentally investigated by the technique of tying up the animal so that it cannot move. Ability to "cope" with stress was studied in so-called "executive monkeys." One monkey of a pair was able to press a lever that avoided a strong, unsignaled shock for an indefinite period, provided the animal continued to press the lever. But the other monkey (in the pair of "yoked" monkeys) also received a shock every time the "executive" failed to press the lever. So the pair each received the same number of shocks, but one of the pair was the "executive" agent. In each of four pairs, the "executive" monkey developed ulcers and died. Unfortunately, subsequent attempts to replicate this experiment failed, and until recently the reason for the failure remained a mystery. It is now understood that the "executive" monkey in each original pair was chosen because it was a frequent responder; in addition, since the shock was unsignaled, the "executive" monkey had no way of receiving "relevant feedback" from some pattern of signals. So the combination of a "high-

strung" monkey·and an unpredictable or insoluble problem was what produced the gastric ulcer.

Still another set of experiments has focused on the extent to which an
animal can express the aggression that is evoked by an experimental situation. Animals which were shocked together, so that they fought with each
other and wounded each other, actually developed less severe lesions than
animals that were shocked an equal number of times but alone. Moreover,
those animals which displayed fighting behavior but actually could not hurt
each other physically also showed less severe lesions than the animals
shocked alone. Expressing the aggressive response thus reduced the gastric
lesions, although it remains unclear whether these results were not in some
way a product of the social conditions among the "fighting animals" as opposed to the lone condition of the controls.

Finally, there is a series of experiments which suggest that early maternal separation increases the risk of gastric ulcer in rats (Ackerman, Hofer,
and Weiner, 1978). Rats separated from their mothers at 15 days and then
placed in restraint for 24 hours developed ulcers much more often than
animals separated even one week later. The actual mechanisms by which
early maternal separation makes rats vulnerable are being uncovered; an experiment recently reported in *Science* shows that a fall of body temperature
is responsible for ulcer formation in the early-separated group, and early-
separated rats kept warm do not develop as many gastric erosions in
restraint as do the pups whose temperature falls.

It will be apparent from this brief review of experimental studies of the
role of emotions in gastric damage that the experimental studies in
psychosomatic medicine have transposed the search for specific noxious affects from the human domain to the animal kingdom (in which emotions
may be manipulated). As the experiments have grown more and more
precise (distinguishing, for example, between upper and lower parts of the
stomach, between erosions and lesions, between signaled and unsignaled
shocks), the intellectual distance between this kind of experimental work and
the human emotions that are specific to hysterical symptoms has increased.
Yet each of the emotional analogues has direct reference to a human situation: separation from mother, inability to cope (helplessness), unpredict-
ability, unexpressed aggression (helplessness), immobility, insoluble conflict
between needs — all evoke acutely painful emotional states which are, since
Freud's work, commonly observed to be pathogenic for neurosis. It is an
ironic footnote to the history of ideas that experimental animal
psychologists, like the rest of their academic colleagues, are often unaware
of Freud's role as a source of their work. So, for example, the very valuable
review of psychological factors in gastrointestinal lesions from which I have
been quoting has only the most tangential reference to the psychoanalytic

origins of the field. Similarly, as we shall see in Chapter 4, the researchers (Friedman and Rosenman, 1974) who formulated the "Type A" personality — ambitious, irritable, hurried, money-seeking — are apparently unaware that their "Type A" and Freud's "anal character" have many features in common.

In recent years, the knowledge that physical illness often accompanies times of emotional stress has made the term "psychosomatic illness" almost a household word. The term is used to cover not only physical illnesses with a possible emotional component, like ulcer or asthma, but hypochondriacal symptoms and any illness which physicians cannot diagnose. Thus the understanding of hysteria, which increased our knowledge of a close tie between emotional stress and physical illness, has, paradoxically, tended to obscure the fact that hysterical symptoms need to be taken seriously — and that they require therapy.

It sometimes happens that people today have to insist on a thorough-going physical examination because their symptoms, if at all mysterious, are all too easy to diagnose as "psychosomatic." This diagnosis has sometimes become an elegant term for what is often regarded as "faking" by the patient. It is a diagnosis which also carries a powerful threat of "put-down." And since now, as in the past, hysterical symptoms much more often afflict women than men, women are more often caught in this bind. On the one hand, they have a physical symptom which is worrisome and debilitating; on the other hand, it threatens them with the mortification of being thought fakes. As to the latter possibility, the women themselves are not always sure.

CHAPTER 3

Phobias

The Problem of Anxiety

In his analysis of the case of Little Hans, Freud (1909a) extended his hypothesis that the symptoms of hysteria are transformations of forbidden sexual longings to phobic symptoms as well. In fact, it was Freud who first suggested (1909a, p. 115) that phobia be named "anxiety-hysteria"[1] because of the similarity between the psychological structure of phobia and hysteria, namely, that both are products of transformed libido. The single but decisive difference that Freud observed between hysteria and phobia is that in phobia the transformed libido is "set free" in the form of another affect, anxiety, while in hysteria it is "converted" from the "mental sphere into a somatic innervation" (p. 115).

Freud (1926a) later abandoned his view that anxiety is transformed repressed libido. He substituted, instead, a view that anxiety is an inherited affective state — the affective symbol of danger to the individual's physical survival. The case of Little Hans thus played a pivotal role in Freud's thinking; he returned to it with problems — which are in fact still unsolved today. Freud's reason for changing his theory was that he found it impossible to account for the dynamics of the forbidding agency, that is, for the very existence of repression without postulating the existence of anxiety in the first place. How can anxiety be the *effect* or product of repression when it can

[1]Freud's term, "anxiety-hysteria," has not found wide acceptance outside of psychoanalytic circles because its implication that *all* phobias are symbolic transformations of emotional conflicts has not been accepted by psychiatry. Marks (1969) provides an excellent summary of present-day information on phobias.

63

also be seen — in the case of Little Hans for one thing — to be the *cause* of repression coming into play? Freud did not pretend that he had the solution to this puzzle. On the contrary, he expressed his puzzlement by invoking the Latin phrase *"non liquet."*

With the renewal of interest in affective states of shame and guilt (Lewis, 1971) and with a theoretical perspective that regards these affective states (along with the emotions in general) as modes of maintaining and restoring human attachments, Freud's puzzle about whether anxiety is cause or effect can be better understood as an essentially false issue. I think it can be demonstrated that Freud's problem of conceptualizing anxiety as cause or effect of repression resulted from the absence in his time of a viable concept of human nature and human emotions. To have postulated, for example, that affective states of shame and guilt are prime movers of behavior was not an acceptable scientific stance for Freud, even though his account of Little Hans's behavior, like his accounts of his obsessional and hysterical patients, was full of references to these powerful emotional states. In turn, this deficiency in the theory of emotions was (and still is) the result of a concept of human nature which based it only on individualistic instincts and their ideational representatives.

Before turning to a detailed discussion of Hans's phobia, Freud's reformulation of it, and subsequent developments in the field, it is useful to pause and consider how many different issues about child development and human behavior in general were first raised in the case of Little Hans. These more general issues will be more fully discussed in Volume 2. But it is instructive at least to note some of them at this point; if only because the wealth of clinical material Freud presented in the case becomes more apparent.

"FIRST" OBSERVATIONS ABOUT CHILDREN IN THE CASE OF LITTLE HANS

Reading the case of Little Hans some seventy years after it was published is not only a most illuminating exercise in pinpointing theoretical issues, but a reminder of how many "first" observations Freud made in this "first" child analysis. In fact, observations about Hans's sexual behavior were being collected by Hans's father and sent to Freud since before Hans was three years old, well before the unexpected outbreak of the child's phobia. Freud had been encouraging his pupils to make observations about the "sexual life of children — the existence of which [had been] cleverly overlooked or deliberately denied" (p. 6). Hans's parents had both been Freud's analysands. Both parents were also committed to the principles of respect for children's feelings and intelligence and of gentleness, that is, for "enlighten-ment" in child-rearing for which Freud stood.

Cognition and Affect

It was in his observations about children's intellectual functioning con-tained in the case of Little Hans that Freud raised the issue of affective in-fluences on the development of children's cognitions. A first observation, relayed by Hans's father, was that Hans, not yet three years old, nevertheless had a lively curiosity about whether or not his mother had a penis. Hans had his own term for his penis: In German it was his *"Wiwimacher," "Wiwi"* being the nursery term for urine, so, literally, his urine-maker. (The translators have chosen to render this term into the English, "widdler," although "wiwi" is a nursery term for urine also in English: thus "wiwi-maker" could have been more literal.)

Here is the text of Hans's father's note to Freud: "Hans: Mummy, have you got a widdler, too? Mother: Of course. Why? Hans: I was only just thinking" (p. 7). Another note about Hans from the same age reported that Hans, seeing a cow being milked, thought that the milk was coming out of its "widdler." As Freud puts it, "the cow's udder . . . is in its nature a *mamma* [Freud's italics], and in its shape and position a penis" (p. 7). Hans's misperception of the udder as a penis was thus to be understood not only as a function of the incomplete cognitive development of a young child but of the similarity in "gestalten" inherent in percepts of the breast and penis which could be misleading. Freud understood adult pleasure in sucking a penis as a product of this originally "innocent" (and understandable) confusion be-tween breast and penis.

Still another observation about Hans's intellectual interest in widdlers suggests that Hans connected them with being alive. Making an error, based this time on overgeneralization, Hans remarked reflectively when he was 3¾ years old: "'A dog and a horse have widdlers; a table and a chair haven't.' He had thus got hold of an essential characteristic differentiating between animate and inanimate objects" (p. 9). (Freud ought actually to have said *some* instead of all animate objects.)

Hans's curiosity about who has a widdler and who doesn't also led him to question his father directly (at this same age of 3¾) about whether father had one. When father replied that he did, Hans remarked that he had never been able to see it while father was undressing. When he questioned his mother on the same subject, in fact, staring at her to "see if you'd got a wid-dler too" (p. 9), Hans's mother told him that of course she did have a widdler.

"Mother: 'Didn't you know that?' Hans: 'No. I thought you were so big you'd have a widdler like a horse.'"

This conversation clearly had implications for the development of Hans's phobia many months later. The child was responding to his mother's false information about having a widdler by apparently agreeing with her that he *did* know she had a penis, and at the same time describing her penis as big enough to fit a horse. In this complicated reply he is "putting her on" as he "accepts" her misinformation. The conversation thus reflects the fact that a very young child is capable of responding with disguised or transformed hostility to information that he senses is false.

Another observation about Hans describes his reaction to seeing his mother immediately after the new baby's birth. It emphasizes the child's doubts that a baby was really brought by a stork, the story Hans's father had given him about pregnancy and childbirth. It details the child's jealous behavior, including his open declaration: "I don't *want* a baby sister" (p. 11). It also documents Hans's efforts to accommodate his perception of his sister's genitals to the information his mother had given him that females have widdlers. Hans said, watching his sister being bathed: "But her widdler's still quite small. . . . When she grows up it'll get bigger all right." Freud is here describing not only that the child was capable of doubting misinformation given him by his parents, but that he evolved cognitive compromises designed to enable him to assimilate disagreeable information. Her penis was pronounced little (rather than nonexistent), but would grow in the future.

Freud's comment on this misperception by Hans reflects his awareness of the "opposition" to his views. Why is it, he asks, that "these young enquirers did not report what they really saw — namely that there was no widdler there? . . . As a matter of fact [Hans] was behaving no worse than a philosopher of the school of Wundt. In the view of that school, consciousness is the invariable characteristic of what is mental, just as in the view of little Hans a widdler is the indispensable criterion of what is animate. If now a philosopher comes across mental processes whose existence cannot but be inferred, but about which there is not a trace of consciousness to be detected . . . instead of saying that they are *un*conscious mental processes, he calls them *semi*conscious. The widdler's still very small!" (pp. 11–12, footnote).

Thus far, Freud had made observations which he generalized as reflecting a sexual basis for intellectual curiosity. Hans's sexual curiosity "roused the spirit of inquiry in him and enabled him to arrive at genuine abstract knowledge" (p. 9). If Freud had left his generalization at this level, which includes a concept of "genuine abstract knowledge," less controversy might have been generated. But he went on to make an overgeneralization when he wrote, on the same page, that "thirst for knowledge seems to be inseparable from sexual curiosity" (p. 9). Sexual curiosity may evoke a thirst for knowledge, but not all of this thirst is necessarily based on sexual curiosity. It was this kind of overgeneralization in theory that Hartmann (1950, 1951) corrected in his concept of "conflict-free ego functioning."

Even more important, however, than his infelicitous theorizing is the fact that Freud was raising a fundamental question about the motivational underpinnings of intellectual functioning — a question that has occupied psychology greatly since his day. Since Freud's time, such theorists as Tomkins (1962, 1963) and Izard (1975, 1977) have formulated the hypothesis, partly in response to Freud's observations, that emotional states do motivate intellectual processes. In this formulation, emotions have an independent status as "movers" of intellectual processes.

In his observations about Hans's intellectual functioning, Freud was also calling attention to the distortions of perception born out of emotional needs. Once again, Freud raised an issue that has claimed a great deal of attention in modern psychology: the extent of the influence of affective states on cognitive functioning. As might have been expected, cognitive functioning has turned out to be more robust in its own set of laws than Freud might have predicted. It is also true, however, that "defensive" distortions of everyday perceptions have become a commonplace observation in the folk wisdom of modern times.

Infantile Sexuality

Hans's father also sent observational notes suggesting that Hans's interest in his widdler was, as Freud says, "by no means a purely theoretical one" (p. 7). Hans, at 3½ years, was much gratified by the sensations he was able to elicit by touching his penis. Once again the text of the observation from Hans's father is worth quoting. Hans's mother had "found him with his hand on his penis. She threatened him in these words: 'If you do that, I shall send for Dr. A. to cut off your widdler. And then what will you widdle with?' Hans: 'With my bottom'" (pp. 7–8). (Note at this point Hans's defiant reply to his mother's threat.)

In spite of this threat from his mother, Hans continued to be interested in masturbating, in masturbation games (such as inventing a pretend W.C. in which he played with his penis), and in inviting his mother to touch his penis. For example, one day when Hans was 4¼ years old, and he was being given his daily bath by his mother and as she was powdering around his penis, Hans said: "'Why don't you put your finger there?' Mother: 'Because that's piggish.' Hans: 'What's that? Piggish? Why?' Mother: 'Because it's not proper.' Hans (laughing): 'But it's great fun'" (p. 19).

It was probably these observations suggesting the existence of childhood sexuality that caused Freud the most difficulty with his contemporaries. And lest it be thought that Freudian enlightenment with respect to sexuality has since taken a firm hold on modern thinking, it should be remembered that the publication of Kinsey's work on human sexual behavior in the middle of this century created a sense of outrage in many segments of America. Most particularly, Kinsey's publication of his work on sexuality in the human female evoked a storm of hostile reactions that, according to his biographer (Pomeroy, 1972), contributed to Kinsey's early death.

Studies of infancy have since shown that two- to three-day-old infants have regularly recurring erections of their penes accompanying their REM periods. Erections of the penis are also regular accompaniments of the REM period in adult sleep. Freud's guess about sexuality as one underpinning of human behavior may have been overgeneralized, and it can perhaps be more suitably framed as involving many affects, not just one, but it clearly correctly predicts observable phenomena. As to the role of masturbation both in childhood and in adult life, actually very little is known beyond Freud's speculations that masturbation is "normal," but somehow potentially harmful.

Gender Identity

Another important issue raised by Freud in his observations about Little Hans was the origin and functioning of gender identity. Impressed by the tenacity with which Hans clung to the idea that every person has a penis, Freud deduced that boys' ideas about their masculine gender are heavily influenced by castration anxiety. Some present-day experimental psychologists have taken strong issue with that view. Kohlberg (1966), for example, suggests that the process of forming gender identity is not "determined by instinctual wishes and gratifications, but is a part of the general process of conceptual growth" (p. 98). Kohlberg is here explicitly dissociating himself from a psychoanalytic view of the question, maintaining instead that gender identity is a "cognitive-developmental" phenomenon. He suggests further that the child "engages in 'spontaneous' evaluations of his own worth to himself, to seek worth and compare his worth with that of others and to evaluate others" (p. 108). It is most instructive to realize that Freud, while describing an emotional base for gender identity, by no means excluded cognitive operations from its formation. For example, he speaks of Hans's "need *for making a comparison* [Freud's italics] which impelled him [to want to see his parents' genitals]. The ego is always the standard by which one measures the external world; one learns to understand it by means of a constant comparison with oneself" (p. 107). If this Freud quotation and the Kohlberg quotation were offered to a judge without knowledge of their sources, it is very likely that both quotations would be ascribed to the latter author. The issue of the cognitive versus emotional basis for gender identity and the experimental work that has grown out of their joining will be more fully discussed in Volume 2 of this work.

Shame and Guilt in Young Children

In the course of documenting what he perceived as the child's early sexuality, Freud also observed that Hans, a precocious little "libertine," had clear feelings of shame, and less clearly apparent feelings of guilt. These affects are described by Freud as occurring even before the outbreak of the child's phobia. Thus, for example, Freud describes four-year-old Hans's somewhat exaggerated "long-range love" for a little neighbor girl, suggesting that perhaps the child's excessive feelings grew out of his having at the moment no playmates of his own age. "Spending a good deal of time with other children clearly forms part of a child's normal development" (p. 16).

Hans's behavior gave his parents "a good deal of entertainment, for Hans has really behaved like a grown-up person in love. For the last few days a pretty little girl of about eight has been coming to the restaurant where we have lunch. Of course Hans fell in love with her on the spot. He keeps constantly turning around in his chair to take furtive looks at her; when he has finished eating he stations himself in her vicinity so as to flirt with her, but if he finds himself being observed he blushes scarlet. If his glances are returned by the girl, he at once looks shamefacedly the other way" (p. 18).

When he was 4¼ years old Hans also had a dream which can be interpreted as "distorted," that is, reflecting his guilt over wanting to be masturbated by some older little girls with whom he had been playing the game of forfeits. In the dream, "Someone said: Who wants to come to me? Then someone said: I do. Then he had to make him widdle" (p. 19). The dream thought that he had to be made to widdle was interpreted as a (guilt-induced) distortion of the wish to be masturbated.

During the outbreak of his phobia, Hans had a frightening dream about a big giraffe and a crumpled giraffe. In the dream, Hans took the crumpled giraffe away from the big one, which "called out" against this. "Then it stopped calling and I sat down on the top of the crumpled one" (p. 37). Hans accepted the interpretation that the two giraffes were his father and mother, not only in their differing anatomies, but in terms of a familiar matrimonial scene in which Hans's father regularly remonstrated against the mother's taking Hans into their bed. Hans himself at first refused to tell his mother this dream, even though she had begged him to tell her what was frightening him. In his own words, he "felt ashamed with Mummy." (p. 41), although he did not quite know why. Whether he was ashamed of his longing for his mother, or of calling attention to her crumpled condition — in which case he would be ashamed *for* her — is entirely speculative. But shame is clearly described in the young child's behavior, and in a way that makes intuitive sense to an adult.

Thus, in his rich and accurate clinical account of the child's behavior, Freud noticed the very early presence of the complicated social affects of shame and guilt. But it was impossible for him to use them as the foundations of his theoretical system.

FREUD'S 1909 ACCOUNT OF THE GENESIS OF PHOBIA

Let us turn now to the actual outbreak and treatment of the phobia.

Outbreak of the Phobia

In the midst of the observations Hans's father was sending to Freud about the child's sexuality, Hans had an entirely unexpected outbreak of phobic behavior. The father's account to Freud is worth quoting:

'My dear Professor, I am sending you a little more about Hans — but this time, I am sorry to say, material for a case history. As you will see, during the last few days he has developed a nervous disorder, which has made my wife and me most uneasy, because we have not been able to find any means of dissipating it. . . .

'No doubt the ground was prepared by sexual over-excitation due to his mother's tenderness; but I am not able to specify the actual exciting cause. He is afraid *a horse will bite him in the street* [Freud's italics], and this fear seems somehow to be connected with his having been frightened by a large penis. As you know from a former report, he had noticed at a very early age what large penises horses have, and at that time he inferred that his mother was so large she must have a widdler like a horse.

'I cannot see what to make of it. Has he seen an exhibitionist somewhere? Or is the whole thing simply connected with his mother? It is not very pleasant for us that he should begin setting us problems so early. Apart from his being afraid of going into the street and from his being in low spirits in the evening, he is in other respects the same Hans, as bright and cheerful as ever' (Freud, 1909, p. 22).

Varied Emotional States "Connected" to Phobia

Freud's trial-and-error clinical interventions speak graphically of the variety of affective states that he supposed might be "causing" the phobia. His first intervention was an implied suggestion to Hans that his "nonsense" (symptom) resulted from his wanting to masturbate. This led to the giraffe dream and to a worsening of Hans's phobic symptoms. Freud recorded this failure and his retreat from the intervention. Freud's second intervention was the interpretation to Hans that the horse was a symbol of father. It was more relieving, since it forgave Hans his hostility to father and also led to the child's communication to his father of how much retaliatory fury the child had felt toward mother and sister at Hanna's birth. Hans's father was now able to interpret Hans's complicated fantasies expressing his rage at mother and longing for her. Hans's father also had the gratification of successfully interpreting, for the first time, some of Hans's fantasies as symbols of Hans's "sibling rivalry." Freud had mentioned rivalry between siblings in his cases of hysteria — notably in the case of Elisabeth von R. — but this was the first case account in which forbidden hatred of siblings was central to symptom formation and could also be demonstrated in a young child. One can empathize with the father's gratification at his own insight and Freud's pleasure in acknowledging his pupil's interpretive skill. With the interpretation of his pregnancy fantasies, Hans evolved a prideful fantasy of himself as a father, tenderly caring for his own children, and Hans lost his phobia.

Although Freud thoroughly explored the child's conflicting feelings about the three members of his family — mother, father, sister — he placed a selective emphasis on the child's hostility to his father. Freud's emphasis in "explaining the symptom" was on the conflict between Hans's dread of his father and his sexual longing for his mother. This emphasis specifically identified the proximal stimulus to Hans's phobic behavior as the fear of castration by father. Sexual longing for mother was the more distant stimulus, operating to maintain the dread of father. This emphasis was chosen by Freud without an explicit reason for failing to give at least equal weight to the child's humiliated fury at his mother's unavailability, especially after the arrival of a baby sister. The emphasis on dread (hatred) of the father as the proximal stimulus is even more puzzling, since a careful reading of the case account also reveals a clear statement of the most immediate event before the outbreak of the phobia. It was that "the child's affection for his mother [had become] enormously intensified" (p. 25).

Freud's self-analysis, completed in the course of preparing his book on dreams, had had as its principal outcome his discovery of his own castration complex; here, too, there was much less emphasis on Freud's hatred of his mother for her faithlessness. Whether because of this slant in his own understanding of himself or for other reasons, the affects of humiliated fury or shame-rage evoked by "loss of love" were fully described in the case account but not emphasized in the discussion of the genesis of the symptom. The resulting neglect of humiliated fury or shame-rage foreshadowed a hierarchical ordering of affects in which shame was not only neglected, but devalued as representing a more primitive state than guilt.

The emphasis on guilt arising out of castration fear was partially redressed in later work by a growing attention in later psychoanalytic theory to so-called "pre-Oedipal" traumatic experiences in a child's life. But this redress, undertaken in the spirit of inquiring into earlier and earlier life experiences, had the effect also of rigidifying the notion that affects other than guilt and castration anxiety must be "earlier" and therefore more primitive. So humiliated fury or shame-rage at mother for her neglect was regarded as an "earlier" or more "primitive" affective state — without any evidence that this is, in fact, the case.

Freud's overemphasis on castration anxiety was also redressed by Melanie Klein's (1957) efforts to apply his theoretical system of Eros and Death Instincts to the psychic life of infants. In this kind of account the metaphors or images used to describe the infant's affective life reflect the struggle between affection and hostility. The arena of struggle, moreover, is entirely "intrapsychic." There is no possibility of considering castration anxiety as a response to "realistic" external danger as Freud maintained in his 1926 account. Rather, the infant's self is conceptualized as adopting at first a "paranoid" attitude and then a "depressive" attitude, representing its earliest encounters with the experiences of "bad mother." While this viewpoint implied a developmental scheme for affective states, it also implied the possibility that affective states of shame and guilt (or precursors of these states) are possible in six-month-old infants.

Although Freud took for granted in his clinical account that ambivalent or contradictory feelings for the same person are an intrinsic stimulus to the formation of anxiety, he did not really use this avenue of explanation. Freud described Hans's ambivalent feelings about each family member in great detail, describing in each instance how the ambivalent feelings would be experienced as anxiety. But in theorizing about the genesis of the phobia, he relied only on the boy's conflict of feelings toward his two parents, rather than on the conflicts within the boy's relationship to each parent and to his sister.

A theoretical system which postulates that contradictory affects breed anxiety can, for example, assume that on the cognitive level there are contradictory "appraisals" or messages from the same source, and that this cognitive contradiction creates, at the very least, restless ideation. In this theoretical system, noxious effects of contradictory affects "within person" as well as "between persons" can be assumed to have a cumulative effect, the system thus gaining more power in its prediction of anxiety.

Let us look at Freud's actual descriptions of the boy's relationship to each family member, to see how clearly he was describing the contradictions of affect toward each separate person. As already indicated, in his very careful description of the actual moment at which Hans's phobia erupted Freud saw as the "fundamental phenomenon in his condition" that the child's "affection for his mother [had become] enormously intensified" (p. 25). In fact, Freud entertained the idea that the horse was a substitute for mother (p. 27), but regarded this as a superficial interpretation since it would not account for Hans's fear that the horse would come into his room. It is amazing that the man who argued so convincingly for the multiple determination of symptoms could not also have allowed the horse to represent mother as well as father — this in spite of the fact that the child had himself dubbed his mother a horse when he was angry with her (cf. p. 66). It is particularly significant that an event preceding Hans's phobia by one day was his remark to his mother (at bath time) that his aunt (unlike mother) had admired his widdler. One can assume that Hans's humiliated feelings were reverberating (and righting themselves) in this challenging comment to his mother.

Here, briefly, are some of the many reasons Freud detailed (in the case account) as to why Hans's affection for his mother should have coexisted with a great deal of anger at her. She had threatened him with castration if he did not stop touching his penis; she refused to masturbate him when he asked her to; she had misinformed him about having a penis herself (at which point he actually referred to her as a horse); she had ridiculed his wish to sleep with an older playmate, Mariedl, and teased him with a threat of abandonment if he preferred Mariedl to herself; and, above all, she had given birth to a baby sister whom he did not want. Furthermore, she (along with his father) had deceived him about childbirth and conception with the story about the stork. The circumstances of childbirth Hans witnessed were such as to make him distrust her: he heard her groans during the delivery and he saw all the blood that it involved. Thus, the specific angry affect that Hans could easily have felt toward his mother was, in addition to suspicion, humiliated fury at being both rejected and ridiculed as a young lover. Hans himself spoke of his "sadistic" wish to beat his mother as she beat him (with a carpetbeater) when she was angry with him.

When we turn to the material on the boy's relation with his father we find an explicit statement that contradictory feelings evoke anxiety. Freud had already had the gratification of suddenly seeing, as the boy and his father sat together in Freud's consulting room, that the father's eyeglasses and mustache made his facial configuration like that of a horse. So the interpretation was made that being afraid of a horse was really being afraid of his father (because he was so fond of his mother). He was also reassured that father was not angry with him in return. This reassurance the boy instantly contradicted, accusing his father of having hit him that very day. (That an accidental blow by Hans to his father had happened that day was overlooked by both the boy and his father until that moment.)

Some weeks later, in the course of a struggle not to come into father's bed because of anxiety in the mornings, Hans said: "Why did you tell me I'm fond of *Mummy* and that's why I'm frightened, when I'm fond of *you*?" (Freud's italics). Freud comments at this point that the little boy was "displaying an unusual degree of clarity" since he was "bringing to notice the fact that his love for his father was wrestling with his hostility toward him . . . and he was reproaching his father for not yet having drawn his attention to this interplay of forces *which was bound to end in anxiety*" [my italics]. Freud goes on to speak of Hans's anxiety as having two components: "There was fear *of* his father and fear *for* his father. The former was derived from his hostility toward his father and the latter from the conflict between his affection, which was exaggerated at this point by way of compensation, and his hostility" (p. 45). It should be noted in passing that Freud had also understood the child's "enormously intensified" affection for his mother as a secondary compensation for his hostility toward her.

That the child was conflicted over his hostility toward his sister is also clearly described. Hans, for example, refused to sit down in the big bath, and this anxiety was traced to his wish that his mother drown Hanna in her bath. "Hans: 'I'm afraid of her letting go and my head going in.' I (father): 'When you were watching Mummy giving Hanna her bath, perhaps you wished she would let go of her so that Hanna should fall in?' Hans: 'Yes.'" (p. 67). Hans's anxiety about his own drowning thus represents his conflict between loving and hating his baby sister. On another occasion, Hans reported: "I thought to myself Hanna was on the balcony and fell down off it" (p. 68). Hans had been cautioned lest Hanna go too near the balustrade. When his mother asked him if he would rather Hanna were not there, he replied in the affirmative. Once again, Freud reports that Hans's dislike of Hanna is "overcompensated by an exaggerated affection" (p. 68).

Thus, Freud actually took for granted, without spelling out the process, that ambivalent feelings toward the same person are an intrinsic stimulus to the formation of anxiety. If, in addition, we make the fundamental assumption that the maintenance of affective ties with caretakers is a continuing biosocial necessity for the acculturated human being, ambivalent feelings toward a parent are particularly difficult to sustain. Hatred involves the threat of losing the affectional tie; longing involves the threat of humiliated frustration, which, in turn evokes hatred. Moreover, as Freud so clearly observed, frightening hatred can intensify longing. These feelings of "mingled apprehension and longing" (p. 26, footnote) can become "pathological anxiety." In this kind of theoretical system, forbidden, ambivalent, or contradictory affects rather than instincts are the "causes" of anxiety.

That a pattern of contradictory emotions such as longing for and apprehension of (the same person) could be powerful enough to cause anxiety was not theoretically acceptable to Freud, precisely because he based his theory on an individualistic concept of human nature. In such a concept it is physical survival rather than social attachment that is primary in motivation. Even more important, since the instinct for survival was prepotent in Freud's system, he ultimately based his theory of anxiety not on conflicted or transformed sexual longing but on "Realangst," or physical threat. Ever since Freud's work, in fact, there has been a tendency in psychology to base anxiety on fear, as behaviorists do, and to keep the term "fear" for responses to realistic dangers, while the term "anxiety" is reserved for responses to less "realistic" threats to the self. However, if as we now theorize the self is a much more social product than late nineteenth-century psychology imagined, anxiety and fear can both be rooted in ambivalent, contradictory emotions toward significant others, not just in threats to physical survival.

Consulting the dictionary for definitions of fear and anxiety makes clear how indistinct are the differences between the two states in common usage and experience. *Webster's Dictionary* defines fear as "(1) a painful emotion marked by alarm; dread; disquiet. (2) anxious concern." The second meaning of fear thus makes it synonymous with anxiety, which itself is defined as "a painful uneasiness of mind over impending or anticipated ills; solicitous desire." "Uneasiness of mind" and "disquiet" are very similar states in both fear and anxiety. The dictionary's reference to "solicitous desire" as anxiety clearly refers to a social function of anxiety. It is also true that we do experience fear in such anxious moments. The conventional psychological distinctions between fear and anxiety thus do not hold in common usage and experience.

Neither do they hold up physiologically: a person in a state of nameless anxiety is often as frightened physiologically as someone facing direct physical assault. In musicians' stage fright, for example, the physiological responses are similar to the "fight and flight" responses to physical danger. Adrenalin is released into the bloodstream, where it travels to beta receptors and initiates sweating, palpitation, tremors, dryness of the mouth, and other symptoms. "The sudden hyperactivity may have been useful for our ancestors in facing saber-toothed tigers, but it interferes severely with musical performance" (Brantigan, 1979).

THE 1926 REVISION OF THE CASE OF LITTLE HANS

Perhaps the easiest way to pinpoint the issues with which Freud was dealing is to look at his own retrospective explanation for his change in the concept of anxiety. He tells us that when he formulated his concept of anxiety as transformed libido he had been much struck by the frequency with which the symptoms of hysteria accompanied the interruption of sexual discharge in coitus interruptus. This co-occurrence of symptoms and dammed-up discharge had been so striking that he was convinced some cases of neurosis should be thought of as "actual neuroses" rather than as true cases of hysteria. Actual neuroses seemed to Freud to be thinly disguised transformations of the sexual experiences of heavy breathing, increased heart beat, sweating, and the like. (It was only later that these became known as indicators of autonomic arousal.) Freud's description of anxiety as transformed repressed sexual longing was thus modeled upon what he thought of as a physiological actuality: undischarged sexual excitement "converts" into a hysterical symptom, an abdominal pain, or a dyspnea. Moreover, Freud (1926a) continued to assert the validity of this *description* of symptom formation. "The observations that I made at the time hold good" (p. 110).

But his analyses of cases since Little Hans — principally the cases of obsessional neurosis — and his reanalysis of his thinking about Little Hans persuaded Freud that although his description was accurate, his metapsychology was wrong. His new view was that anxiety does not arise out of repressed libido but as a signal of *"Realangst"* — a perceived danger of threatened castration arising in the *ego*. Anxiety thus produces repression rather than resulting from it.

> It is no use denying the fact, though it is not pleasant to recall it, that I have on many occasions asserted that in repression the instinctual representative is distorted, displaced, and so on, while the libido belonging to the instinctual impulse is transformed into anxiety. But now an examination of phobias, which should be best able to provide confirmatory evidence, fails to bear out my assertion; it seems, rather to contradict it directly. The anxiety felt in animal phobias is the ego's fear of castration while the anxiety felt in agoraphobia (a subject that has been less thoroughly studied) seems to be fear of sexual temptation — a fear which after all must be connected in its origins with the fear of castration. As far as can be seen at the present, the majority of phobias go back to an anxiety of this kind felt by the ego in regard to the demands of the libido. It is always the ego's attitude of anxiety which is the primary thing and which sets repression going. Anxiety never arises from repressed libido. If I had contented myself earlier with saying

that after the occurrence of repression a certain amount of anxiety appeared in place of the manifestation of libido that was to be expected I should have nothing to retract today. The description would be correct; and there does undoubtedly exist a correspondence of the kind asserted between strength of impulses that has to be repressed and the intensity of the resultant anxiety.[2] But I must admit that I thought I was giving more than a mere description. I believed I had put my finger on a metapsychological process of direct transformation of libido into anxiety. I can now no longer maintain this view (p. 109).

It should be noted, also, that embedded in this formal retraction of Freud's earlier theory of anxiety, there is an important clinical observation and a suggestion for further study about the difference between animal phobias and agoraphobia. As we shall see later in this chapter, the difference between animal phobia and agoraphobia had turned out to be salient clinically (Marks, 1969). Also, a recent experimental study (Seif and Atkins, 1979) predicted and confirmed that agoraphobics are more field-dependent and less likely to use isolation of affect than people with animal phobias.

As Bowlby (1973) has remarked, Freud's reappraisal of his theory of phobia was "agonizing" for him. Moreover, the editors of the *Standard Edition* point several times to Freud's attachment to the description of anxiety as transformed libido. In this description, anxiety still has "force," instead of being only a cognitive signal. But Freud was now faced with explaining how an affect like anxiety can originate in the ego, which has no intrinsic force or power in it. What energy is being used to create an affect if it arises in the ego? In trying to deal with this "economic" problem, Freud used two lines of speculation, and then simply gave up on the economic problem as "today scarcely of any interest" (1926a, p. 140). (As he wrote this, he also restated his 1909 view: "Of course there is nothing to be said against the idea that it is precisely the energy that has been liberated by being withdrawn through repression which is used by the ego to arouse the affect; but it is no longer of any importance which portion of energy is employed for this purpose.")

The first line of speculation that Freud used involved a denigration of affects as mere "inherited hysterical attacks." The second line of speculation was entirely different: Freud offered the suggestion that affects are appropriate responses to the person's appraisal of his situation. This is a view of affects that is quite familiar to modern-day theorists of emotions, such as Arnold (1960), who speaks of affects as the results of appraisals of one's situation. The first line of speculation continues to root affects in the instincts, as some kind of Darwinian remnant of inherited behavior fostering species survival. The second line of speculation bases itself on cognitions: It is more like a modern-day cognitive theorist's approach to the origin of af-

---

[2]Note how Freud continues to assert the "correspondence" between repressed impulse and resultant symptom.

fects. That Freud could not reconcile these two lines of speculation is no wonder — they start from opposite premises. The difficulty is not so much that one view starts with instincts and the other with cognition, but that the instinct theory is an individualistic one, rather than a theory that human behavior is *social* by biological origin. Even more important, both instinct theory and cognitive theory fail to give emotions a primary place in the motivation of behavior.

Let us look more closely at Freud's (1926a) theory of affects as inherited hysterical attacks.

> Anxiety is not newly created in repression; it is reproduced as an affective state in accordance with an already existing mnemic image. If we go further and inquire into the origin of that anxiety — and of affects in general — we shall be leaving the realm of pure psychology and entering the borderland of physiology. Affective states have been incorporated in the mind as precipitates of primaeval traumatic experiences, and when a similar situation occurs they are revived like mnemic symbols. I do not think I have been wrong in likening them to the more recent and individually acquired hysterical attacks and in regarding them as its normal prototypes (p. 93).

This is a view of emotions as inherited by-products of trauma. It is a view of affects as inherently "primitive" and disorganizing. As Leeper (1968) has so persuasively shown, this concept of emotions as disorganizing and "something to outgrow" not only dominates much of present-day psychology but was an outgrowth of an age of "scientific" rationalism in which emotions were devalued. It was, moreover, an outgrowth of what Leeper calls an "antique tradition" (p. 188), in which cognition, conation, and affection (thinking, willing, and feeling) were separate departments of the mind and in which feeling and thinking in particular were inherently opposed to each other.

Freud's concept of instincts had no independent place for affects. His concept involved a split or separation between instinct and its ideational representatives (affects being neither prime movers nor ideational representatives). This artificial separation between instinct (force) and idea followed the opposition between body and mind, passion and reason, or between "sexual instincts" and "ego instincts" which Freud's psychology inherited from theology.

To follow the fate of forces and of ideas was most important to Freud in his clinical description of neurotic symptoms. Not only did he distinguish carefully and accurately between hysteria and phobia on this basis, but he also postulated that obsessional symptoms arose out of a still different fate of ideas separated from their "force": the separated ideas return to consciousness but deprived of their affective charge. Theoretically, however,

Freud was in trouble because he was not actually describing "instincts" or psychological forces, but *affects,* and there was no viable theory of affects; they were neither instincts nor ideas.

Freud's second line of speculation that anxiety is an ego response involved an uncharacteristic clinical inaccuracy. In speculating about how castration anxiety arises, for example, Freud simply adopted the very un-Freudian notion that the danger of castration was "realistic," as if every boy's father must *literally* threaten him. It is interesting to note, in passing, how difficult this German term *"Realangst,"* was for Freud's translators to render (p. 108, footnote). Clearly, Freud was treating the "danger of castration" as a metaphoric representation of a feeling-state, since he labeled it an *"Angst"* or anxiety. On the other hand, he was treating it as if it were a realistic or objective danger, to which the ego responded appropriately. Freud had thus not separated "real" from metaphoric, or affectively perceived danger.

Speculating about anxiety as an ego signal, Freud worked out a developmental scheme in which anxiety varies in its content in an age-appropriate way. He suggested that the earliest form of anxiety is separation from the mother, the next stage, castration anxiety, and that "castration anxiety develops into moral anxiety — social anxiety — and it is not so easy now to know what anxiety is about . . . (since) the formula 'separation and expulsion from the horde' applies only to the later portion of the superego, not to the nucleus of the superego" (p. 139). Clearly, he was willing to base anxiety on its earliest form, separation from mother. But its later form — a dread of social ostracism — necessarily puzzled Freud because his fundamental concept of human nature was narcissistic. Freud thus could not assume that separation anxiety, especially in its earliest form, was a social phenomenon.

> The first experience of anxiety an individual goes through (in the case of human beings, at all events) is birth, and objectively speaking birth is a separation from the mother. Now it would be very satisfactory if anxiety, as a symbol of separation, were to be repeated on every subsequent occasion on which a separation took place. But unfortunately we are prevented from making use of this correlation by the fact that birth is not subjectively experienced as separation from the mother, since the foetus, *being a completely narcissistic creature,* is totally unaware of her existence as an object (p. 130) (my italics).

With hindsight today, it is possible to see that the problem with which Freud was struggling required the formulation of a social theory of human nature, and with it, a concept of the biosocial nature of the affects. A theory in which emotions and thinking are inherently in opposition (and in which thinking should be the governor) created an uneasy framework for Freud's compelling clinical observations that emotions are very powerful forces. Recognizing that affects such as anxiety are appropriate reactions to danger seemed to require that he give up his first theory of the origin of affects in "libido." Moreover, that affective states are simultaneously "movers" of behavior *and* cognitive structures appropriately reflecting the individual's appraisal of his connection to significant others is a concept of emotions that is only now slowly emerging in present-day psychology.

This deficiency of theory has been partially redressed by the work of Bowlby and his students, who postulate that the organism has a built-in "attachment system" in which anxiety operates as a signal for maintaining or restoring the attachment. Similarly, smiling, pleasure, and joy cement the social bond. In turn, these formulations rest on our newer knowledge of infancy, which suggests that infants are much better organized and much more socially capable than we had previously supposed. Affects may be understood as expressing human social connectedness, including separation anxiety, as well as the positive affects which accompany attachment. In this theoretical framework, in which the assumption is made of human nature as biosocial, the "superego" affects — that is, the affective states of shame and guilt, may also be conceptualized as products of the attachment system and similarly designed to maintain and restore it (Lewis, 1979).

DEVELOPMENTS SINCE 1926

In the years that have followed Freud's account of Hans's phobia and his agonizing reappraisal of the theory of anxiety, two main lines of work can be distinguished. One line of development is within the psychoanalytic system and has tended to follow Freud's clinical lead rather than his theory. Very careful accounts of the multiplicity of ambivalent affects underlying phobia have been developed, centering more on "separation" from loved figures than on castration anxiety. These developments have led to attempts to reformulate Freud's theory in more social and less individualistic terms — in terms of "object-relations" rather than in terms of instincts. Important work along these theoretical lines has been developed by Spitz (1965) and Mahler (1968), without specific reference to phobia. Also prominent in this line of development has been the influential work of Bowlby, and from it, the empirical observations of anxiety in normal infants by Ainsworth (1969, 1979), Sroufe (1979), and many others.

Antipsychoanalytic Approaches to Phobias

A second line of development since the case of Little Hans has been the appearance of overtly antipsychoanalytic researchers, most prominently Wolpe (1958) and Eysenck and Rachman (1965). Before discussing the developments within psychoanalytic theory and its revisions, it will be useful to consider the work of the antipsychoanalytic researchers, whose criticisms of Freud have been manifold and sharp. One reason for considering the behaviorists' antipsychoanalytic framework is that the theoretical difficulties engendered by the evidence they have amassed seem to point to just the same hard places that gave Freud so much difficulty. Specifically, without a thoroughgoing reliance on affects as prime movers, anxiety, itself an affect, is difficult for them to understand except in terms of the conditioned responses that evoke it.

Two major lines of criticism are offered: first, that the genesis of phobia has been overcomplicated by symbolic interpretations, and second, that the treatment of phobia should be much more straightforwardly aimed at dissipating the phobic symptom than psychoanalytic theory would allow. This second line of criticism of the psychoanalytic theory of the origin of phobia comes from plentiful evidence which the behaviorists have supplied that phobic symptoms may be substantially relieved by a variety of deconditioning techniques — systematic desensitization, flooding, and the like. The behaviorists argue that if phobias are easily treated by conditioning techniques their origin in unconscious sexual and aggressive conflicts cannot be supported. A behavioristic framework is offered in opposition to the psychoanalytic framework, in which it is assumed that phobia develops as a learned conditioned response. An unconditioned or "natural" fear response becomes linked, by contiguity, similarity, or other accidental reasons to non-fear-evoking situations. Phobias are responses, for which it is not necessary to hypothesize symbolic meanings, and for which it is not necessary to unravel the emotional antecedents that they symbolically represent. Behavior theorists argue that since phobias or irrational fears are evolved by conditioning, they may also be deconditioned, that is, treated by various techniques that aim at pairing the noxious phobia stimulus with a new "positive" set of responses. Their argument is furthermore, that since deconditioning works to relieve the symptom, psychoanalytic theory of the origin of the symptom is disconfirmed. In this error of logic they are, unfortunately, joined by the psychoanalysts themselves, who have argued that the genesis of phobia in emotional conflict requires the unraveling of the causal emotional conflict as its treatment. In fact, psychoanalysis has predicted, on the analogy of a hydraulic pressure system, that symptom eradication could yield new symptoms, since the emotional complex which produced them has not been resolved. As I have shown elsewhere (Lewis, 1971), psychoanalysts have committed the genetic fallacy of confounding technique of treatment with theory of origin of symptom. But some behaviorists also make the same error.[3] Just because deconditioning works as treatment is no proof that phobia originates in a conditioned response.

For convenience let us consider first the behaviorists' criticism of Freud's theory of the origin of phobias, and then turn back to their criticism of psychoanalysis for its technique of treatment. Two of the workers most prominent in the antipsychoanalytic movement have offered a spirited critique of Freud's case of Little Hans (Wolpe and Rachman, 1960), which one of them (Rachman, 1978) has summarized. They regard as unsupported the following of Freud's contentions: "that the child had a sexual desire for his mother, that he hated and feared his father and wished to kill him, that his sexual excitement and desire for his mother were transformed into anxiety, that his fear of horses was symbolic of his fear of his father, that the purpose of his illness was to keep him near his mother, and finally, that his phobia disappeared because he resolved his Oedipus complex" (Rachman, p. 218). Rachman prefers the little boy's own explanation of his phobia, which was that it started when he witnessed a street accident in which a horse collapsed.

Wolpe and Rachman's criticism of Freud's contentions is that they are unsupported by evidence, and specifically that evidence obtained by Freud "third-hand" (that is, from the boy's father) is bound to be defective. They point out that the boy misled his interlocutors, gave conflicting reports, and, most important of all, that the father in effect suggested the interpretations that Freud adopted. It should be noted, in passing, that each of these points of criticism of the evidence was raised and dealt with by Freud in his case account; the disagreement arises over how damaging each of the evidentiary circumstances is to Freud's concept that the boy was in a state of emotional ambivalence toward the principal people in his family. The issue that needs to be decided is not whether the sources of evidence are impeccable, but whether there is indeed evidence that *emotional stress* preceded witnessing the accident, which then provided a trigger for the phobia outbreak. It is this point that Wolpe and Rachman seem to ignore. In any event, Rachman regards the "monograph on little Hans (as) a poor product" which cannot be relied upon (p. 219), and on this point, as Rachman says, reading the case account is the only way to make up one's mind.

Behavior Theory's Account of the Genesis of Phobias

When we turn to the difficulties encountered by conditioning theory in

[3]By no means all behaviorists make this error. Rachman (personal communication) comments that the "effectiveness of the method of treatment does not, of itself, tell us anything about the origin of the fear."

accounting for the genesis of phobia, it seems clear that the theory suffers from its failure to make room for the power of affects. Let us look at the account of his own intellectual progression from conditioning theory given by Rachman (1978). He tells us that his (and Wolpe's) original formulation read as follows: "Any neutral stimulus, simple or complex, that happens to make an impact on an individual at about the time that a fear reaction is evoked, acquires the ability to evoke the fear subsequently ʼ. . . there will be a generalization of fear reactions to stimuli resembling the conditioned stimulus" (p. 174). Reviewing the six arguments that accumulating evidence urged against the acceptance of this theory, he lists the following:

Argument 1. People fail to acquire fears in theoretically fear-evoking situations, such as air raids. "The observations of comparative fearlessness enduring despite repeated exposures to intense trauma, uncontrollability, and uncertainty are contrary to the conditioning theory of fear acquisition. People subjected to repeated air raids should acquire multiple conditioned responses and these should be strengthened with repeated exposure" (p. 186).

Although Rachman does not consider this explanation, a psychoanalyst might suggest that the persons who did not acquire phobic responses during repeated air raids were *not* in a state of emotional ambivalence toward the significant persons in their personal lives. (This might include, at another level of experience, a state of wholehearted loyalty toward their own country under attack.)

Argument 2. A thorough attempt to condition fear in normal infants was a failure. This is consistent with the adult's failure to develop fears under air raids. And it is also consistent with evidence that patients treated with electrical aversive therapy do not develop fear under the course of treatment. A psychoanalyst might ask if the reason for these failures was not that there prevailed, in all the circumstances, a fundamentally benign emotional attitude toward the purveyor of electric shock (or other fear-evoking stimulus).

Argument 3. Not all stimuli have equipotentiality to evoke phobias. This is perhaps the most significant difficulty with conditioning theory. There is ample evidence that some stimuli are indeed much more potent than others in inducing fears. Observations about phobias suggest that they are "largely restricted to objects that have threatened survival, potential predators, unfamiliar places, and the dark" (Seligman and Hager, 1972, p. 465). This view suggests that some "prepared" fears are the remnants of a biological inheritance, and that prepared fears have a greater potential than unprepared ones to develop into phobias. It is worth noting that this view is identical with Freud's second theory about anxiety: namely, that it is a signal operating in the ego of an archaic danger to survival. Freud also suggested (very much earlier than the behaviorists) that a child's fear of large animals is what behaviorists now call a "prepared" fear. Freud rested this notion both on the Darwinian idea of emotional survivals from archaic dangers and on a "transfer" from the differences in size between a little child and surrounding adults, which the child might easily experience as intimidating. Once again, however, the question that arises in attempting to explain "prepared" fears is whether they are to be conveniently explained as biological inheritances or whether their origin might not be better explained as arising out of the vicissitudes of the child's universally contradictory, ambivalent emotional experiences with significant adults.

Arguments 4 and 5. The distribution of fears within both a normal and a psychiatric population does not coincide with predictions from the equipotentiality theory. For example, the fear of snakes is just too common to be explained on the basis of the probable frequency with which people have been exposed to frightening experiences with snakes. In an epidemiological study of a Vermont city, Agras, Sylvester, and Oliveau (1969) showed that fear of snakes occurred in 390 of every 1000 people but fear of dentists in only 198 of every 1000. Clearly people in a Vermont city are likely to visit the dentist oftener than they are likely to encounter snakes. Similarly, the prevalence of snake fears was five times greater among 30-year-old people than that of fear of injections, although the likelihood of exposure to the latter is much greater than exposure to the former.

Not only is the epidemiology of fears inconsistent with the notion of equipotential stimuli, but patients' own reports of the onset of their phobias often show *no* apparent trauma which might have initiated the phobia. It is in fact very difficult, as clinicians well know, to find a convincing precipitant of a phobia. Taken together, all this evidence about the distribution of specific fears and the absence of convincing precipitants in clinical phobias suggests that "forbidden" emotional states might be underlying phobic symptoms. Snakes, spiders, and heights might be metaphors for these forbidden affective states, as psychoanalytic theory suggests.

It is interesting to note in this connection, that two kinds of fears emerge as predominant in most surveys. These are, first, a fear of social situations, and second, fear of animals or insects which might do bodily harm. In a psychiatric sample (Lawlis, 1971), the major fear factor comprised social situations: patients were afraid of the loss of approval, loss of status, feelings of rejection, and feelings of humiliation. A second factor comprised fears of animals — snakes, spiders, rats, insects. Although Rachman does not explicitly say so, it is indeed difficult to imagine how an explanation which does not take account of underlying emotional state could account for the development of social anxieties. We have already seen the difficulties encountered when conditioning theory attempts to explain the distribution of animal phobias.

Rachman's case account (1978) of a woman suffering from a severe "unprepared" phobia is a fascinating study which studiously avoids even considering psychoanalytic ideas, even though the case is presented as totally puzzling. Mrs. V. was admitted to a hospital with a powerful fear of chocolate, and with compulsive rituals to ensure that she did not come into contact with chocolate. Since chocolate has no biological significance, and is therefore not a "prepared" stimulus, Rachman finds it hard to understand the genesis of the patient's very severe phobia. She avoided brown objects, would never sit on furniture that had anything brown about it, once walked up many flights of stairs because there was a brown stain near the elevator button, and finally became so phobic that she was house-bound.

According to both the patient and her husband, her psychiatric involvement with chocolate began after the death of her mother, to whom she was "inordinately attached" (just like Little Hans). Before her mother's death she had been very fond of chocolate; for four years after her mother's death she grew increasingly phobic about anything connected with chocolate.

The case of Mrs. V. calls to mind Spitz and Wolf's (1949) finding that one-year-old infants who had experienced adequate mothering for several months and then were abruptly deprived of it by sudden loss were particularly inclined to autoerotic "fecal play," that is, playing with their feces in a dreamy state. In this dream state they were "out-of-touch," but clearly enjoyed fondling their feces. Spitz interpreted "fecal play" as the infant's symbolic representation of the maternal "object," fondled in substitution for maternal loss. Following this kind of lead, one might imagine that Mrs. V.'s inordinate attachment to her mother occasioned many fantasies about her mother in death including the imagery of decay, and of disgust such as is associated with feces. The brown of chocolate can easily be generalized from the brown of feces. In any case, whether or not this line of "explanation" has any relation at all to Mrs. V.'s experience, psychoanalytic symbolism is available for consideration. What is even more important, however, is the possibility that, as any psychoanalyst might imagine, along with an inordinate attachment to mother, there might well be forbidden hostility which, especially now that mother is dead and guilt cannot be directly expiated, requires a check on Mrs. V.'s former gratifications.

Argument 6. The conditioning theory of phobia has also suffered a major setback because behavior theorists now know, principally from the work of Bandura (1977), that fears may be transmitted vicariously. The discovery of vicarious fear transmission does indeed make it difficult for conditioning theory since there is the possibility that one may become afraid of something one has never actually encountered, merely through the agency of vicarious experience. Vicarious experience is, of course, a prime example of human social attachment, which makes it possible for people to experience themselves in another person's activities and which is the stuff of which social interactions are made. Once again, as in each of the arguments that Rachman summarizes against conditioning theory, we are led to the realization that what is missing is an adequate theory of human emotions. This is the same deficiency that made it necessary for Freud to theorize about his observations in terms of instincts — an enterprise that led him back into reliance on biological inheritance instead of on the power of human social, affective interactions.

In a most instructive review of the common features of all major psychotherapeutic approaches, Andrews (1966) points out that in their case accounts, behavior therapists describe their phobic patients in much the same human emotional terms as do dynamic theorists. For example, Mary Cover Jones (1960), describing the case of Peter (the behaviorists' equivalent of Little Hans), focused specifically on the issue of Peter's emotional separation from his mother. She wrote: "He is the recipient of much of the unwise affection of his parents. . . . His mother is a highly emotional individual who cannot get through an interview, however brief, without a display of tears. . . . In an attempt to control Peter she resorts to frequent fear suggestions. 'Come in, Peter, someone wants to steal you.' To her erratic resorts to discipline, Peter reacts with temper tantrums" (p. 52).

Andrews also calls attention to the fact that in Wolpe and Lazarus' case accounts, very frequent mention is made of the phobic patients' dependent attitudes toward their overprotective parents (or spouses). And as we shall see in a moment, behavior therapists, although disavowing an emotional basis for phobic symptoms, do take active steps to free their phobic patients from noxious emotional situations that might be causing emotional stress.

Behavioral Critique of Psychoanalytic Theory of Phobias

Let us return now to the behaviorists' criticism of psychoanalysis for unraveling emotional conflict as its technique of treating phobias. We may quickly dispose of the logical fallacy that the success of learning techniques in curing phobias is a demonstration that phobias originate by "learning" rather than being "emotionally determined." A cure may be effected by very different mechanisms than the unraveling or retracing of the mechanisms that produced the symptoms. To argue the etiology of a symptom from the results of treatment is incorrect, whether it is behaviorists or psychoanalysts who do so. And while behaviorists would surely not explicitly endorse this error they implicitly accept it in dealing with psychoanalytic technique. For example, Rachman (1978), responding to the psychoanalytic concept that the spider phobia is a "representative of the dangerous (orally devouring and anally castrating) mother," offers the "comfort . . . that a fear of spiders can be desensitized in five sessions" (p. 214). Rachman tells us further that the process of spider phobia deconditioning is at times boring. And while the implied sarcasm in response to heavy psychoanalytic jargon is understandable, Rachman's main point — that spider phobia is *not* emotionally determined — cannot be accepted even on the encouraging evidence that only five sessions of treatment are needed.

There is a substantial body of evidence now accumulated by behavior therapists which suggests that behavioral learning techniques that focus directly on phobic symptoms are effective, particularly with phobias in "nonpsychiatric" (relatively normal) people, and more often in treating specific animal phobias than in treating nonspecific phobias, such as are commonly classed as "agoraphobias." Let us pause at this point to review the highlights of the behaviorists' successful technique. As we shall see, the behaviorists' own accounts of their work contain many places in which they indicate that people's emotional conflicts are directly or indirectly involved in the therapeutic work. Andrews' (1966) review of commonalities in all psychotherapies is particularly enlightening in this respect. Furthermore, as we shall see, the areas in which direct behavioral modification techniques are less effective are precisely those in which the person's "defenses" against emotionality are less active. Specifically, agoraphobics are more likely to use repression, while animal phobics use isolation of affect (Seif and Atkins, 1979). It is with persons who have animal phobias that behavior modification has had its most outstanding successes; agoraphobics are less susceptible to behavior modification (Marks, 1969). It seems reasonable to suppose that people whose affects are managed by isolation of affect and intellectualization, and whose phobia is specific rather than diffuse, would benefit more from a learning procedure that plays down affects.

Emotional Components in Behavioral Techniques

The most widely used of the behavior modification techniques is systematic desensitization, which, as Rachman (1978) tells us, has provided at least 100 empirical studies of phobic symptom relief. This technique was devised by Wolpe (1958) after a series of experiments on the artificial induction and reduction of experimental "neurosis" in cats. Once again, as we saw also in discussing hysteria (Chapter 2), experimenters turned to animal behavior in their search for understanding.

The principle evolved by Wolpe from his animal work is called "reciprocal inhibition." He describes it as follows: "If a response antagonistic to anxiety can be made to occur in the presence of anxiety-provoking stimuli so that it is accompanied by a complete or partial suppression of the anxiety responses, the bond between the stimuli and anxiety responses will be weakened" (p. 71). In addition to "reciprocal inhibition" of anxiety, Wolpe made use of the findings by Edmund Jacobson (1938) that "progressive relaxation" of the musculature can provide direct relief of the experience of body tension in anxiety.

Rachman's (1967) description of the technique of systematic desensitization is very concise and clear:

> The patient is relaxed and then requested to imagine the anxiety-producing stimuli in a very mild and attenuated form. When the image is obtained vividly, a small amount of anxiety is usually elicited. The therapist then relaxes the patient and instructs him to stop imagining the scene and to continue relaxing. The full sequence is: relax, imagine, relax, stop imagining, relax. The superimposition of relaxation on the anxiety reaction produces a dissipation of anxiety (reciprocal inhibition). The process is then repeated with the same stimulus or with a stimulus which is slightly more disturbing. . . . With each evocation and subsequent dampening of the anxiety response, conditioned inhibition is built up. Eventually the patient is able to imagine even the previously most anxiety-producing stimulus with tranquility and this tranquility generalizes to the real-life situation. . . . Naturally, before the systematic desensitization proper commences, various preliminary steps have to be taken. In the first place a full history of the patient's current disorder and general history are obtained. Second, an attempt is made to *reduce or eliminate any conflicts of anxiety-provoking situations which prevail at the time of treatment. If, for example, the patient's parents or spouse are exposing him to anxiety-provoking situations, an attempt is made to alter their behavior* [my italics]. Third, the patient is trained in methods of progressive relaxation as described by Jacobson. Fourth, a hierarchy or group of hierarchies containing the anxiety-provoking stimuli is established by the therapist and the patient as a result of detailed therapeutic discussions. In these discussions, the therapist, with the aid of the patient, builds up a series of situations which might produce anxiety in the patient. The patient is then required to rank them from the most disturbing to the least disturbing situation. When all these steps have been completed the desensitization itself may proceed (p. 94).

Two other techniques have been evolved which, along with desensitization, are the main behavioral learning procedures used in the treatment of phobias. These are "flooding," a technique of "implosive therapy" evolved ty Stampfl (1970) in which patients are required to imagine extremely distressing scenes derived from psychoanalytic explorations of their past, and "therapeutic modeling" (Bandura, Blanchard, and Ritter, 1969), in which a phobic person watches a nonphobic one approach the frightening stimulus. In this latter technique, emulation of another person is the central agent of change, with the implication that courage may be "learned" through vicarious experience of another person's calm in the face of the phobic person's dreaded stimulus. Bandura et al. (1969) provide evidence that participant modeling, that is, the patient's real-life participation in the other person's approach to snakes, is even more effective than systematic desensitization, imaginary modeling, or a control condition.

It is instructive to consider also the pioneer experiments of Lang and Lazovik (1963) on snake phobia and the follow-up study by Lang, Lazovik, and Reynolds (1965). In their 1963 study, Lang and Lazovik compared the effects of systematic desensitization with those of a control procedure on severe snake phobia in an otherwise "nonpsychiatric" college student. Their studies were designed as experimental analogues for work with clinical patients. Both on subjective report and on objective measures of overt avoidance behavior, students treated by systematic desensitization were significantly improved. Muscle relaxation and hypnosis were not responsible for the change, nor was the suggestibility of the subjects. There was, moreover, no evidence that the snake phobia had been replaced by a substitute symptom.

In their subsequent study, Lang et al. (1965) were at pains to examine the influence of the patient–therapist relationship on their subjects' improvement. In pursuit of the "therapeutic placebo" effect, they instituted a control procedure called "pseudotherapy." In this procedure, the students assumed that they were in psychotherapy. (The deception was not unmasked by any student during the experiment.) In pseudotherapy, the subject was hypnotized, relaxed, and asked to imagine previously described pleasant scenes. These scenes were starting points for discussion between therapist and student. But no discussion of the phobia was permitted in these "pleasant" talks. Students were informed that they were getting a "better understanding" of themselves, and close and empathetic relationships between therapist and student did emerge. Nevertheless, as predicted, systematic desensitization was more effective than "pseudotherapy," which was not much more effective than the control procedure. Lang et al. conclude that the effects of systematic desensitization do not depend on the patient–therapist relationship but on the specifics of the deconditioning procedure.

It is also instructive to note that Paul (1966) demonstrated the effectiveness of treating the fear of public speaking by systematic desensitization, and found this technique more effective than "insight psychotherapy" or control. Clearly, then, behavioral learning techniques can be applied (in a nonpsychiatric population) to social anxiety as well as to specific animal phobias.

Finally, as Rachman (1978) summarizes the present state of behavior therapy, not only has the imagination of fearful scenes in a state of relaxation been shown to be a "robust technique" for treating fears, but the attack on the symptom does not lead to symptom substitution. As for the patient–therapist relationship, Rachman looks forward to the expendability of the therapist. "While we need not discount the contribution a sympathetic therapist might make to reducing someone's fears, a wholly satisfactory explanation of desensitization effects must take account of the expendability of a therapist" (p. 162).

The question to which we now return is that of understanding the basis for these therapeutic effects. They are said to be the result of a learning program, in contrast to a psychoanalytic view that a therapeutic relationship and an unraveling of the underlying emotional conflict are required. But it may be that the two approaches are not so far apart as they appear. In his clinical account of the case of Little Hans, Freud sought to unravel the child's emotional conflicts. But Freud did not neglect techniques by which Hans would learn to master his phobia. Hans's father repeatedly persuaded him to go with him on Sunday excursions to the grandparent (p. 29); real improvement in the phobic behavior was reckoned by the degree of persuasion needed to make Hans leave the house and by the fact that the "radius of his circle of activity with the street-door as its center grows ever wider" (p. 53). Nor was there an absence of attention to what would in behavioral language of today be called a "hierarchy." Hans's most terrible fear was of a horse's bite; he also had fears that horses would fall down and somewhat lesser fears of horse-drawn carts and furniture vans. Commenting specifically on the technique of treating phobias, Freud (1910) wrote:

> These patients cannot bring themselves to bring out the material necessary for resolving their phobias so long as they feel protected by obeying the condition which it lays down. . . . One must therefore help them by interpreting their subconscious to them until they can *make up their minds* [my italics] to do without the protection of their phobia and expose themselves to a now greatly mitigated anxiety (p. 145).

In other words, psychoanalytic technique for phobia, as clinically described, consists of a combination of learning and emotional unraveling techniques. Fenichel (1945), who is acknowledged as a major exponent of Freudian psychoanalytic thinking, summarizes the position in even more clear-cut terms. "After the framework of the neurosis has been loosened enough by the analysis, the analyst must actively intervene in order to induce the patient to make his first effort to overcome the phobia" (p. 215).

We can also ask the same question in other ways. Do behavior modification techniques involve *only* a special learning program? Specifically, can anything like a similar constellation of *emotional* and learning factors be discerned in behavioral modification techniques? Are the components of the learning program really to be understood only as a simple pairing of a positive stimulus with a negative one in reciprocal inhibition of the latter by the former? Or does the positive stimulus have a taken-for-granted emotional meaning far deeper than the apparent one of just relaxing muscles?

The state of emotional being in muscle relaxation is surely connected (if only by associative conditioning) to states of satisfaction. An early Freudian would call the state "sexual satisfaction"; a Jungian would call it "union" of the self with the "life-force"; a neo-Freudian would call it "security"; Bowlby calls it "attachment." I find it close to the mark to equate the benign state of muscle relaxation with Nirvana — the absence of shame and guilt, or "inner peace." From the phenomenological standpoint, the absence of shame and guilt usually does entail relaxed muscles (although this proposition is unfortunately not reversible). In any event, the benign effects of muscle relaxation may themselves be products (happily evoked during systematic desensitization) of our human attachment system. The therapist who induces such a state — even if by tape-recorded message — would be symbolic of a "good mother." In behavioral terminology, muscle relaxation is a "prepared" stimulus — an emotional one, prepared by a lifetime of social connectedness.

The attitude of a person entering any kind of therapy, including systematic desensitization for phobia, is also a highly emotional factor which operates silently during the procedure. There is an attitude (an emotional state) of shame, or at least self-dislike for having a symptom in the first place. As Lang et al. (1965) suggest, the positive feedback from the step-to-step mastery of the hierarchy of fears must operate tacitly to relieve the subject's shame and thereby increase his or her courage to face the noxious stimulus. As Rachman (1978) points out, patients need great courage to encounter their fears. They do not acquire courage only by reciprocal inhibition, but also by an alteration in their emotional attitude toward themselves which results from the mastery of a learning program. In turn, this learning program makes use of special relaxation techniques which communicate symbolic emotional support. As we shall see in Chapter 7, there is indeed evidence that patients in behavior therapy resemble patients in psychotherapy in designating the patient–therapist relationship as an important factor in change (Sloane, Staples, Whipple, and Cristol, 1977).

It is instructive to realize that psychoanalytic writers, beginning with Freud, accepted the fact that nonanalytic techniques of symptoms removal can work. Freud (1909a), for example, clearly accepted the possibility that "the boy would have gone out for walks soon enough if he had been given a sound thrashing" (p. 100), but he suggested that the psychic damage from such harsh treatment might have been considerable. Fenichel (1945) devoted considerable attention to the possible mechanisms by which nonanalytic therapies work. "Many therapists have great skill in applying threats and reassurances one after the other, thus combining the two types of influence and treating patients with a 'Turkish bath method' — one day hot, next day cold" (p. 559). Fenichel quotes Ferenczi as discussing the effectiveness of this method in taming a horse, clearly anticipating Wolpe's animal experiments pairing anxiety with reassurance. Fenichel, moreover, suggested that the efficacy of nonanalytic techniques be systematically investigated from a psychoanalytic point of view. He described both Glover's and his own interpretations of the emotional meaning of each of many commonly used "behavioral" modification techniques. He looked forward to the day when each of these nonanalytic techniques might have its explanation in what he called psychoanalytic terms, that is, in terms of their emotional significance.

One of the most sophisticated and successful attempts to explain the efficacy of systematic desensitization in emotional terms has been that of Andrews (1966). As mentioned earlier, Andrews' review of the literature revealed a strong consensus among all viewpoints, including the behavioral, in describing phobic persons as "overdependent" on significant other persons. Andrews points out that behavioral treatment suits this personality. It is a "highly structured and directive arrangement. The nature of the patient's problem is defined at the start and the procedure consists of very specific routine which the patient is expected to follow obediently . . . this stance places the patient in the complementary role which calls for docile-dependent behavior" (pp. 467–468). The therapist, in other words, establishes himself in the directive role normally "pulled" by phobics from other people. The procedure also involves muscle relaxation and/or hypnosis, both of which emphasize the nurturant role of the therapist. The behavioral procedure thus provides the social context of directiveness and nurturance familiar to phobic people at least in relation to their phobic symptoms. And it is in this social context that the phobia is deconditioned. This is not to say that the specific deconditioning procedure itself is unimportant; on the contrary, it speaks to the wisdom of a focus on symptom removal. But in this version of events, learning and relaxation also have emotional components that behavioral theorists deny although behavioral practitioners often make use of them. This is parallel to the situation in psychoanalysis: Psychoanalytic theory denies the wisdom of a focus on removing the symptoms while its practitioners are clearly aware that, especially in the case of phobia, a direct attack on the symptom may be necessary.

The Value of Symptom Removal

We come now to the last and perhaps most important question that divides psychoanalysis and behavior modification theory: the value of symptom removal. It is in this area that one can see most clearly the difficulties created for psychoanalytic theory by the absence of a viable theory of human emotions. We can also observe that the same difficulty afflicts behavioral theory.

The remarkably rigid attitude of psychoanalysis to symptom removal becomes somewhat clearer in its historical context. Although we have already seen that psychoanalysis accepted the efficacy of nonanalytic techniques of symptom removal and even attempted a psychoanalytic explanation (Fenichel, 1945), the more pervasive attitude toward symptom removal became a denigration of its importance. The grounds for denigration were at first empirical, namely, that symptom removal was only temporary and unstable. As nearly as can be determined, the evidence for this point mainly concerned the removal of hysterical symptoms by hypnosis (Freud, 1916–1917, p. 451). Freud's experience with hypnosis — applied as suggestion only, without emotional catharsis — had been (see Chapter 2) that the symptom, that is, the mother's inability to nurse, had recurred and had had to be rehypnotized or suggested away with each childbirth. Somewhat later, the reason for denigrating symptom removal came to be "theoretical," namely, that symptom removal without removing the emotional cause of the symptom was *bound* to lead to symptom recurrence or symptom substitution. This proposition is entirely unfounded since it assumes that the etiology of neurotic symptoms is known. But one is struck, especially in reading the case account of Little Hans (Freud, 1909a), with how frequently Freud asserted his ignorance of the actual etiology of the child's phobia:

> It is hard to say what the influence was which . . . led to the sudden change in Hans and to the transformation of his libidinal longing into anxiety . . . whether the scales were turned by the child's *intellectual* inability to solve the difficult problem of begetting children and to cope with the aggressive impulses that were liberated by his approaching its solution or whether the effect was produced by a *somatic* incapacity, a constitutional intolerance of the masturbatory gratification in which he regularly indulged (whether, that is, the mere persistence of sexual excitement at such a pitch of high intensity was bound to bring about a revulsion) (p. 136) [Freud's italics].

It should be noted further, that Freud continued to reiterate our fundamental ignorance of the etiology of neurosis not only in his 1926 rethinking of the case, but also in the final publication (1940) of his life. Clearly, if the etiology of phobia is unknown, symptom removal cannot be predicted to result in symptom replacement.

The proposition about symptom removal finally came to have the meaning that only the psychoanalytic technique of analyzing resistance and transference was capable of finding the emotional cause of the symptom. It also came to have the meaning that only psychoanalytic technique can relieve the cause, an excellent example of begging the question. As to this latter meaning, Freud was accustomed to making the distinction between symptom removal and removing the emotional cause of illness. But, at least on some occasions, he was careful to distinguish between the *method of finding* the emotional reason for illness and the *method of curing* it! Freud describes

. . . a causal therapy . . . [as] a procedure which does not take the symptoms of an
illness as its point of attack but sets about removing its *causes* [Freud's italics].
Well, then, is our psychoanalytic method a causal therapy or not? The reply is not
a simple one, but it may perhaps give us an opportunity of realizing the worthlessness of such a question framed in this way. In so far as analytic therapy does
not make its first task to remove the symptoms, it is behaving like a causal
therapy. In another respect, you may say, it is not. For long ago we traced the
causal chains back through the repressions to the instinctual dispositions in the
constitution and the deviations in the course of their development. Supposing
now that it was possible, by some chemical means, perhaps, to interfere in this
mechanism, to increase or diminish the quantity of libido present at a given time
or to strengthen one instinct at the cost of another — this then would be a causal
therapy in the true sense of the word, for which our analysis would have carried
out the indispensable preliminary work of reconnaissance. At present, as you
know, there is no question of any such method of influencing libidinal processes
(Freud, 1916–1917, pp. 435–436).

In this paragraph Freud is clearly treating psychoanalysis as a method of
reconnaissance and assuming that any method of interrupting the causal
chain would be acceptable to psychoanalysis. It is noteworthy that Freud
(1937) reiterated these thoughts in one of his last publications. These careful
statements by Freud, however, tended to be forgotten because they were
embedded in the larger context of Freud's own denigration of therapeutic
aims (and successes). Especially in the case of Little Hans, it is clear that
Freud (1909a) was caught between the conflicting demands of psychoanalysis as a research tool and as a therapeutic agent. So, for example, in one place
he says that psychoanalysis is "not an impartial scientific investigation but a
therapeutic measure" (p. 104), and in another place he says that "therapeutic
success is not our primary aim" (p. 120). We know, also, that as his work
progressed, Freud emphasized his own research interests to the neglect of
therapeutic success. As a result, problems of therapeutic technique were not
only not directly pursued, but they were downgraded. By a familiar (Freudian) mechanism called rationalization, an atmosphere was created in which
the possibility that therapeutic success could be achieved without depth
analysis was denied, or if admitted, rendered the success trivial because inherently unstable! Moreover, in another compensatory development to
justify the downgrading of therapeutic aims, Freud began to speak of
psychoanalysis as having higher aims than mere symptom removal, suggesting that after psychoanalysis, the patient's "mental life remains protected
against fresh possibilities of falling ill" (Freud, 1916–1917, p. 451).
Psychoanalysts today no longer affirm this claim; on the contrary, they freely admit that analyzed patients are subject to a return of symptoms. But,
once again, this admission is made with the implicit attitude that symptoms
are relatively trivial events. Unfortunately, the patients who suffer from
symptoms cannot readily agree with this evaluation.

On the side of the behaviorists there is the very compelling argument, which psychoanalysts have no theoretical reason for disputing, that symptom relief itself may generalize into improved psychic health. Although the behaviorists do not especially say so, symptom relief may make a profound alteration in what psychoanalysts call the person's emotional economy. A symptom, once formed, clearly involves the patient in what Freud described as an expenditure of psychic energy. As Freud put it, symptoms deplete the psychic economy. On the face of it, therefore, symptom removal itself should be enough to improve psychic functioning if only by releasing the "quantities of libido" held in check by the symptom. One probe into this question (Kamil, 1970) did, in fact produce some slight evidence of psychodynamic changes (in response to the TAT) as a consequence of systematic desensitization.

More specifically, having an uncontrollable symptom always involves the patient in the shame of his or her inadequacy. Release from the shame of having a symptom into the feeling of competence in having mastered it is progress not to be denigrated.

The most important reason for the neglect of symptom removal by psychoanalysts, however, is Freud's formulation of his cases in terms of instincts and psychic structures rather than in terms of affects. Since the patients' symptoms are ascribed to instinctual or structural malfunctioning, the remedy seems to lie in an instinctual or structural reorganization rather than in an emotional one. Freud's need to transform his observations about affective states into theories about instincts is particularly apparent in the case of Little Hans. Even though he described in exquisite detail a multiplicity of the child's affects, Freud compressed these into a system of instincts. He summarized the case not in terms of affects but by saying that the essence of Hans's illness was dependent on the nature of the instinctual components that had been repressed: the symptom was a victory for the forces of inhibition over Hans's sexuality. In such a formulation, the symptom loses its connection to the ambivalent affects that have most immediately preceded its formation. In contrast, an intervention (like that of behavior modification) which specifically focuses on the affect of anxiety can produce a diminution of it. That the behavior therapist also plays down the emotional factors in his success is a product of the same intellectual atmosphere which pushed Freud to downplay affects.

Advances in Psychoanalytic Concepts of Phobias

We come back, now, to the developments in our understanding of phobia that have occurred within the psychoanalytic system. Classical psychoanalysts who worked with children's phobias (Bornstein, 1935, 1949; Schnurmann, 1949; Sperling, 1952) have been uniformly impressed by the phobic child's inability to bear separation from its mother. Bornstein (1949), for example, in her account of the analysis of a 5½-year-old phobic boy, offers a moving description of the profound loneliness unconsciously expressed by the child's play during his opening session. These clinical phenomena of sadness and loneliness in phobic children were formulated as "pre-Oedipal" traumata — oral and anal fixations underlying the castration anxiety postulated by Freud for Little Hans.

In more recent years, Bowlby (1973) has offered a reformulation of phobic behavior which rests on his abandonment of Freud's instinct theory in favor of an ethological view of the infant and mother as biologically attached. In this theoretical reformulation, Freud's observations about affects have a framework in which the affects associated with attachment and separation are the "prime movers" since they reflect the state of the "given" (biological) affective bond between mother and child. Phobia is conceptualized as the result of the unavailability of internalized models of attachment figures. The phobic person makes the forecast that his or her attachment figures will be unavailable and this forecast is a "fair reflection of the types of experience he has had . . . and may perhaps be still" (p. 258). Bowlby provides an excellent summary of the empirical work on phobias in the course of his reformulation.

One principal outcome of Bowlby's reformulation is his suggestion that the majority of cases of so-called school refusal (a better term than school phobia) are results of one or more of four main patterns of pathological *family* interaction. These are as follows:

Pattern A — mother, or more rarely father, is a sufferer from chronic anxiety regarding attachment figures and retains the child at home to be a companion.

Pattern B — the child fears that something dreadful may happen to mother, or possibly father, while he is at school and so remains at home to prevent its happening.

Pattern C — the child fears that something dreadful may happen to himself if he is away from home and so remains at home to prevent that happening.

Pattern D — mother, or more rarely father, fears that something dreadfulwill happen to the child while he is at school and so keeps him at home.

These patterns are, of course, not incompatible; one or more of them may be dominant in any particular case. Pattern A is the most common, although it may be combined with the others.

Bowlby also implicated these four patterns of pathological family interaction in many cases of diffuse phobic reactions — the so-called agoraphobias, or situation phobias. As Bowlby's reformulation suggests, dynamically-based family therapy is an appropriate mode of treatment for phobias. Bowlby reviews both Little Hans's and the behaviorists' Peter's family situation and shows that the family system in each classic case was pathological.

Another development within the framework of psychoanalysis has been a reformulation of phobias in terms of the defenses employed in generating the symptom. Beginning with Glover (1939), many psychoanalytic observers have been impressed with the obsessional character of phobic symptoms and with the extent to which isolation of affect rather than repression is central to symptom formation. Salzman (1965) emphasizes the importance of isolation of affect in phobias. It should be noted, in passing, that the controversy over central defenses in phobia rests, in part, on the fact that early in his writings Freud used the term "repression" to cover all kinds of defenses (Madison, 1961), while only later, as clinical observations increased, were the many varieties of "repression" specified.

An important recent experimental study (Seif and Atkins, 1979) has suggested that the controversy over repression versus isolation of affect in phobia might be a reflection of a difference in kind of phobia. Specifically, the hypotheses evolved were that persons with animal phobia might be more likely to use isolation and intellectualization as defenses, and that they would be more likely to be field-independent in their cognitive style. Conversely, agoraphobics, or as the authors call them, "situation" phobics, would be more prone to use repression (in the narrower sense of repression of ideas), displacement, and projection as defenses and to be more field-dependent in their cognitive style. These predictions were confirmed. Situation phobics, whose phobia generalizes more freely than animal phobics, and for whom there is a relative diffuseness in the way the phobia is experienced, are more field-dependent persons.

Another line of development within the psychoanalytic framework is my own attempt to understand the fact that women are more likely to become phobic than men. The evidence for this preponderance of women phobic patients is strong and conclusive, especially in the case of agoraphobia (Marks, 1969; Mendel and Klein, 1969). It is congruent with the strong evidence that "normal" women are more prone to all forms of anxiety than men (Maccoby and Jacklin, 1974), as well as with the evidence that women report themselves as experiencing more pathological anxiety than men — more nightmares, palpitations, fears of dying, fainting, nervous breakdown, and the like (Chesler, 1972). The greater proneness of women to fear apparently begins in childhood (Maccoby and Jacklin, 1974).

From my own psychoanalytic perspective, the greater proneness of women to phobia is best understood as a function of women's greater proneness to the affective state of shame (Lewis, 1971, 1976). Conceptualizing shame as the proximal state in phobia depends on a network of linkages; women are more field-dependent than men, and there is a linkage between field-dependence and proneness to shame as well as a linkage between female gender and proneness to phobias. Very briefly, shame is conceptualized as the affective state accompanying "loss of love," or separation from attachment figures. Female infants, reared by a same-sex caretaker in what may be a smoother bonding than is the case with male infants (Moss, 1974), have closer early attachment figures than males. The culture deepens this closer attachment by its encouragement of girls and women to be more nurturant and affectionate than men, which indeed they do become (Maccoby, 1966). On this ground alone, separation from attachment figures should be more difficult for women than for men. If, in addition, as Bowlby (1973) has pointed out, it "seems childish, even babyish, to yearn for the presence of a loved figure or to be distressed during her (or his) absence" (p. 80), women are more likely than men to experience shame on separation.

Furthermore, the culture, although encouraging the affectionateness of women, nevertheless places a higher value on "masculine" attributes of competitiveness, aggression, and self-assertion. Women, moreover, are also more often second-class citizens in the world of work. On this ground, also, women are more likely than men to experience shame. The phenomenological characteristics of shame — that it is an affect directly about the self, that it involves self-directed hostility, that it is experienced as an acute paralysis or helplessness of the self — are all congruent with the experience of phobia in which the self is threatened with "annihilation." Clearly, of course, this formulation of shame as the proximal state in phobia is more likely to be true of agoraphobia than of snake phobias. It should not be difficult to put to empirical test a hypothesis that people with agoraphobia are more shame-prone than people with animal phobias, but this has not yet been done.

This review of the developments in our understanding of phobia within both the psychoanalytic and the behavioral traditions leaves us with the realization that the exact etiology of phobia is as elusive today as it was for Freud in 1909. A phenomenon that depends on a specific constellation of emotions which may be reached in a great variety of ways will not easily be specified. Freud was conveying this in the case of Little Hans by saying that "no sharp line of distinction can be drawn between 'neurotic' and 'normal' people — whether children or adults . . . our conception of 'disease' is a purely practical one and a question of summation, that predisposition and the eventualities of life must combine before the threshold of the summation is overstepped so that a number of individuals are constantly passing from the class of healthy people into that of neurotic patients, while a far smaller number also make the journey in the opposite direction" (pp. 145–146).

When Freud speaks of "summation" and the "eventualities of life" he is referring in his typically nonemotional theoretical style to the emotional blows that life affords. This is clearly not a medical model of mental illness, but something much closer to George Engel's (1977) "biopsychosocial" model. From this standpoint it is small wonder that the etiology of phobias is still unknown. For adherents of this broad biopsychosocial model, the useful scientific course is the careful examination of the complicated emotional situations in which people become enmeshed, both through family and through larger social systems. What is badly needed for this task is a less contentious attitude among both "learning" and "psychoanalytic" theorists, and an increased attention to the psychology of human emotions.

CHAPTER 4

Obsessional Neurosis
The Problem of Sadism

In his introduction to the case account of the Rat-Man, Freud (1909b) observed that an obsessional neurosis was much less easy to understand than a case of hysteria. He found it puzzling that this should be so, since "the language of the obsessional neurosis — the means by which it expresses its secret thoughts — is . . . only a dialect of the language of hysteria. It is moreover, a dialect in which we ought to find our way about more easily than in hysteria, since it is more nearly related to the forms of expression adopted by our conscious thought than is the language of hysteria. Above all, it does not involve the leap from a mental process to a somatic innervation — hysterical conversion — which can never be fully comprehensible to us" (p. 156).

What Freud was alluding to in this puzzle was the fact, now familiar to us because of his work, that obsessional neurotics can describe their forbidden thoughts, and can even perceive them as "crazy," but are powerless to stop them from intruding into awareness. In contrast, in hysterical patients the forbidden ideas implicated in their symptoms are totally lost. In any rational system, knowing that ideas are "crazy" should be adequate to demolish them, but in the obsessional neurosis the patient's intellect is powerless to do more than observe his "craziness." In cases of hysteria and phobia, as we have just seen, the emotional situation of the patient is relatively obvious: There is distress in relation to parent, sibling, lover, or spouse. But in obsessional neurosis the emotional circumstances of the patient are less obvious. The patient suffers from "isolation of affect": Affects

101

are visible to an observer (including the patient) in the form of "crazy" ideas, but the affects are not fully experienced.

It is to Freud's everlasting credit that he grasped the essential similarity between hysterical and obsessive symptoms — that they were indeed both based in emotional conflict — even though the configuration of the affects is so different in the two illnesses. One is reminded of the extent of Freud's contribution in this respect by his own footnote (1909b, p. 163) to his description of the Rat-Man's symptoms: "Yet attempts have been made to explain obsessions without taking the affects into account!"[1] Freud's insight into the similarities between hysteria and obsessional neurosis and thus into paranoid (obsessive) ideation with its links to schizophrenia offered psychiatry its first unified theory based on emotional conflict.

Even in his earliest descriptions of the obsessional neurosis, Freud specified the emotion that is "repressed," namely, the "affect of self-reproach," or guilt. This description, which Freud never altered, has been overlooked principally because Freud himself shifted his formulations from the universe of affects to the universe of instincts. Let us look, now, at how Freud (1895) put the first case he reported. In the passage I shall quote at some length, Freud is distinguishing between two versions of obsessional neurosis. In version one the affect is simply "indefinite unpleasure" in connection with the content of the obsessional ideas, although one would expect the affect to be self-reproach. In the second form, the affect of self-reproach actually forces its way (from repression) into consciousness but is connected to irrelevant although not incompatible ideas.

> The affect of self-reproach can, by means of mental addition, be transformed into any other unpleasurable affect. When this has happened there is no longer anything to prevent the substituted affect from becoming conscious. Thus self-reproach (for having carried out some sexual act in childhood) can easily turn into *shame* (in case some one else should find out about it), into *hypochondriacal anxiety* (fear of the physical injuries resulting from the act involving the self-reproach), into *social* anxiety (fear of being punished by society for the misdeed), into *religious anxiety*, into *delusion of being noticed* (fear of betraying the act to other people), into *fear of temptation* (a justified mistrust of one's own moral powers of resistance), and so on (Freud, 1895, p. 171).

Freud goes on to describe the secondary defenses against these obsessional ideas: *"obsessional brooding"* which regularly deals with abstract and *suprasensual* things (in defense against sexuality); a *compulsion to test things*

---

[1] A memoir by the Wolf-Man (1958) of his treatment by Freud contains a moving account of the "desolate situation" he experienced before starting treatment with Freud in 1910. "The neurotic went to a physician with the wish to pour out his heart to him and was bitterly disappointed when the physician would scarcely listen to his problems, much less try to understand them. . . . The treatment of emotional illness seemed to have got into a dead end street" (p. 349).

and a *doubting mania,* as diversions away from the obsessive thoughts. Freud also described other protective measures against "obsessional *affects: penitential* measures (burdensome ceremonials, the observation of numbers), *precautionary* measures (all sorts of phobias, superstition, pedantry, increase of the primary conscientiousness); measures to do with the *fear of betrayal* . . . or to ensure *numbing* (of the mind) (dipsomania). Among these obsessional acts and obsessional impulses, phobias, since they circumscribe the patient's existence, play the greatest part" (p. 173). In this quotation we can see the power that Freud ascribed to the affect of self-reproach, in phobia and alcoholism as well as obsessional neurosis. Although the affects always played a major role in his subsequent clinical accounts, they were secondary in his theoretical formulations.

Three related themes emerge from a review of Freud's work on obsessional neurosis in the light of modern developments. The first theme has to do with the increasing duration of treatment, particularly the recalcitrance of obsessional neurotics. It was in connection with the obsessional neurosis that Freud (1923a) observed the "negative therapeutic reaction" which he attributed to the force of unrelenting guilt. The second theme is the prominence of guilt as the affective state in obsessional neurosis; "misplaced" guilt is an accurate description of the content of obsessional symptoms since the commands, prohibitions, and ideas of harming others for which the patient feels responsible (guilty) are so patently absurd. In Freud's view, however, guilt must be appropriate to something that had happened in the past — and not just to forbidden sexual longings as in hysteria and phobia — but to *regressed* sexual longings. From desire for sexual union the obsessional patient had already regressed in his childhood to sadism and anal-erotism. It is these horrifying anal-sadistic impulses that make the obsessional neurotic so endlessly (and in the last analysis, so Freud thought, appropriately) guilty. The third theme is thus the prominence of sadism in obsessional case accounts, the linkage between sadism and anal-erotism as instinctual developmental stages and the consequent neglect of the affects of humiliation or shame and guilt. As the reader will have seen, the sadism which is the presumed basis for obsessional neurosis is no longer conceptualized as sadistic fantasy or sadistic longing, but as sadism "in reality." The distinction between fantasy and "reality" is lost when an instinctual stage of development is postulated.

It was Freud's use of psychoanalytic technique to search for instinctual developmental stages and the *origins* of guilt that led him away from the phenomenology of the affects of guilt and shame. As a result, the experiential connection between these affects and obsessive symptoms became obscured. My own work (Lewis, 1971, 1979) has demonstrated that there are phenomenological similarities between guilt and obsessive ideation, and that, at least in some instances of obsessional symptoms, it is bypassed shame that functions to keep guilt from being resolved. The fact that the very same affective configurations may have occurred in childhood is not the relieving insight. But when the patient experiences the way in which his bypassed shame vis-à-vis the therapist has thrown him into an insoluble, guilty dilemma (of what to do or what to think) then obsessional symptoms can be resolved.

OBSESSIONAL NEUROSIS AND THE INCREASING DURATION OF TREATMENT

The expected duration of treatment of obsessional neurosis seems to have lengthened during Freud's lifetime and to have increased enormously as the work of his followers progressed. Freud "cured" the Rat-Man in eleven months of intensive, daily treatment beginning October 1, 1907. The success lasted at least seven years; the patient was killed in the First World War. Before the 1909 report, Freud published fragmentary accounts of five cases of obsessional symptoms that he treated successfully (Freud, 1894–1895). Although no specific durations are reported in this early analytic work, the impression is unmistakable that the emotional unraveling and accompanying symptom relief were accomplished in a very short time.

Freud's (1918) second major report of a case of obsessional neurosis, the Wolf-Man, was contained in an account of the Wolf-Man's infantile neurosis and did *not* describe the adult obsessional symptoms that had brought the patient into treatment. Freud was, in fact, so little interested in giving an account of the adult case that he leaves us in some confusion about the actual presenting symptoms. Freud tells us that the case had previously been misdiagnosed as a case of manic-depressive insanity. He says, somewhat vaguely, that the case "is to be regarded as a condition following on an obsessional neurosis which has come to an end spontaneously but has left a defect behind it after recovery" (p. 8). There is no question that the illness, whatever the exact symptoms, was severe. The patient had become "entirely incapacitated and completely dependent on other people" (p. 7) for years after a gonorrheal infection. The patient himself wrote later on (Wolf Man, 1958) of his recurring depressions. And Muriel Gardiner (1964), in her account of correspondence with him, also speaks of his depressions. Freud, however, because his interest in writing the account was only in the reconstruction of the patient's past, described only the patient's obsessional symptoms in his childhood. Whether because of this focus of interest or as a coincidence, the therapy lasted not eleven months but four years, and the patient suffered relapses. Freud's deprecation of short treatment, already apparent in the case of Little Hans, had grown even stronger by the time of the Wolf-Man. He wrote:

> Analyses which lead to a favorable conclusion in a short time are of value in ministering to the therapeutist's self-esteem and substantiate the medical importance of psycho-analysis; but they remain for the most part insignificant as regards the advancement of scientific knowledge. Nothing new is learnt from them. In fact they only succeed so quickly because everything that was necessary for their accomplishment was already known. Something new can only be gained from analyses that present special difficulties. . . . Only in such cases do we succeed in descending into the deepest and most primitive strata of mental development. . . . And we feel afterward that, strictly speaking, only an analysis which has penetrated so far deserves the name (p. 10).

It is clear from this paragraph that reconstructing the patient's past had become synonymous with "analysis" and that analysis as a technique for the therapy of symptoms had been downgraded.

Freud's attitude toward the duration of treatment, however, must also have been influenced by a considerable amount of exasperation with the patient. He tells us that the Wolf-Man was "unassailably entrenched behind an attitude of obliging apathy. His unimpeachable intelligence was, as it were, cut off from the instinctual forces which governed his behaviour. . . . His shrinking from a self-sufficient existence was so great as to outweigh all the vexations of his illness" (p. 11). Specifically what evoked Freud's impatience with the Wolf-Man's behavior as a patient was his attitude of doubt. "We know how important doubt is to the physician who is analysing an obsessional neurosis. It is the patient's strongest weapon, the favorite expedient of his resistance. The same doubt allowed our patient to lie entrenched behind a respectful indifference and to allow the efforts of the treatment to slip past him for years together. Nothing changed, and there was no way of convincing him" (p. 75).

It was under the press of this exasperation that Freud set a termination date for the analysis, without first obtaining the patient's consent.

> Under the inexorable pressure of this fixed limit his resistance and his fixation to the illness gave way, and now in a disproportionately short time the analysis produced all the material which made it possible to clear up his inhibitions and remove his symptoms. All the information, too which enabled me to understand his infantile neurosis is derived from this past period of the work, during which resistance temporarily disappeared and the patient gave an impression of lucidity which is usually obtainable only under hypnosis (p. 11).

Many years later Freud (1937) pronounced his insistence on a termination date to have been a technical mistake which contributed to the Wolf-

Man's several relapses, as well as paranoid symptoms. Freud's explanation of these relapses was that some aspects of the transference had not been resolved. As I have shown (Lewis, 1971) one unresolved aspect is bypassed shame in the ongoing patient–therapist relationship; this can easily be overlooked, especially if it becomes absorbed in analytic zeal for reconstructing the past. I think it is possible to interpret the Wolf-Man's "lucidity" as if under "hypnosis" as an instance of such analytic zeal for the past. One can speculate further that the paranoid symptoms which later emerged were also by-products of bypassed shame at Freud's "rejection" of him, which the unilateral decision to terminate had evoked.

The patient's attitude of "obliging apathy" or "doubt" is also easily understood as an (unconscious) retaliatory posture of hostility toward the therapist. The "indifference" which Freud confronted is inherently insulting without being overtly anything more than a neutral attitude. And if, as happened during the reconstruction of the past, the present symptoms were not immediately experienced in relation to the affective states which they represent, doubt or neutrality is a cognitively appropriate attitude for the patient to have. It is, however, inevitably humiliating to the therapist's investment in his own wisdom. No wonder Freud wanted to get finished with this patient and then later assumed responsibility for his relapses!

In recent years, the recalcitrance of many patients with obsessional symptoms to psychoanalytic treatment and the long duration which this recalcitrance requires, has been ascribed, following a lead of Freud's, to the fundamental narcissism of these patients (Kernberg, 1975; Kohut, 1971). Freud had hinted at this idea in his statement that the Wolf-Man "fell ill . . . as a result of a *narcissistic* 'frustration'" (p. 118). Freud was referring here to the attack of gonorrhea which precipitated the Wolf-Man's adult illness. He speaks also of the "excessive strength of his narcissism" as a reason for his illness. As I have suggested (Lewis, 1980a), a simpler solution may lie in the failure to analyze bypassed shame in the patient–therapist relationship, specifically, a failure to recognize the presence of unacknowledged shame as a force maintaining guilty, obsessive ideation.

As for psychoanalysis as a therapy of obsessional symptoms, the attitudes Freud expressed in his account of the Wolf-Man — derogation of short treatment or of anything less than "deep" analysis of childhood events — were little short of disastrous. Classically trained psychoanalysts, for example, encountering the notion of a focus on the phenomenology of shame and guilt in neurosis are always careful to tell me that they are willing to try things out in psychotherapy, but reluctant to interfere with the course of an analysis! In any case, one cannot be surprised that obsessional symptoms remain resistant to a treatment which deprecates the aim of relieving them.

GUILT AND THE OBSESSIONAL NEUROSIS

Freud's other line of explanation for the long duration and unsatisfactory outcome of treatment in obsessional neurosis was the presence of a "'moral' factor, a sense of guilt, which is finding satisfaction in the illness and refuses to give up the punishment of suffering. We shall be right in regarding this disheartening explanation as final. But as far as the patient is concerned this sense of guilt is dumb; it does not tell him that he is guilty; he does not feel guilty, he feels ill. This sense of guilt expresses itself as a resistance to recovery which is extremely difficult to overcome. It is also particularly difficult to convince the patient that this motive lies behind his continuing to be ill; he holds fast to the more obvious explanation that treatment by analysis is not the right remedy for his case" (1923a, pp. 49–50).

In his theoretical treatment of this sense of guilt Freud (1923a) had come to regard it as a manifestation of sadism turned against the ego, that is, of the operation of the death instinct. Powerlessness to affect the course of instinctual drives or to effect changes in their childhood expression is not too difficult to understand. This line of explanation was also invoked for melancholia as well as for obsessional neurosis. In obsessional neurosis, the "reproaches of conscience" are an "interminable self-torment," but the sense of guilt cannot altogether justify itself to the patient, so that he tries unsuccessfully to "repudiate it." Moreover, in obsessional neurosis, the patient is aware of the distinction between himself and the "object" or "other" whom he hates. In melancholia, in contrast, the sense of guilt can literally drive a person to suicide and is thus a "pure culture of the death instinct" (p. 53). The melancholic person, moreover, has incorporated the hated object into the ego and so has lost distinction between the self and the other. Freud is, as usual, making a most important clinical distinction here between melancholia and obsessional neurosis in the "boundary" between self and other. The distinction is congruent with later findings which suggest that melancholics or depressives are likely to be field-dependent in their cognitive style; while obsessional neurotics are more likely to be field-independent (Witkin, 1965; Lewis, 1978). At the same time that Freud is making an accurate clinical distinction, he is dealing with the sense of guilt not as an affective state but as a "pure culture of the death instinct."

When we turn back to Freud's early accounts of short treatments of obsessional cases, and especially when we read his account of his success with the Rat-Man's fulminating obsessional symptoms, which had escalated into a two-day "delirium," we find a very different picture. The unraveling of the obsessional symptoms is a marvel of psychoanalytic insight. It relates them to the sense of guilt, tracing the primary-process transformations of guilt into "crazy commands." The unraveling not only makes intuitive sense, but we marvel also at the distortions by which a human being will try to keep himself emotionally attached to the people he loves. I have called attention (Lewis, 1971), in a reinterpretation of the Rat-Man's case, to the role of unacknowledged or bypassed shame in the maintenance of his guilty obsessional thoughts. These are reinterpretations which rely on Freud's descriptions of conflicted affective states as the source of primary-process ideational transformations.

FREUD'S EARLY CASES OF OBSESSIONAL NEUROSIS

Let's look first at Freud's descriptions of some cases of obsessional neurosis in 1894 and 1895. The reports make it clear that an overwhelming sense of guilt was the immediate stimulus to symptom formation, and that relief of guilt relieved symptoms. Also present in the emotional situation of the patient is the shame associated with illicit sexual activity. Here is an example from Freud's paper on *The Neuro-psychoses of Defence (1894)*.

> A girl suffered from obsessional self-reproaches. If she read something in the papers about coiners, the thought would occur to her that she, too, made counterfeit money; if a murder had been committed by an unknown person, she would ask herself anxiously whether it was not she who had done the deed. At the same time she was perfectly conscious of the absurdity of these obsessional reproaches. For a time, the sense of guilt gained such an ascendancy over her that her powers of criticism were stifled and she accused herself to her relatives and her doctor of having really committed all these crimes. (This was an example of a psychosis through simple intensification — an *'Überwältigungspsychose.'*) Close questioning then revealed the source from which her sense of guilt arose. Stimulated by a chance voluptuous sensation, she had allowed herself to be led astray by a woman friend into masturbating, and she had practised it for years, fully conscious of her wrong-doing and to the accompaniment of the most violent, but, as usual, ineffective self-reproaches. An excessive indulgence after going to a ball had produced the intensification that led to the psychosis. After a few months of treatment and the strictest surveillance, the girl recovered (pp. 55–56).

Another case illustrates the continuity between obsessive and phobic symptoms.

> A girl had become almost completely isolated on account of an obsessional fear of incontinence of urine. She could no longer leave her room or receive visitors without having urinated a number of times. When she was at home or entirely alone the fear did not trouble her. Reinstatement: It was an obsession based on temptation or mistrust. She did not mistrust her bladder, but her resistance to erotic impulses. The origin of the obsession shows this clearly. Once, at the theater, on seeing a man who attracted her, she had felt an erotic desire, accompanied (as spontaneous pollutions in women always are) by a desire to urinate.

> She was obliged to leave the theater, and from that moment on she was a prey to
> the fear of having the same sensation, but the desire to urinate replaced the erotic
> one. She was completely cured (1895, p. 77).

Again, as in the case of phobia, Freud was uncertain about the etiology of obsessional symptoms, both in his early publications and in his later writings. Reviewing the evidence accumulated since Freud's time Nagera (1976), a classical psychoanalyst, deplores the scarcity of original findings. In her foreword to this work, Anna Freud describes the obsessional neurosis as "displaying the human quandary of relentless and unceasing battles between innate impulses and acquired moral demands" (p. 9). This description does not go beyond Freud's earliest formulations.

What Freud provided in both his earliest publications and in later case accounts was a clinical description of the psychic or emotional alchemy out of which obsessional symptoms form. Although by his own account this description was "figurative," it nevertheless made obsessional symptoms understandable as transformations of thought and feelings occurring under the press of forbidden desires. Let us look at his 1896 formulation: "*Obsessional ideas* are invariably transformed *self-reproaches* which have emerged from *repression* and which always relate to some *sexual* act that was performed with pleasure in *childhood*" (p. 169) (Freud's italics). In his 1909 publication Freud changed this formulation only a little. His criticism of it was that it was too much of a generalization to speak of "obsessional ideas," since this phrase covers many heterogeneous psychical structures (p. 221). (It is amusing that Freud rather testily placed the blame for this overgeneralization on the obsessional neurotics themselves.) "Obsessional thinking" would be a better term, he says, since that would cover obsessional "wishes, temptations, impulses, reflections, doubts, commands or prohibitions, distinctions which patients endeavor to tone down" (p. 222). But in a footnote Freud goes on to say that the fault in this definition was corrected in that same early paper when it went on to say that the "reactivated memories, however, and the self-reproaches formed from them never re-emerge into consciousness unchanged: what becomes conscious as obsessional ideas and affects and take the place of the pathogenic memories so far as conscious life is concerned are structures in the nature of a compromise between the repressed ideas and the repressing ones. In the definition, that is to say, especial stress is to be laid on the word 'transformed'" (1909b, p. 221).

THE CASE OF THE RAT-MAN

The transformations which Freud retranslated from obsessional symptoms back into the repressing and the repressed are particularly instructive in his account of the Rat-Man (Freud, 1909b). Let us look more closely at the clinical situation which Freud faced in this case, and at the unraveling of symptoms he performed there entirely unaided by any previous understanding of such complicated emotional transactions.

An intelligent, university-educated young man applied to Freud for treatment of obsessional ideas that "something would happen" to his father and to his fiancée if he (the patient) did not fulfill certain admittedly absurd commands. It should be noted that the overt emotional state the patient was describing in connection with his obsessional ideas was not specifically a *feeling* of guilt. As we have already seen, Freud had carefully distinguished between obsessional patients who experienced overt self-reproaches or overt feelings of guilt and obsessional patients who experienced only an affect of "indefinite unpleasure" (1896, p. 170) or "uncanny apprehensions" (1909b, p. 165) in connection with their ideas. The Rat-Man seems to have been one of the latter kind. But in describing himself as a person to Freud, in their very first psychoanalytic session, the patient volunteered that he had been for years accustomed to go to a friend of his when "tormented by some criminal impulse and ask him whether he despised him as a criminal. His friend used then to give him moral support by assuring him that he was a man of irreproachable conduct" (p. 159). Thus, although the patient does not explicitly identify his *affect* during obsessional ideas as guilt — it is rather a state of "uncanny" feeling — he is aware that his "criminal" impulses have something to do with guilt. He keeps asking his friend for reassurance that he is not to be "despised" as a criminal. As we shall see a bit later on in the case, when this same issue arose between the patient and Freud, this reassurance covered both the "objective" fact that the patient was not guilty, which he already knew, and the more "subjective" reassurance that he was not to be "despised" for his thoughts. In this latter reassurance there was a need (which Freud missed) to relieve feelings of shame.

In this same first session, the patient dated the beginning of his illness to the time when he was six years old and "suffered" from erections. He used to have an "uncanny feeling" as though "something might happen" if he thought such things as wishing to see girls naked, and he must do everything he could to prevent it. Once again, in this description of his earliest obsessions, the patient did not explicitly speak of a feeling of guilt, but rather a state of uneasy vigilance to prevent his own (wrong or bad) thoughts. To an observer, the patient is in a state of guilt about his sexual wishes, but it is a state that the patient experiences as anxiety that something will happen if he does or does not *do* something.

As Freud points out, the "inventory of neurosis" thus includes, as it does in phobia and hysteria, "an erotic instinct and a revolt against it; a wish which has not yet become compulsive, and struggling against it, a fear which is already compulsive; a distressing affect and an impulsion toward the performance of defensive acts" (p. 163).

We come now to Freud's account of the actual obsessive symptoms which brought the patient to treatment and which he began to describe in his second session. Freud's account is so dramatic that it is worth reprinting almost in toto (pp. 165–170). The outbreak of symptom occurred when the patient was in the army, which he hated, unlike his father, who had been a bluff and hearty upholder of army values.

"I had been suffering and tormenting myself with all kinds of obsessional thoughts, but they had quickly passed off during the manoeuvers. I was keen to show the regular officers that people like me had not only learned a good deal but could stand a good deal too. One day we started from ____ on a short march. During the halt I lost my pince-nez, and, although I could easily have found them, I did not want to delay our start so I gave them up. But I wired to my opticians in Vienna to send me another pair by the next post. During that same halt I sat between two officers, one of whom, a captain with a Czech name, was to be of no small importance to me. I do not say he was a bad man, but at the officer's mess he had repeatedly defended the introduction of corporal punishment, so that I was obliged to disagree with him sharply. Well, during this halt we got into a conversation, and the captain told me he had read of a specially horrible punishment used in the East"

Here the patient broke off, got up from the sofa, and begged me to spare him the recital of the details. I assured him that I myself had no taste whatever for cruelty and certainly no desire to torment him, but that naturally I could not grant him something that was beyond my power. He might just as well have asked me to give him the moon. The overcoming of resistances was a law of the treatment, and on no consideration could it be dispensed with. . . . I went on to say that I would do all I could, nevertheless, to guess the full meaning of any hints he gave me. Was he perhaps thinking of impalement? – "No, not that . . . the criminal was tied up. . . ." He expressed himself so indistinctly that I could not immediately guess in what position. . . . – 'The criminal was tied up . . . a pot was turned upside down on his buttocks . . . some *rats* were put into it . . . and they . . ." – he had got up again and was showing every sign of horror and resistance. . . . "*bored their way in . . .*" into his anus, I helped him out.

Once again, although Freud does not explicitly identify the patient's feelings while he was trying to describe his obsessional ideas, it is clear that the patient was in an agony of shame at exposing his thoughts. Freud speaks only of the "overcoming of resistances"; shame is, however, phenomenologically the most acute affective "resistance" to overcome.

At all the more important moments while he was telling his story his face took on a very strange, composite expression. I could only interpret it as one of *horror at pleasure of his own of which he himself was unaware.* He proceeded with the greatest difficulty: "At that moment the idea flashed through my mind *that this was happening to a person who was very dear to me*" [Freud's italics]. In answer to a direct question he said that it was not he himself who was carrying out the punishment, but that it was being carried out as it were impersonally. After a little prompting I learnt that the person to whom this "idea" of his related was the lady he admired.

He broke off his story in order to tell me that everything which followed in their train had passed through his mind with the most extraordinary rapidity. Simultaneously with the idea there always appeared a "sanction," that is to say, the defensive measure which he was obliged to adopt in order to prevent his phantasy from being fulfilled. When the captain had spoken of this ghastly punishment, he went on, and these ideas had come into his head, by employing his usual formula (a "but" accompanied by a gesture of repudiation, and the phrase "whatever are you thinking of?") he had just succeeded in warding off *both* of them.

This "both" took me aback and it has no doubt also mystified the reader. For so far we have heard of only one idea — of the rat punishment being carried out upon the lady. He was now obliged to admit that a second idea had occurred to him simultaneously, namely, the idea of the punishment also being applied to his father. As his father had died many years previously, this obsessive fear was much more nonsensical even than the first, and accordingly it attempted to escape being confessed for a little while longer (pp. 165–168).

Once again, although Freud does not explicitly label the patient's affect as shame, it is clear that an even more "nonsensical" idea is even more shameful than the first one, and so "seeks to escape being exposed."

The rest of the patient's next two sessions were taken up with his description of how the lost pince-nez became involved in a set of contradictory sanctions about paying 3.80 kronen. In brief, the patient was handed his new pince-nez by the "cruel" captain, who told him that the charges were to be paid to Lieutenant A. Immediately, a sanction formed in his mind that he must *not* pay Lieutenant A the money — or "it" would happen; and immediately, as usual, the inner command came that he *must* pay Lieutenant A the money or else it would happen! This absolutely insoluble dilemma of action — specifically, of how to absolve himself of the guilt or responsibility for what might happen to his beloved and to his father (in the next world) — consumed the patient's activities for the next few days. His first attempt at solution was foiled by the discovery that the captain had given him wrong information: Lieutenant A refused payment because he had not laid out the 3.80 kronen. (Later on in the account it developed that he had actually known all along that Lieutenant A was not to be paid, because it was actually the woman in charge of the post office who had laid out the money.) In spite of this information, he was "incessantly tormented by his vow" (p. 170) and his actions in order to fulfill it took him on a long fruitless train journey to the place to which Lieutenant A had been sent. Finally, in desperation, he betook himself to the home of the friend who was accustomed to reassure him, told him the whole story, was reassured and got some sleep! But the next day the obsessions resumed their ferocity. A chance happening that put one of Freud's books (*The Psychopathology of Everyday Life*) into his hands determined him to seek Freud's help.

Freud was able to unravel the emotional significance of each detail of the content of the patient's obsessive episode. The cruel Czech captain was, of course, a father-surrogate. The patient was aware only of loving his father very much; awareness of hatred of father was inaccessible to the patient. Freud tells us that the patient could become convinced of the other side of his feelings only in a painful transference experience.

> He began heaping the grossest and filthiest abuse upon me and my family, though in his deliberate actions he never treated me with anything but the greatest respect. His demeanor as he repeated these insults to me was that of a man in despair. "How can a gentleman like you, sir," he used to ask, "let yourself be abused in this way by a low, good-for-nothing fellow like me? You ought to turn me out, that's all I deserve." When he talked like this, he would get up from the sofa and roam about the room — a habit which he explained at first as being due to delicacy of feeling; he could not bring himself, he said, to utter such horrible things while he was lying there so comfortably. But soon he himself found a more cogent explanation, namely, that he was avoiding my proximity for fear of my giving him a beating. If he stayed on the sofa, he behaved like someone in desperate terror trying to save himself from castigations of terrific violence; he would bury his head in his hands, cover his face, jump up suddenly and rush away, his features distorted with pain, and so on. He recalled that his father had a passionate temper and sometimes in his violence had not known when to stop (p. 209).

We should note that in this "transference" experience, the patient's expressed "delicacy of feeling" as he was insulting Freud was probably a feeling of embarrassment for Freud's possible humiliation (if Freud were to take the insults personally). The patient, however, emphasized his fear of retaliation or retribution from Freud, a position which is less damaging to Freud's feelings.

The connections that the patient and Freud were able to establish between an insoluble dilemma of paying for a pince-nez and rats boring into the anus of his beloved father and lady are wonderfully complex and yet obviously related either metaphorically or by associative continuity to the patient's emotional conflicts. The primary-process transformations that Freud uncovered in dream content are also at work in the content of obsessional symptoms, as they are in phobia and hysteria.

Paying the kronen as the "cruel" captain had told him to do hit the patient in what Freud, following Jung's terminology, calls a "complexive sensitiveness." When the patient's father was a noncommissioned officer in the army, he had gambled with company funds and lost. He would have been in serious trouble had not one of his comrades raised the money for him. The patient's father had tried to trace his comrade after their service but had not managed to do so. "The recollection of this sin of his father's youth was pain-ful to him, for, in spite of appearances, his unconscious was filled with hostile strictures upon his father's character. The captain's words . . . had sounded to his ears like an allusion to this unpaid debt of his father's" (pp. 210–211).

We may observe, in understanding the emotional basis of this sensitivi-ty of the patient's, that it rested on a loving identification between the patient and his father, as well as on "hostile strictures" against the latter's character. The loving identification can make it come about that the patient can feel or be threatened by shame for his father's failure as if it were his own. This vicarious feeling makes him vulnerable to a "complexive sensitivity."

The patient's father had been a *"Spielratte,"* literally a play-rat, which is a German colloquial term for a gambler. In this instance, a pun on words, that is an accidental linkage of meaning or "verbal bridge" was the basis for a connection between paying a debt and rats. From the idea of "rats," the con-nections to paying money are very numerous.

In addition, by the verbal bridge between *"Raten,"* meaning "in-stalments" of feces or money, and *"Ratten,"* meaning "rats," a connection ex-isted between rats and anal excitations. For instance, Freud learned six months after the analysis began, that when the patient was told the amount of the fee, he responded with the thought, "so many florins, so many rats." This same train of thought applied to prostitutes, who charge "so many florins."

Direct connections between rats and painful affects of shame and guilt were also experienced by the patient. For example, the patient remembered that at his father's funeral he had seen a rat coming out of the grave. He assumed that it had just had a "meal off his corpse. The notion of a rat is in-separably bound up with the fact that it has sharp teeth with which it gnaws and bites. But rats cannot be sharp-toothed, greedy, and dirty with impuni-ty; they are cruelly persecuted and mercilessly put to death by man, as the patient had often observed with horror. He had often pitied the poor creatures. But he himself had been just such a nasty, dirty little wretch, who was apt to bite people in a rage and had been fearfully punished for doing so [by his father]" (pp. 215–216).

In his childhood, also, the patient had been troubled frequently by in-testinal worms, which had had to be pulled out of his anus. The experiences of disgust and shame connected with this illness, as well as the erotic feelings which had been stirred by the excitation are direct emotional connections to the story of rats in the anus. As Freud puts it, the experience with worms in childhood had stirred the patient's anal-erotism.

But only when Freud and the patient understood that "rats" also meant "children" to the patient could still another essential emotional connection be made. Freud tells us that it was when the "Rat-Wife" in Ibsen's *Little Eyolf* came up in the analysis that the metaphoric connection between rats and children became clear. Ibsen's Rat-Wife first enticed the town's rats into the water and then, by the same means, lured the children out of the town, never to return. The patient, in fact, had been hesitant about marrying his beloved lady, not only because his father had deprecated his choice of her (terming him a fool for wanting to marry her), but because she was unable to bear children — and he was "extraordinarly fond of children." The same ambivalent set of feelings as existed about his father thus existed about his lady — and she was also the person to whom the rat-punishment would be administered if the patient did not pay his debt.

Summarizing the unraveling of the patient's emotional state at the moment when he was handed the pince-nez by the "cruel" captain, Freud tells us that "out of the stirrings of his father-complex . . . there formed in his mind some such answer as 'Yes, I'll pay back the money to A. when my father and the lady have children.' In short, a derisive affirmation attached to an absurd condition." Freud goes on to state, in a footnote, that "absurdity signifies derision in the language of obsessional thought, just as it does in dreams" (p. 218). And, he tells us, "when we reached the solution . . . the patient's rat delirium disappeared" (p. 220).

THE PROBLEM OF SADISM

When it came to formulating his theoretical conception of obsessional neurosis, Freud was struck by the sadism being warded off by the crazy, contradictory "moral imperatives." It was the horror of the patient's sadistic fantasies that led Freud to speak of the "extraordinary part played by impulses of hatred and anal-erotism in the symptomatology of obsessional neurosis" (1913b, p. 321), citing also Jones's confirming observations in support of this emphasis. In his paper on the *Disposition to Obsessional Neurosis*, Freud (1913b) describes the clinical experience that led him to postulate a specific instinctual basis for sadism and anal-erotism: namely, "a stage [in development] in which the component instincts have already come together for the choice of an object and that object is already something extraneous to the subject's own self, but in which *the primacy of the genital zones has not yet been established*. On the contrary, the component instincts which dominate this *pregenital organization* of sexual life are the anal-erotic and sadistic ones" (p. 321) (Freud's italics).

The reader will have noticed that "hatred" and "sadism" are here used synonymously by Freud, although there is considerable difference in meaning of the two terms. Hatred is an aversive affect; the dictionary defines it as "a strong aversion coupled with ill will." "Sadism" it defines as "a sexual perversion in which gratification is got by torturing the loved person" or, in a second meaning, as "love of cruelty, conceived as manifesting sexual desire." Sadism involves sexual arousal, hatred does not; sadism thus fuses sexual arousal and the ill will of hatred into a love of torture. It was Freud's insight that the "obsessional idea 'I should like to kill you' . . . means at bottom nothing other than 'I should like to enjoy you in love' . . . these impulses apply to those who are nearest and dearest to the patient" (1916, pp. 343–344).

Moreover, it was Freud's clinical observation that the anal-erotic sadistic form of loving could be evoked out of a frustration of "genital" or more ordinary forms of loving. As we shall see in a moment, this was what had happened in the case which was the basis for his theoretical formulation. In that case, the patient's obsessional symptoms developed when her husband, whom she loved — he was "the only man of whom there could be any question for her" (p. 320) — became impotent.

But in his theoretical formulation, Freud was less interested in the way in which the affects of love can turn into the affects of aversion with ill will than he was in the instinctual stages of development that must be assumed. A correct statement of these instinctual stages seemed to him to hold out the promise of predicting which neurosis a patient might develop. He had already formulated an autoerotic stage in which there are "component instincts" depending on the functioning of the body, a "narcissistic" stage in which the self is the "object" of the libido, and a stage of "genital primacy." Now he was adding a "pregenital" stage, in which anal-erotic sadistic impulses are predominant. Obsessional neurotics could be people who never got beyond an anal-sadistic organization of the libido, and those, like the woman patient he described, who had achieved genital primacy, only to regress to sadism when genital activity was frustrated.

It should be noted at this point that Freud put forward his theory as "a small new fragment of theory" which although apparently linked to just one case, was "based on a large number of earlier impressions." In spite of the modesty of this presentation, Freud's formulation was thereafter treated as the authoritative psychoanalytic theory of obsessional neurosis. The gravity of a regression to an early instinctual developmental stage, and the even more serious implication that some obsessional patients never went beyond this stage contributed to the acceptance within psychoanalytic theory of obssessional neurosis as a most intractable disorder requiring many years of treatment.

But perhaps the most important difficulty that resulted from Freud's focus on a regression to sadism is, as mentioned earlier, the blurring of distinction between sadistic behavior and sadistic fantasy. Clearly what Freud's patients were doing — as patients do today — was driving themselves crazy about their horrible sadistic fantasies, which are just as intolerable as if they were actions. When Freud reformulated castration anxie-

ty as a biologically given ego-signal, the distinction was lost between castration as a metaphor for an affective state and castration anxiety as response to
realistic danger; just so the assumption of sadism as a developmental stage
tended to focus on sadism as behavior rather than as affective state.

An examination of the case material which formed the basis for Freud's
theoretical statement reveals only a fragment of a case account; the usual
restrictions for the sake of the patient's privacy were in force. The case
began, Freud tells, "after a traumatic experience, as a straightforward anxiety hysteria and retained that character for a few years. One day, however, it
suddenly changed into an obsessional neurosis of the most severe type" (p.
319). Freud continued:

> Up until the time of her falling ill the patient had been a happy and almost com-
> pletely satisfied wife. She wanted to have children, from motives based on an in-
> fantile fixation of her wishes, and she fell ill when she learned that it was impossi-
> ble for her to have any by the husband who was the only object of her love. The
> anxiety hysteria with which she reacted to this frustration corresponded, as she
> herself soon learned to understand, to the repudiation of phantasies of seduction
> in which her firmly implanted wish for children found expression. She now did all
> she could to prevent her husband from guessing that she had fallen ill owing to the
> frustration of which he was the cause. But I have good reason for asserting that
> everyone possesses in his own unconscious an instrument with which he can inter-
> pret the utterances of the unconscious in other people. Her husband understood,
> without any admission or explanation on her part, what his wife's anxiety meant.
> He felt hurt without showing it, and in his turn reacted neurotically by — for the
> first time — failing in sexual intercourse with her. Immediately afterwards he
> started on a journey. His wife believed that he had become permanently impotent,
> and produced her first obsessional symptoms on the day before his expected
> return.
>   The content of her obsessional neurosis was a compulsion for scrupulous
> washing and cleanliness and extremely energetic protective measures against
> severe injuries which she thought other people had reason to fear from her — that
> is to say, reaction-formations against her *anal-erotic* and *sadistic* impulses. Her
> sexual need was obliged to find expression in these shapes after her genital life had
> lost all its value owing to the impotence of the only man of whom there could be
> any question for her (p.320) (Freud's italics).

It is when we read this clear description of the delicacy of feeling with
which the patient was trying to keep her husband from feeling mortified on
her account, and the wordless exchanges by means of which each was trying
to avoid his own and the other's humiliation that we get the sense of how
much Freud lost when he put his theory in terms of regression to partial instincts. The origins of humiliation are by no means less obscure than the
origins of sadism. The solution to both problems will have to await a better
understanding of the nature of human nature. But at least following the affects where they lead makes the formation of symptoms more understand-

able and, what is perhaps as important, makes their treatment easier if only because the symptoms are not regarded as so ominous.

This is well illustrated if one reviews Freud's account of the phenomenology of the sadistic fantasies he encountered, which were also the clinical material on which his theoretical formulations rested. In fact, the patient mentioned in *The Disposition to Obsessional Neurosis* used to have beating fantasies in her childhood. *A Child Is Being Beaten* (1919) is a clinical account of long-standing beating fantasies observed in six cases, four women and two men. Since Freud's account of them, beating fantasies have been very frequently observed among patients (Niederland, 1958; Joseph, 1965). Kris is reported to have found them "routine" in women patients and also very frequent among men. In his account, Freud takes for granted that a deprivation of love is the equivalent of a humiliation, and that fantasies of being beaten are an appropriate cognitive content of a feeling of humiliation. "One soon learns that being beaten (as a child), even if it does not hurt very much, signifies a deprivation of love and a humiliation" (p. 187).

As I have shown in reviewing these fantasies from the point of view of shame (Lewis, 1971), many characteristics of the shame experience are present in these fantasies. In the first place, the feeling of humiliation which evokes the (retaliatory) beating fantasies can come suddenly. "Many children who believed themselves securely enthroned in the unshakable affection of their parent . . . are cast down . . . by a single blow" (p. 187). There is, in other words, a sudden reorganization of the perceptual field in which a feeling of humiliation or shame suddenly emerges out of a feeling of being loved. In my own therapeutic experience, this was dramatically illustrated by a sudden shift in a patient's perception of himself as a "fool" — a "moral prig" instead of a morally scrupulous person — a shift which resulted from an unconsciously cruel remark by his beloved (Lewis, 1971, pp. 466–471). In immediate sequence the patient began to develop obsessive ideation about himself which culminated in sexual impotence.

The patient's confession of beating fantasies always evokes "shame and a sense of guilt" (Freud, 1919, p. 187), just as the Rat-Man's fantasies did. Shame characteristically evokes additional shame in the presence of the other. Patients are also characteristically in a state of guilt for these fantasies as evidenced by the fact that real experiences of watching someone being beaten evoke an excited feeling of "repugnance"; often the real experience of seeing someone beaten is "intolerable." It is, in fact, a condition of these fantasies that no irreparable or fatal injury occur. The childhood experience of these patients actually involved very infrequent beatings; the rod was spared.

Another similarity in phenomenology between beating fantasies and the shame experience is the characteristic vagueness of the perception of the self.

The actual identity of the participants in the fantasy is vague, including both the identity of the person doing the beating and the person being beaten. The position of the self is perceived as that of "spectator," except at the moment of sexual release at which time the self is clearly a participant in an intense affective experience.

It was this connection between beating fantasies and sexual excitement that Freud set out to explain; his solution was to postulate the existence of a primary "aggressive" or "death" instinct which is constantly modifed by Eros or "life" instincts. Sexual pleasure in cruelty was a developmental stage in which the "death" instinct was only partly defused.

I have followed, instead, a path which tries to understand sadistic fantasies as a product of as well as a stimulus to shame. In fantasies, the self can become so absorbed in thoughts about the "other" in relation to the self that it is momentarily "lost." Shame is an acute affect in which the boundaries of the self are painfully affirmed; the acute experience is described, however, by phrases such as "I could die" with shame, that is, in terms of a "loss" of the self. But the "loss" refers either to the vicarious experience of being in another's position in fantasy or to the boundary experience of resuming one's own position after having been "lost." Shame is a vicarious (actually a fantasy) experience of the other's scorn of the self. It is this phenomenological characteristic of vicariousness that helps to explain how a feeling of scorn in someone else's eyes can "right itself" as a feeling of gratification in someone else's humiliation. In any case, it is probably a universal experience that a feeling of humiliation leads to the agreeable, retaliatory idea that someone else, specifically the humiliator, is humiliated instead of the self. Triumphant feeling over someone else is a "natural" relief of shame feeling, and can simultaneously regenerate the experience of shame when the fantasied triumph ends. That sexual arousal should accompany both the fantasy and the restorative ideas is a reflection of the fact that longings for union with the beloved "other" are operating. Sexual arousal is symbolic of such union; the orgasm that results is the same as if there had been union. The sexual arousal accompanying the fantasy experiences of triumph and humiliation is an affirmation of the self, especially at the orgastic climax. The acuteness of the immediately ensuing shame experience is also a reminder to the self that its previous experience was only vicarious instad of "real." (Pressed to understand why they should have so much shame over masturbatory fantasies patients often say that the experience was only a poor substitute for the real thing.)

This concept of sadistic fantasies as affective sequences stemming from feelings of humiliation at loss of love is not too different from Freud's equation: "I should like to kill you" means "I should like to enjoy you sexually." But by shedding the theoretical implication that this equation necessarily represents a regressive debasement to an infantile developmental stage of life, we avoid a view of patients with obsessional defenses against sadistic fantasies as gravely and intractably ill.

Tracing sequences from the affect of shame and back into it also rests on different assumptions about human nature than Freud made. One basic assumption is that human beings are social by biological origin, and that the maintenance of affective ties is a fundamental condition of human existence. Shame, like guilt, is a means of maintaining affective ties even at the expense of the self.

As we have seen before (Introduction), Freud's adoption of an instinct theory was a progressive intellectual step in keeping with the Darwinian tradition, and independent of theological tradition. But his instinct theory committed Freud to an individualistic concept of human nature. The developmental stages of his instinct theory took account, by implication, of the relation between the person and others, but the two earliest stages — the autoerotic and the narcissistic — conceptualized the young child as an asocial creature. The anal-erotic stage although social, nevertheless demonstrated that "in the order of development hate is the precursor of love." Freud here quotes with approval Stekel's remark (which he once found "incomprehensible") that "hate not love is the primary emotional relation between men" (1913, p. 325). It is small wonder that Freud at first found this statement incomprehensible; his clinical observations all demonstrated the passionately loving behavior of very young children. And we now know that infants are not only better-organized selves, but much more social creatures than Freud had any way of knowing (see Chapter 3, Volume 2).

Sadism and the Marquis de Sade

Before leaving the subject of sadism, it is instructive to consider briefly the history of the term itself. The Marquis de Sade, a nobleman with revolutionary political views, spent almost thirty years of his life in prisons, both before and after the French Revolution. During his imprisonments, which were essentially political, he wrote a number of pornographic works, detailing sexual fantasies which would be unspeakable brutalities if actually performed (Sade, 1966). It is clear from his own account that during these fantasies he masturbated to orgasm. It is his record of the combination of sexual fantasies and cruel tortures that has given his name to a sexual perversion.

It is generally agreed that his works are extremely repetitive: as his critics agree, obsessively so. In one of them for example, *Philosophy in the Bedroom*, there is repeated, rhythmic alternation between sadistic sexual fantasies and dissertations on morality and religion. The alternation seems to parallel a coming to orgasm on sexual fantasy followed by a philosophical discussion of moral issues. Sade's position in these discussions is that of an anarchist. The purpose of the brutalities is didactic: It is to rid people's heads of false notions of religion and morality which a hypocritical, corrupt society has instilled. Two of his works, *Eugenie de Franval* and *Justine*, are called "moral tales." As Paulhan (1966) remarks, in a critical essay on Sade's works, they may be called the Gospel of Evil.

The tortures and punishments actually inflicted on heretics and witches during the Inquisition of preceding centuries are little different, either in quality or in content, from the Marquis' fantasies. Those tortures and punishments were justified by a code of morality which imposed them for crimes against God. In fact, tortures are still inflicted today in the name of political morality. They remind us of the unexplained paradoxes of human behavior which morality has generated over the centuries of civilized existence. Sade's *Gospel of Evil*, written a century before Freud, was part of the secularization of a philosophy of morality in which Freud joined, and which has formed the basis for modern psychiatry. Sade's sexual fantasies contained a derision of morality. As Freud saw in his careful analysis of the Rat-Man's obsessional symptoms, these also are a derisive version of moral imperatives. Schreber's delusion also expressed his derision of God, as we shall see in Chapter 5.

Sade's behavior in reality was sexually promiscuous, but otherwise governed by a high standard of personal ethics. While he was a prisoner in the Bastille (at the instigation of his wife's family) he wrote to his wife:

> I am a libertine, but neither a *criminal* nor a *murderer* [Sade's italics], and since I am compelled to set my apology next to my vindication, I shall therefore say that it might well be possible for those who condemn me as unjustly as I have been might themselves be unable to offset their infamies by good works as clearly established as those I can contrast to my errors. I am a libertine, but three families residing in your area have for five years lived off my charity. . . . I am a libertine, but I have saved a deserter from death. . . . I am a libertine, but at Evry, with your whole family looking on, I saved a child at the risk of my life — who was on the verge of being crushed against the wheels of a runaway horse-drawn cart. . . . How therefore do you presume, that from so innocent a childhood and youth I have suddenly arrived at the ultimate of premeditated horror? No you do not believe it. And you who today tyrannize me so cruelly, you do not believe it, either; your vengeance has beguiled your mind, you have proceeded blindly to tyrannize, but your heart knows mine, it judges more fairly, and it knows full well it is innocent (Sade, 1966, pp. viii–ix).

In an interesting account (Bach and Schwartz, 1972) of one of Sade's dreams, an attempt was made to understand his cruel sexual fantasies. The account, although phrased in the language of "narcissism," also relies on an inevitable sequence from humiliation to triumph and back again. They describe the fantasies, "written during years of incarceration when Sade felt himself persecuted and abused as a cry of outrage by a man who turned his life into a rage against extinction" (p. 461). The "grandiose self," the term used for feelings of pride, can be shattered so that the self feels "shredded, mutilated . . . silenced" — in my phrasing, in the affective state of shame. Orgasm, in contrast, is a strong affirmation of the boundaries of the self. The sexual fantasies of cruelty are thus attempts to cope with "narcissistic decompensation" (p. 473) by "restitution and triumph" (pp. 473–474). This seems to be the same sequence which I have described in affective terms as a sequence from humiliated fury or shame-rage into retaliatory triumphant, vicarious experiences of the other's humiliation. It should be noted that as far as can be determined Sade did not suffer from the classical symptoms of obsessional neurosis — that is, an insoluble dilemma of obeying absurd, conflicting, trivial commands. Bach and Schwartz suggest that he suffered from a psychotic disorder, but they are also impressed by the qualities that allowed him to survive long years of imprisonment, to maintain his unique sense of identity and to produce his extraordinary work. The dream which they reproduce is full of tenderness and grief at the loss of his mother. It attests, along with Sade's passionate political beliefs, to his high "ego-ideals." The sadistic fantasies that he occupied himself with writing down expressed his shame-rage at his unjust imprisonment and gave him repeated sexualized retaliatory gratification in the fantasized brutal tortures inflicted on "good" people. His own "acceptance" of these fantasies at least to the extent of writing them down in detail (and shedding "tears of blood" at the loss of some of his manuscripts in the fall of the Bastille) would be congruent with a relative absence of shame and guilt about them. This, in turn, would "explain" the absence of obsessional symptoms. In any case, Sade's account in *The 120 Days of Sodom* of all the varieties of torture fantasies on which one could come to orgasm, was an encyclopedic document which its author thought was a more honest account of human nature than Rousseau's, Voltaire's or Diderot's!

SHAME, GUILT, AND OBSESSIONAL SYMPTOMS

In his clinical description of the patient's obsessive commands Freud characterizes them as "derisive." Clearly, Freud was picking up the ridiculing or shaming quality of the moral imperatives contained in his patient's obsessional commands, but without emphasizing this aspect of them. The affinity between ideas of the "black mass" during Inquisition days and the "black comedy" that the Rat-Man's conscience was making him play out is clear in a reworking of the case from the point of view of shame. As I have tried to demonstrate (Lewis, 1971), the patient was not only in a state of shame about his "crazy" symptoms, but bypassed shame, not central in his awareness, was operating to create both his sadistic fantasies and the obsessive symptoms that emerged about them. Unlike the case of Dora (Chapter 2), however, in this case it is necessary to dig for evidence of shame in the Rat-Man's emotional situation at the time of each obsessional outbreak.

Let us consider some of the evidence about the operation of bypassed shame in the formation of obsessional symptoms that can be seen in the case of the Rat-Man (Freud, 1909b). In this brief review, Freud's published account will be supplemented by his "original record," that is his daily notes of the case. Events which could evoke mortification or shame occurred in connection with each outbreak of obsessional symptoms even before the major episode which brought the patient to Freud. The specific content of the obsessions can be related to the content of the shaming events. This is close to Freud's description of events, but it emphasizes the state of shame, which Freud does not. For example, Freud says: "They [obsessional impulses] arose as a reaction to a tremendous feeling of rage, which was inaccessible to the patient's consciousness and directed against someone who had cropped up as an interference with the course of his love" (p. 189). We know that the patient's father had shamed him for his choice of a woman. Although Freud does not explicitly say so, we can reinterpret him to mean that it is a shaming person who evokes a tremendous feeling of (inaccessible) shame-rage. In short, it can be seen that the torturing obsessional commands are warding off unbearably humiliating events — both to the persons involved in the fantasies and to the patient who thinks them.

As we saw earlier, the patient opened his analysis with a statement of his need to go to his friend for assurance that he should not be "despised" as a (guilty and shameful) criminal. This pattern of needing reassurance was a continuation of one that existed earlier in his life, when he was fourteen or fifteen years old. An older student, who was a tutor in the patient's house, "had taken a liking to him and had raised his self-esteem to an extraordinary degree, so that he appeared to himself to be a genius. . . . [The tutor] had suddenly altered his behavior and begun treating him as though he were an idiot. At length he noticed that the tutor was interested in one of his sisters, and had realized that he had only taken up with him in order to gain admission into the house. This had been the first great blow of his life" (pp. 159–160).

The patient is here clearly describing the sudden humiliation of perceiving that he has been used. This is the kind of realization which is exquisitely calculated to evoke mortification — and, moreover, mortification suffered in silence, since the patient was aware that his own vanity had been one source of his downfall. Moreover, Freud tells us that the patient had also been relying on this tutor for relief of guilt feelings, in the same way that he now relied on his friend. The background for the patient's mortification is thus his own chronic sense of guilt.

In this same first session, the patient proceeded to tell Freud, "without any apparent transition," of similar humiliations evoked during his childhood. When he was four or five years old, a "pretty" governess (Fräulein Peter) had acceded to his desire to finger her genitals — which he found "queer" — "so long as I said nothing to anyone about it" (p. 160). Subsequently, he was left with a burning and tormenting desire to see girls naked, including a subsequent governess, Fräulein Lina. He also had a fear, which was already obsessional , that he had "spoken these thoughts aloud." In this context, he remembers Lina saying that "'it could be done with the little one [Paul's younger brother] but Paul . . . is too clumsy, he would be sure to miss it.' I did not understand clearly what was meant, but I felt the slight and began to cry" (pp. 160–161).

A linkage between the obsessive fear of *speaking* his thoughts and the original condition laid down by Fräulein Peter that he *tell* no one about fingering her genitals is apparent. While he had been in complicity with her in an illicit, triumphant act of fingering her genitals, he had noted that they felt "queer." The puzzlement experienced at this moment of triumph can be connected to the obsessive "tormenting" curiosity to see other girls naked, as well as to repeat the triumph. But this curiosity is also illicit — both guilty and shameful. In this context he is totally shamed by hearing Fräulein Lina's aspersions on his sexual prowess and begins to cry. Lina takes him into bed with her, allows him to fondle her, and the stage is set for a renewal of sexual fantasies which also evoke guilt: They give him the "uncanny feeling as though something must happen if I thought these things, and *as though I must do all sorts of things to prevent it*" (p. 162).

Let us suppose that the "something which will happen" is that the self will be "lost," that the person will "die" of shame if his fantasies are exposed. The patient reports that he had an "uncanny feeling" that he must mobilize himself to prevent this: He must *do something* or else he would be responsible for a nameless disaster. The sense of guilt has been mobilized to prevent the loss of the self in shame.

As I have shown in detail (Lewis, 1971), the affective structure I have described was in operation at the time of each obsessional outbreak reported by the patient before he came to Freud with his major episode. For example, the theme of shame of his own cowardice was to the fore at the time of the outbreak of his great obsessive episode. The pince-nez, which the patient had lost during the halt at which he heard the cruel captain's story, was connected verbally to an incident in which the patient had failed to meet a challenge to a duel. The patient was "keen to show" what a good soldier he was; in previous army service he had been "apathetic and ineffective" and he had a lieutenant who was a bully and who struck him with the flat of his sword. "The patient had a number of fantasies of challenging him to a duel, but gave it up. In some ways he was glad his father was no longer alive . . . as an old soldier he would have been very much upset [presumably at the patient's cowardice]" (p. 304).

It is perhaps in the patient's transference behavior that we get the clearest picture both of the extent of shame with which he had to cope and of the complexity of the psychical operations connected with shame. Freud describes the "deep depression" (p. 281) which the patient suffered when he was obliged to tell Freud "frightful" thoughts about Freud. The theme of almost all these fantasies which the patient found so acutely shameful to tell was that of Freud's humiliation. One fantasy, for example, was that Freud's daughter was practicing fellatio. Another was of Freud being ordered by the patient to bring his daughter into the room so that he could "lick the *Miessnick*" [the ugly one]. Still another was of the humiliation Freud's mother would feel at witnessing the hanging of her son as a criminal. The patient had a dream in which he was marrying Freud's daughter for her money, not for her beautiful eyes. Still another fantasy was of copulating with Freud's daughter by means of a stool from her anus. It was during these recitals of his fantasies that the patient was unable to remain on the couch on account of his "delicacy of feeling" toward Freud.

The patient was also unable to bear praise from Freud: "He said that whenever I praised any of his ideas he was always very much pleased; but that a second voice went on to say 'I snap my fingers at the praise' or more undisguisedly, 'I shit on it'" (p. 315). We may interpret that the patient was not only too guilty but too proud to be able to bear "caring about" the "other's" praise. Realizing that one is vulnerable to someone else's opinion can make even praise feel shameful.

A most illuminating instance of how bypassed shame operated during the sessions to create new obsessional ideas comes from Freud's account of the sessions immediately following upon the patient's recital of his obsessive ideas about rats. We know that those sessions had involved acute shame for the patient in the telling of the details of his fantasy. The patient had begun the next hour by telling Freud that he had been pursued by relentless self-reproaches for being absent at the moment of his father's death . . . "the only thing that had kept him going at that time had been the consolation given him by his friend who had always brushed aside his self-reproaches as idle on the ground that they were grossly exaggerated." "Hearing this," Freud says, "I took, the opportunity of giving him a first glance at the underlying principles of psychoanalytic therapy" (p. 175). Freud contrasted that attitude of the analyst with that of the lay person, who says that the affect is exaggerated, therefore the inference that the patient is a criminal is false. The analyst knows better than this: "The affect is justified. The sense of guilt is not open to further criticism. But it belongs to some other content" (by which Freud meant some *childhood* act). Freud concluded by "admitting that this way of looking at the matter gave immediate rise to some hard problems; for how could he admit that his self-reproach of being a criminal toward his father was justified, when he must know that as matter of fact he had never committed any crime against him?" (p. 175).

In the next hour the patient "ventured to bring forward a few doubts" about Freud's theories. Specifically the patient wondered why "knowing that self-reproach was justified could have a therapeutic effect" (p. 176). In the ensuing discussion, the patient told Freud that a "sense of guilt can arise from a breach of one's own moral principles and not from that of external ones." Freud says that he agreed with the patient, as indeed he might have since the patient was restating Freud's version that the sense of guilt is not open to further criticism. But, the patient continued, if the sense of guilt is not open to further criticism, how can Freud's method work against it any better than a friend's consolations? And if Freud is right, then the patient must be suffering from a *"disintegration of personality"* (Freud's italics) and it is doubtful that he can ever be helped. The session ended by Freud's reminding him that his "youth was very much in his favor, as well as the intactness of his personality. In this connection I said a word or two upon the good opinion I formed of him and this gave him visible pleasure" (p. 178). (We may imagine that the thought "I shit on it" may have crossed the patient's mind in response to this reassuring condescension.)

In the patient's logical difficulties and doubts about therapy we may discern the operation of the sense of shame at needing help. This feeling drives him to a wish for Freud to be in theoretical difficulties. Having stated this doubt, however, which implies that the therapy on which he is relying is useless, the patient quickly shifts the burden of difficulty back to the disintegration of his own personality, manages to evoke a reassurance from Freud, and so is again in the position of the shameful patient. I have shown at some length, in the transcripts of psychotherapy sessions, that this current of unacknowledged shame which the patient experiences vis-à-vis the therapist is likely to become involved in derogatory thoughts about therapy and thence back into the formation of new obsessive symptoms (Lewis, 1971).

Sequences from Bypassed Shame into Obsessive, Paranoid Ideas

A particularly instructive example of a sequence from bypassed shame into guilt and thence into obsessive, paranoid ideation comes from the transcript of a field-independent male patient whose therapist had been interpreting (with some quiet derision) the grandiosity of the patient's ego-ideal. It is easy for an observer to be amused by another person's ego-ideal and also easy to evoke shame in the person whose ego-ideal is under inspection, especially since it is difficult to spell out a rationale for one's own strivings.

The patient had entered treatment for chest pains that had no organic base. He himself connected his symptoms with an "ego-ideal or something that I'm setting up." The patient had a characteristic way of describing his chest pains: he kept saying that he "receives" the pain. The patient had been arguing with the therapist that his ambitions were necessary and inevitable in his life circumstances. In the midst of their dispute about the wisdom of ambition, the therapist called the patient's attention to his peculiar mode of speech about the pains. The patient laughed (most likely with embarrassment, although he did not say so) and several times assured the therapist that he, the patient, knew no one was giving him his pains. At the end of this hour, the patient was suddenly moved to ask the therapist about the microphone in the room. This in spite of the fact that the microphone had been discussed at the opening session of the therapy and this was now the third session.

The patient opened his next hour by telling the therapist the following: "I was sort of curious last week about that microphone." It developed, on questioning, that the patient had had a fantasy, which he himself labeled as "weird," "illogical," and "improbable," to the effect that the therapist had sent a copy of the transcript of the therapy session to the school where the patient studied. His exact words are important because they pick up the theme of sending and "receiving" that had been a particular focus of the patient's embarrassment and had evoked the patient's need to reassure the therapist that he, the patient, was not crazy, since he knew he was not "receiving" chest pains from anyone. Here is the text of the patient's primary-process ideation about the therapist's betrayal made necessary out of "duty":

> P. Well, yeah, I just thought that maybe you were drawing severe conclusions and that someone should know about it at school. And some administrative officer should know about me . . . mm. And I was just wondering, 'cause no one's ever known that I sort of . . . ah . . . had funny ideas of what (laugh) (inaudible). Just a normal human being . . . and now . . . the picture's changed. I just thought that maybe, uh, I just thought that maybe you were sending them out of duty or something . . . some way (laugh) (inaudible) some way 'cause what's gonna happen if he does do it though.

The patient's shame and humiliated anger had been evoked by the therapist's interpretation, but it is hostility that has no "rationale" since the therapist is benign. The patient is in a state of guilt vis-à-vis the therapist for the patient's own shame-rage. The outcome is a paranoid fantasy that is very compelling, in spite of the patient's better judgment. And the content of the fantasy concretizes "receiving" and "sending" information about the severe conclusions that the therapist must be drawing about the patient's peculiarities and that the therapist is compelled to make known on pain of the therapist's being in a state of guilt toward the authorities who should be notified. In this compelling fantasy, both patient and therapist are in an insoluble dilemma of guilt.

CURRENT STATUS OF FREUD'S CONCEPT OF OBSESSIONAL NEUROSIS

As mentioned earlier, a recent review of obsessional neurosis from within the psychoanalytic framework (Nagera, 1976) reported very little progress. A review of obsessional states (Beech, 1974) representing both antianalytic and nonaligned viewpoints also concludes that the illness remains very puzzling. In contrast, Freud's views on the normal "anal character" as the core of (normal) obsessional personalities have found their way into folk wisdom. Freud's concept of the anal character and its connections with obsessional personality has had mixed results, as we shall see in Volume 2, but with considerable substantiation for Freud's insights, considering the methodological difficulties of experimental work with such concepts. This path was made easier by Fromm's (1955) brilliant translation of anality as a metaphor for the bourgeois character. Fromm's revision and broadening of Freud's insight resulted in the widespread dissemination of an image of "tight-assed," "rigid" personalities as adaptive to the structure of life as an organization man. As a relatively recent example, the formulation of coronary-prone Type A personality (Friedman and Rosenman, 1974) — the hard-driving, money-conscious, irritable man — was made from clinical observations, without any acknowledgment either to Freud or to Fromm. It has formed the basis for some of the ideology of the counterculture — as presaged by Sade. As a consequence of this widespread cultural absorption of psychoanalytic views, attention has been diverted away from the study of obsessional neurotic symptoms as a separate entity. Patients entering treatment for a variety of hard-to-specify dissatisfactions with themselves and their lives are often prey to obsessional symptoms much less florid than the Rat-Man's. But they are afflicted with rational-appearing "insoluble dilemmas" which are in fact obsessive symptoms. One consequence of the diversion of attention away from obsessional neurotic symptoms has been a neglect of them. In contrast to the almost ubiquitous obsessional personality presumably inhabiting Western culture, few cases of actual obsessional neurosis are diagnosed in psychiatry. (This is actually one example of Freud's lesser influence on psychiatry than he has had on the intellectual life of our times.) Obsessional neurosis is relatively uncommon; rough estimates of prevalence vary from 0.1% to 4.6% (Black, 1974).

Freud's description of the anal character in relation to obsessional neurosis also raised the empirical question as to whether or not obsessional neurotics do or do not show anal character traits prior to falling ill. Moreover, Freud's "anal triad" of personality characteristics — orderly, parsimonious, and obstinate — can be judged as both "good" and "bad" characteristics depending on one's viewpoint. As Sandler and Hazari (1960), working within the psychoanalytic framework, put it, "obsessional" is a "term of abuse or approbation used to describe one's friends or colleagues (depending upon whether one finds their behavior irksome or not)" (p. 113).

As to the question of anality a review of investigations of clinically diagnosed obsessional neurotics does show a close correspondence between obsessional illness and prior obsessional personality (Slade, 1974). Slade cites Ingram in a clinical study of 77 inpatients with severe obsessional states which found evidence of premorbid obsessional personality traits in 84% of the patients. These figures may be somewhat vitiated by the retrospective nature of the assessment of previous personality, but they are congruent with the clinical observations of obsessional patients as reflected, also, in psychiatric textbook descriptions of them. Thus, for example, Slade quotes the chapter on obsessional neurosis in a standard textbook on the practice of medicine: "Very many obsessional patients have for years before they become ill shown a rather characteristic mental constitution; they are extremely clean, orderly, and conscientious, sticklers for precision, they have inconclusive ways of thinking and acting; they are given to needless repetition. Those who have shown such traits since childhood are often morose, obstinate, irritable people; others are vacillating, uncertain of themselves and submissive." It should be noted, in passing, that no acknowledgment is made to Freud in the course of this description.

As to the second question — that is, where to draw the line between obsessional personality and obsessional neurosis — psychoanalytic convention has distinguished between trait and symptom on the basis of whether the behavior or thought in question is ego-syntonic or ego-alien. Researchers from other viewpoints have been inclined to agree with this distinction. For example, Marks (1969) distinguished between obsessional symptoms and obsessional traits on the basis of whether the particular behavior helped the individual or hindered him.

In an empirical study of obsessional traits and symptoms as they appear in an unselected population of neurotics, Sandler and Hazari (1960) analyzed the responses of 100 patients (50 males and 50 females) applying to the Tavistock Clinic in London. Sandler's Self-Assessment Inventory was administered to each patient, and 40 items representing obsessional traits and symptoms were extracted from the inventory and subjected to factor analysis. On the basis of the factor loadings, Sandler and Hazari were able to draw two very different pictures of obsessional persons. Factor A represents persons who are exceedingly systematic, methodical, thorough, liking a well-ordered life, consistent, punctual, and meticulous in the use of words. They dislike half-done tasks, and find interruptions irksome; they pay much attention to detail and have a strong aversion to dirt. Factor B, in contrast, represents persons whose daily life is disturbed through the intrusion of un-wanted thoughts and impulses into conscious experience. Thus they are compelled to do things which reason tells them are unnecessary, to perform certain rituals as part of everyday behavior, to memorize trivia and to strug-gle with persistent "bad" thoughts. They tend to worry over past action, to brood over ideas, and find themselves getting behind with things. They have inner difficulty making up their minds and inner resistance to commencing work.

On the basis of their findings, Sandler and Hazari suggest that persons covered by Factor A are "reactive–narcissistic" personalities, a constellation independent of Factor B which represents a continuum between true obses-sional personality and obsessional symptoms. The 40-item obsessionality scale failed, however, to distinguish between patients with obsessional symptoms, patients with obsessional traits, without symptoms, and a con-trol group of patients. Thus, the relationship between the high ideals de-scribed in Factor A and the nagging rituals and obsessions described in Fac-tor B may elude studies which do not relate the two kinds of attitudes to their underlying emotional basis, viz. efforts to ward off the shame and guilt in-herent in a failure of high standards.

One modern nonanalytic theory of obsessional neurosis (Beech and Perigault, 1974) is strikingly similar to Freud's formulation of the affects in-volved. They suggest that "such ordinary and typical misfortunes as a slight or insult, a mild disappointment or criticism . . . seem to have a more pro-found effect (i.e., produce a more serious deterioration in mood state) in obsessional patients than in others. Furthermore, it seems that such changes, once induced, can show an unusual degree of perseveration" (p. 114). Negative mood states, in other words, are the fundamental condition for the formation of obsessional symptoms. The cognitions which appear as part of the obsessional complex are "post hoc accounts offered by the patients as a means of explaining the subjective feeling of disturbance" (p. 115). Beech and Perigault suggest that their account is not incompatible with the details of cases adopting Freud's viewpoint. What they dispute is the symbolic value of the rat story told by the cruel captain as a cue to pathological arousal. Its "undeserved importance in analytical accounts . . . had led to the tortuous, colorful and insubstantial theoretical structure with which the reader is familiar" (p. 115).

Experiments designed to pursue Beech and Perigault's model are concerned with obsessional neurotics' presumed greater sensitivity to emotional arousal — with their perseverative tendencies and their presumed sensitivity to one-time conditioning as the means by which their exaggerated arousal becomes connected to its cognitive content. The authors are quick to point out that the data in support of their theory are extremely limited. But they regard their theory, which focuses on the emotional basis for obsessional symptoms, as closer to clinical evidence than the learning models which Wolpe and Lazarus, the behavior theorists, propose for obsessional neurosis.

Two characteristics of the obsessional neurosis that were puzzling to Freud have been pursued (not necessarily by Freudians) in research since his time, but remain unsolved, although the evidence seems to point in the direction of his guesses. The first is the question of the presumed higher intellectual level of obsessional neurotics as compared with hysterical and phobic patients. Freud speculated that obsessionals were precocious in their ego development and in consequence had been able to form well-defined "objects" but at a time when their libido was still in the anal-erotic sadistic stage. Another line of speculation leading to the same outcome was that in the obsessional neurosis "the instinct for knowledge can actually take the place of sadism" (1913b, p. 324). Precocious ego development and a sadistically based instinct for knowledge should be apparent in a higher level of intellectual functioning in obsessional neurotics than in other forms of neurosis, specifically hysteria and phobia.

In a recent review of the evidence on this point, Slade (1974) tells us that reliable studies, using objective measures of intelligence confirm the general clinical impression that obsessionals function at a higher level than patients with hysterical and phobic symptoms. Specifically, two studies are cited, one by Slater and one by Ingram. The first is of particular significance since the measure used was Raven's Matrices, a measure which correlates positively with tests of field-independence (Witkin, Dyk, Faterson, Goodenough, and Karp, 1962). There is related evidence that obsessionals tend to be more field-independent perceivers than hystericals (Witkin, 1965; Lewis, 1978). There is also some evidence that field-independent patients are more prone to guilt than field-dependent patients (Witkin, Lewis, and Weil, 1968).

A second observation that Freud made was of a sex difference in the frequency of obsessional neurosis. Specifically, he suggested that "hysteria has a strong affinity with femininity, just as obsessional neurosis has with masculinity" (Freud, 1926a, p. 69). In a study of 672 patients in psychoanalysis in Germany (Dührssen, 1951), women patients were found to have more hysterical symptoms, while men had more obsessional symptoms. In a total of 2,566 cases seen in a New York outpatient clinic between 1947 and 1972, men were diagnosed as obsessional-neurotic significantly more often than women (Safer, personal communication). Slade (1974), however, cites much conflicting evidence on the point and suggests that the sex ratio in obsessional neurosis is equal.

As I have suggested in *Psychic War in Men and Women* (Lewis, 1976) there are relatively few studies of sex difference in obsessional neurosis, and that, for a variety of reasons. For one thing, obsessional symptoms, sexual perversions, paranoid ideas in schizophrenia form a continuum of compelling "crazy" ideas. Some obsessional neurotics are sexual deviants; others have also gone "over the border" into paranoia. Men are much more prone to sexual deviations than women; men are also more prone to paranoid schizophrenia.

Another reason why there are few studies of obsessional neurosis is that the spread of psychoanalytic thinking has made the diagnosis go out of fashion. As we saw earlier, the general spread of Freud's ideas, including the notion that each of us is somewhat neurotic, has fostered a general tendency in psychiatry to undertake the enlargement of the general scope of a person's awareness of his inner life or to increase creative capacities rather than to relieve symptoms. Diagnosing disturbed "character" has also tended to obscure the presence of obsessional symptoms.

For example, one of the clearest descriptions by a patient of the experience of an obsessional, "crazy" command is contained in an account by Deutsch and Murphy (1955) of a so-called "envious man." The patient is describing how suddenly, as he is alone on vacation in his hotel room, he is afflicted with the command to jump out of the window. The patient says, "It was like a conscience, practically, like your conscience would say 'go ahead and jump,' and of course, well, I'd know better." The patient, however, was insufficiently sure of whether he would be able to withstand the command to jump, so he sought hospitalization. Working within the psychoanalytic framework, Deutsch and Murphy focus their psychotherapy on a disturbed "sector" of the patient's personality, namely, his envy. But the category in which he was placed was not obsessional neurosis, but a more generalized character-grouping of envious people. One consequence of this categorization is that the connection between envy and the outbreak of obsessional symptoms is obscured.

My own understanding of obsessional neurosis has also emphasized the affects involved, as Deutsch and Murphy's classification system does, but I place specific emphasis on the presence of an insistent guilty state operating in response to bypassed shame. In this connection I have suggested that the life circumstances which make men more likely to be field-independent are also more likely to place them in emotional situations in which they bear a greater burden of guilt for overt aggression than women do, and that their greater proneness to obsessional neurosis is a result.

When it comes to the question of therapy of the obsessional neurosis, there is little or no progress to report either from analytic or from nonanalytic sources. A review of behavioral treatment of obsessive-compulsive disorder (Meyer, Levy, and Schnurer, 1974) suggests at a rough estimation a figure of 30% to 55% of patients improved. Meyer et al. report a new variety of behavioral therapy which they call "apotrepic," a neologism coined from the Greek word meaning to "turn away, deter or dissuade" someone. Very briefly, obsessional patients with severe rituals were hospitalized for a few days of 24-hour staff supervision during which their rituals were persistently restrained — in some cases, with the patient's consent — by mild physical restraint. The therapist visited the patient and staff daily for joint sessions lasting half an hour. Social reinforcement, vicarious reinforcement, and monetary awards were all employed as seemed appropriate. As soon as the total elimination of rituals was achieved under supervision, additional stress was introduced by requiring the patient to confront his ritual-evoking situation. Supervision was gradually diminished, although the patient could ask for it if needed. The patient was sent home with the same instructions — to ask for supervision if ritual behavior threatened to recur. Fifteen patients with hand-washing, cleaning, and dusting repetition–compulsion rituals of many years duration have so far been treated with every patient, except one, showing marked improvement.

From the side of psychoanalysis, as we saw earlier, there has been no impetus for improved methods of therapy since Freud specifically discouraged such an enterprise. Sifneos (1966), however, reports good success in treating outpatients with mild obsessional symptoms of sudden onset. His technique is a short-term anxiety-provoking one. There is no control group reported, nor is there any attempt at quantifying results. Nevertheless, Sifneos's account is encouraging since he relates his success to a concentration on specific areas of emotional conflict rather than on characterological analysis and brings the feelings which result from his insistence on early termination into an analysis of the patient–therapist relationship.

As I have reported (Lewis, 1971), my own emphasis on the sequence from bypassed shame into ideation about a guilty, insoluble dilemma has been very useful to patients with obsessional symptoms. In particular, this sequence is regularly pursued within the patient–therapist relationship, in a vigilant effort to avoid the "negative therapeutic reaction." Although I have no controlled, quantitative evidence for the usefulness of my technique, there is no question that the length of patients' stay in treatment has been considerably shortened and that the success rate has improved. These improvements have resulted from a reliance on Freud's descriptions of how the affects work, rather than on his metapsychology.

SUMMARY

By the time he was analyzing the obsessional Wolf-Man, Freud's interest in the relief of symptoms had diminished. With hindsight, it seems likely that the Wolf-Man's exasperating affect of "indifference" was his means of coping with shame in relation to Freud. Present-day cases of "borderline" or "narcissistic" personalities (Kohut, 1971; Kernberg, 1975) may also be instances which reflect unanalyzed bypassed shame and guilt. These affects clearly governed the appearance of symptoms in the case of the Rat-Man; they suggest the usefulness of formulating sadism in affective rather than instinctual terms. Current work on obsessional neurosis clearly needs to concentrate once again on the way in which obsessive ideation represents a transformation of forbidden affects.

CHAPTER 5

Paranoia

The Problem of Homosexuality

Among the recent developments in the study of paranoia is Colby's (1977) construction of a valid computer simulation of paranoid processes based on a "shame–humiliation" theory. Colby, a psychoanalytically trained researcher, bases his theory (Colby, 1975) partly on Tomkins' (1963) formulation that paranoid information processing is designed to protect the self against humiliation. Colby's theory assumes that shame–humiliation affects are unavailable to the paranoid patient because they are too threatening. As a consequence, when threatened by the activation of shame–humiliation, the paranoid uses a "strategy of blaming others for wronging the self" (p. 56). Although Colby does not use the word "guilt," to blame others for wronging the self is to perceive them as guilty.

Colby's theory of shame–humiliation as the unbearable affect in paranoia is very similar to my own formulation of the role of bypassed shame in the appearance of obsessive, paranoid ideation (see Chapter 4). The two formulations evolved independently; they both suggest the usefulness of pursuing the affects in mental illness. It is significant, moreover, that after several decades of research into the cognitive deficits and distortions in schizophrenia (including paranoid schizophrenia), attention is returning to the pursuit of the affects. A recent study (Knight, Roff, Barnett, and Moss, 1979), comparing the predictive value of diagnosed "thought disorder" with "affective disorder" in assessing long-term outcome

135

(22 years) in cases of (male) schizophrenia, found that measures of "thought disorder" did not predict outcome but measures of affectivity and interpersonal competence did so with high significance. The authors suggest that measures of thought disorder are easier to specify and more reliable than measures of affectivity, and are therefore more attractive to researchers. Especially since in schizophrenia (including paranoia) affect is absent or blunted, affect tends to be overlooked in favor of more prominent ideational distortions. The authors remind us, moreover, that Hughlings Jackson, more than a hundred years ago, suggested the usefulness of distinguishing between "positive" symptoms, meaning disorders of thinking that are active, specific ideas, replacing normal ideation, and "negative" symptoms, principally affects; these latter are silent and so tend to be lost in diagnostic evaluations.

It is to Freud's credit that he was the first to struggle with specifying the relationship between affective and cognitive disorders; in his writings on paranoia (Freud, 1911) he specifically left open the question of how to formulate a relationship between the two systems: "We can no more dismiss the possibility that disturbances of the libido may react upon the ego-cathexes than we can overlook the converse possibility — namely, that a secondary or induced disturbance of the libidinal processes may result from abnormal changes in the ego. Indeed, it is probable that processes of this kind constitute the distinctive characteristics of psychoses. How much of this applies to paranoia it is impossible at present to say" (p. 75).

Freud's (1911) theory of paranoia was that its symptoms were primary-process transformations of forbidden sexual longings, specifically, forbidden homosexual longings. Freud's emphasis in this formulation was on translating the ideational symptom content back into its affective meaning. So, for example, the "click" of the camera that a paranoid woman heard as she was embracing her lover was translated into a clitoral pulse and thence into a "primal scene," signifying earlier forbidden acts or longings (Freud, 1915). As we saw earlier, one affect specific to forbidden longing is guilt for the implied transgression. Frustration or rejection of sexual longings by the beloved person may also trigger the affects of helplessness and shame. Freud, however, dealt with these affects of the "forbidding" agency by implicating them in the ideational content of subsequent symptoms, rather than by direct pursuit of the affective experiences they entail. Analysis of the ideational content particularly with respect to the cognitive distortions which it reflects has since become a major line of research, overshadowing the direct study of the affects.

This line of detective work in solving cognitive distortions is not only congenial to intellectuals, but it fits the affective picture in paranoia. In paranoia, the center of disturbance seems to the patient to be the events (and affects) which are occurring "out there," in the real world. These events involve the person in distress but the noxious affects are not *directly* about the self (as they are in depression and hysteria). We speak of paranoid ideation, not paranoid affect. The ideas are about what to do to remedy things that are amiss or wrong in the world. The self in paranoia is relatively blameless. In paranoia, the ideas, since they are about real events, rather than just about the shortcomings of the self, are well articulated and detailed. In fact, they are often on thei. face convincing to the listener, as they are to the patient. So, for example, the woman patient Freud describes in his 1915 paper was brought to see him by her lawyer who thought she might be paranoid but also understood that she might well be correct in her suspicions, since people do blackmail other people and his client might be so threatened in that way by her fellow employee.

It is a measure of the attractiveness of unraveling cognitive distortions that Colby designed his computer-simulation model as an aid in the *cognitive* therapy of paranoia. Specifically, interventions are recommended to counteract the patient's basic *beliefs* about his own inadequacy at the same time avoiding references that the patient might oversensitively interpret as shaming him, and, finally, "relocating" the source of distress within the patient rather than "out there." Colby is aware, of course, that the paranoid mode of ideation endlessly generates new suspicions and delusions. As an aid in countering this tendency he suggests the search for some kind of psychopharmacological agent that would raise the patient's threshold for shame–humiliation. By Colby's own account, however, the patient is already too little able to bear shaming; an agent that would still further increase his shame threshold would still leave intact or even increase the tendency to employ the strategy of projecting blame (and thus protecting the self) that the paranoid uses. One needs, in strict logic, an agent that would *lower* the threshold for shame–humiliation, at the same time allowing the patient to recognize for himself that these are bearable experiences. This is the conclusion I reached from a phenomenological description of the origin of a patient's paranoid ideas (Lewis, 1971, pp. 333–339).

Colby is aware, also, that deflecting blame back upon the self would increase the patient's depression at the same time that it decreased his paranoia (Colby, 1978, personal communication). In other words, the dilemma in pursuing the cognitive side of mental illness is that it leads to difficult problems in the management of the affects that are fundamental to the cognitive distortions. Colby's sophisticated use of the techniques of artificial intelligence in studying paranoia still leaves unsolved the fundamental questions about paranoia that Freud raised when he included it, along with hysteria, phobia, and obsessional neurosis among the illnesses that are generated by emotional conflict.

Freud's theory of paranoia is actually many-faceted and may conveniently be divided into two closely related parts. The first part is about the projection of unconscious homosexual wishes into paranoid ideation. The second part is about the genesis of homosexuality itself. Since homosexuality arises somewhat differently in the two sexes Freud's clinical descriptions of paranoia are also different for the two sexes. As Freud himself made clear on more than one occasion, however, his model of psychosexual development was essentially a male model, with female sexuality (and homosexuality) a derivative. In the case of paranoia, Freud also reconciled the clinical material from both sexes into a single model based essentially on male experience.

Freud's theory of the role of homosexuality in paranoia has many steps: (1) Paranoia is the result of the "projection" of homosexual longings that are forbidden to become conscious. (2) Since love for the same-sex figure is too disgraceful and too guilt-evoking to become conscious, it is first transformed into hatred of the beloved. (3) But hate itself is too guilt-evoking to be admissible to awareness. It is therefore projected into the hated (loved) figure so that he becomes the hating one: he persecutes and torments the patient because of his evil hatred of the innocent patient.

Freud's (1911) statement of the varieties of ways in which patients retain their innocence by projecting their forbidden sexual longings is worth quoting in full. This theoretical statement is, as usual, cautious, awaiting confirmation from more evidence.

> Nevertheless, it is a remarkable fact that the familiar forms of paranoia can all be represented as contradictions of the single proposition: "I (a man) love him (a man)" and indeed they exhaust all the possible ways in which such contradictions could be formulated.
>
> The proposition "I (a man) love him" is contradicted by: (a) Delusions of *persecution;* for they loudly assert: "I do not *love* him — I *hate* him." This contradiction, which must have run thus in the unconscious, cannot, however, become conscious to a paranoic in this form. The mechanism of symptom-formation requires that internal perceptions-feelings shall be replaced by external perceptions. Consequently, the proposition "I hate him" becomes transformed by *projection* into another one: "He *hates* (persecutes) me and will justify me in hating him." And thus the impelling unconscious feeling makes its appearance as though it were the consequence of an external perception: "I do not *love* him — I *hate* him, because HE PERSECUTES ME" [Freud's italics and capitals]. Observation leaves no doubt that the persecutor is someone who was once loved (p. 63).

Freud also analyzes erotomania, delusional jealousy, alcoholic jealousy, and delusional jealousy in women according to the same formula of a "contradiction" to the forbidden homosexual longing.

As the reader will readily see, guilt and shame are not specifically mentioned but rather implied as the main affective states which govern what longings shall be available to awareness: the paranoid symptoms reflect these unconscious longings in disguised but recognizable (to an observer) forms. It is also clear that the patient is in essentially the same emotional dilemma as the hysteric, the phobic, the obsessional neurotic, and as we shall see in the next chapter, the depressive. A beloved figure is hated but the hatred is too threatening to be borne. In paranoia the hatred is expelled and experienced as hateful events coming from external evil; in depression hatred is taken upon the self in the form of a profound loss of self-regard and a feeling of helplessness.

Freud clearly implies in the formulation just quoted that the person is trying to protect himself from a state of guilt: the paranoid transformation "justifies" the patient in his experience of malevolence coming toward him. As we have seen before, and as we shall see again in the case of depression, Freud's formulation of the self-protection was not directly in terms of the affects involved but rather in terms of a "narcissistic regression" to an infantile stage in which the self is taken as a "love-object." Thus Freud (1911) writes:

> . . . in paranoia the liberated libido becomes attached to the ego and is used for the aggrandizement of the ego. A return is thus made to the state of narcissism (known to us from the development of the libido), in which a person's only sexual object is his own ego. On the basis of the clinical evidence we can suppose that paranoics have brought along with them a *fixation at the stage of narcissism,* and we can assert that the length of *the step back from sublimated homosexuality to narcissism* is a measure of the amount of *regression* characteristic of paranoia (p. 72) (Freud's italics).

Homosexuality, as we shall see in a moment, also involves a narcissistic regression, specifically to the gender of the self rather than the opposite sex as sexually attractive. Paranoia and homosexuality are thus intimately connected with each other in Freud's system. Depression is also, as we shall see in Chapter 6, a narcissistic regression. Once again, attention to the affects of shame and guilt rather than to a structural regression into narcissism may ease some difficult problems. In paranoia, the reason love cannot be acknowledged is that it is homosexual. In depression, it cannot be acknowledged only because it is perceived as lost or unrequited. In the case of paranoia, the patient avoids the affects of humiliation by blaming others; in the case of depression, the patient *accepts* the humiliated feeling as justified by the patient's own worthlessness. We are no closer to a solution today of how these differences may be understood, except in respect to the differing affects that are distinctly involved.

The second part of Freud's theory of paranoia involves the genesis of homosexuality. The theory comprises many steps and the affects involved are not directly mentioned but rather implied. Love becomes homosexual in the first place as a specific solution, usually appearing at puberty, to (the painful, humiliating affects involved in) jealousy of the opposite-sex parent.

The jealous youngster soothes his hurt pride by identifying specifically with the gender of the faithless parent, and by taking a same-sex lover close to the self in age and otherwise "narcissistically" similar to the self, and by loving this same-sex person as tenderly as the faithless parent should have loved the self. Freud thus considered homosexuality to be a complicated set of unconscious maneuvers of Oedipal protest and revenge, but he characteristically described them theoretically in terms of instinctual stages rather than in affective terms.

Freud also considered homosexual longings to be present in every person not only as a product of the universal need for revenge that each of us has but also as a consequence of our bisexual constitution. Social concerns and interests, moreover, are the effect of the sublimated homosexuality present in all of us. By implication, therefore, homosexuals who openly acknowledge their preference and are reasonably satisfied with it were clearly not regarded as particularly neurotic or disturbed. For example, the young woman homosexual sent to Freud by her father (Freud, 1920b) was described as "not in any way ill (she did not suffer from anything in herself), nor did she complain of her condition" (p. 150); "she had never been neurotic, and came to the analysis without even one hysterical symptom" (p. 155).

The simplest way to take Freud's meaning about homosexuality is to quote him directly and in full. The most comprehensive statement is contained in his 1922 paper on jealousy, paranoia, and homosexuality: It is a statement about male homosexuality only, but it represents Freud's theoretical position.

> Recognition of the organic factor in homosexuality does not relieve us of the obligation of studying the psychical processes connected with its origin. The typical process already established in innumerable cases, is that a few years after the termination of puberty a young man, who until this time has been strongly fixated to his mother, changes his attitude; he identifies himself with his mother, and looks about for love-objects in whom he can re-discover himself, and whom he might love as his mother loved him. The characteristic mark of this process is that for several years one of the necessary conditions for his love is usually that the male object shall be of the same age as himself was when the change took place. We have come to know of various factors contributing to this result, probably in different degrees. First there is the fixation on the mother, which makes it difficult to pass on to another woman. Identification with the mother is the outcome of this attachment, and at the same time in a certain sense it enables the son to keep true to her, his first object. Then there is the inclination towards a narcissistic object-choice, which in general lies readier to hand and is easier to put into effect than a move toward the other sex. Behind this latter factor there lies concealed another of quite exceptional strength, or perhaps it coincides with it: the high value set upon the male organ and the inability to tolerate its absence in a love-object. Depreciation of women, and aversion to them, even horror of them, are generally derived from the early discovery that women have no penis. We subsequently discovered, as another powerful motive urging toward homosexual-object-

choice, regard for the father and fear of him; for the renunciation of women means that all rivalry with him (or with men who may take his place) is avoided. The last two motives, the clinging to the condition of a penis in the object, as well as retiring in favour of the father — may be ascribed to the castration complex. Attachment to the mother, narcissism, fear of castration — these are the factors (*which incidentally have nothing specific about them*) that we have found in the psychical etiology of homosexuality; and with these must be reckoned the effect of seduction which is responsible for a premature fixation of the libido, as well as the influence of the organic factor which favours the passive role in love [my italics].

We have, however, never regarded this analysis of the origin of homosexuality as complete. I can now point to a new mechanism leading to homosexual object-choice, although I cannot say how large a part it plays in the formation of the extreme, manifest and exclusive type of homosexuality. Observation has directed my attention to several cases in which during early childhood impulses of jealousy, derived from the mother-complex and of very great intensity, arose (in a boy) against his rivals, usually older brothers. This jealousy led to an exceedingly hostile and aggressive attitude toward these brothers which might sometimes reach the point of death-wishes, but they could not maintain themselves in the face of the subject's further development. Under the influence of upbringing — and certainly not uninfluenced by their own continuing powerlessness — these impulses yielded to repression and underwent transformation, so that the rivals of the earlier period became the first homosexual object choice. Such an outcome of the attachment to the mother shows various interesting relations with other processes known to us. First of all it is a complete contrast to the development of persecutory paranoia, in which the person who before has been loved becomes the hated persecutor, whereas the hated rivals are transformed into love-objects. It represents, too, an exaggeration of the process which, according to my view, leads to a birth of social instincts in the individual. In both processes there is first the presence of jealous and hostile impulses which cannot achieve satisfaction and both the affectionate and social feelings of identification arise as reaction-formations against aggressive impulses.

This new mechanism of homosexual object-choice . . . is sometimes combined with typical conditions already familiar to us . . . . As a rule, however, the new mechanism is distinguished by the change taking place at a much earlier period, and the identification with mother receding into the background. Moreover, in the cases I have observed it led only to homosexual attitudes which did not exclude heterosexuality and did not involve *horror feminae*.

It is well known that a good number of homosexuals are characterized by a special development of their social instinctual impulses and by their devotion to the interests of the community. It would be tempting, as a theoretical explanation of this, to say that the behavior toward men in general of a man who sees in other men a potential love-object must be different from that of a man who looks upon other men in the first instance as rivals in regard to women. . . . In the light of psychoanalysis we are accustomed to regarding social feeling as a sublimation of homosexual attitudes toward objects (pp. 230–232).

One theme that is clear in this lengthy quotation and even clearer in his clinical account of a young woman homosexual brought to treatment by her father (Freud, 1920b) is Freud's recognition that homosexuality is a viable life-style for many persons. As such it is not on a par with paranoia or depression as a symptom; these and other symptoms gravely impede personal functioning. Although psychoanalytic writers since Freud had *all* officially continued to regard homosexuality as pathological (Bieber et al., 1962) the grounds for this categorization are very varied. Even more important, their evidence for the pathology of homosexuality has come from homosexuals who are troubled enough to seek psychiatric treatment. Recognition of this basic fact has led the American Psychiatric Association to delete homosexuality per se as a neurotic symptom from its diagnostic roster. Even though that development was opposed by many psychoanalysts, it could not have evolved without Freud.

Freud's views on the viability of homosexuality as a life-style were in sharp contrast to the prevailing views of his time. These either regarded homosexuality "scientifically" as a form of degeneracy or else morally as a sin. The enlightened treatment of sex that Freud introduced was influential in spurring the work of Kinsey and his colleagues, whose surveys of American sex life showed homosexuality to be much more prevalent than anyone had supposed, especially among men (Kinsey, Pomeroy, and Martin, 1948; Kinsey, Pomeroy, Martin, and Gebhard, 1953). Freud's views on sexuality were also influential in the development of cross-cultural studies of human sexual behavior. Ford and Beach (1951) showed that some form of homosexual behavior among men was found in just about all societies.

However, the question of whether homosexuality is "normal" still remains a subject of debate, often, as might be expected, with considerable passion. Gide (1950), for example, published a famous appeal in his book *Corydon*, to which Beach, a lifelong student of mammalian sexual behavior, directly replied. Beach (1965) later made the useful and clarifying distinction between the term "sexual behavior" which refers to an individual's practices, and "behavior of the sexes," which refers to species-reproduction patterns. Individual sexual behavior is governed by a great variety of idiosyncratic, experiential factors, far removed from any biological determination. For any given individual, his or her sexual behavior ought not to be labeled a perversion since it may represent the "optimum" solution for that person's self-fulfillment. Against the framework, however, of a description of species-reproductive behavior, deviations or perversions may be designated as such. As Beach puts it, "We are at variance with him [Gide] in our belief that the strength of biological forces inclining most individuals toward heterosexual relations is greater than those that tend to produce homosexual alliances" (Gide, 1950, p. 189).

Systematic studies of *normal* homosexuals and heterosexuals have yielded evidence of significant differences between the two groups in familial pattern of affective relationships. Especially in the case of men, homosexuals more often describe being raised in a familial pattern in which the father was hostile and cold, while the mother was "close" and binding (Fisher and Greenberg, 1977). These findings tend to corroborate findings from the large-scale study by Bieber et al. (1962) of homosexuals in treatment as compared with nonhomosexual controls. The evidence from normal women homosexuals also tends to support Freud's hypothesis of exaggerated Oedipal affects (Fisher and Greenberg, 1977), for which homosexuality is a "loving" solution.

This theme of homosexuality as an outcome of exaggerated Oedipal jealousy is also clear in the preceding lengthy quotation from Freud. Reaction-formations of heightened tenderness toward same-sex rivals, as well as heightened (sublimated) social concerns for the welfare of others, help the person to master his jealousy. The problem Freud pinpoints here is why, in some cases, the hated person continues to be loved, in which case we have only homosexuality in quiet reaction-formation; and why, in other instances, the loved person is hated and experienced in projected or paranoid form as a persecutor. A further problem, not specifically noted here but clearly implied, is why, in some instances, the result is neither homosexuality nor paranoia, but depression. Although Freud does not specifically say so, moreover, it is the "hating" that requires defenses — either a reaction-formation, or a projection, or both.

Freud's hypothesis linking paranoia and unconscious homosexuality was most fully expounded in his account (1911) of the Schreber case, which generated much controversy within the psychoanalytic movement. Knight (1940), for example, asked why some people "react so frantically to the dimly perceived homosexual drive" (p. 150), while others successfully repress it without losing their reality testing. Knight's proposed answer was that paranoics have love–hate conflicts not only with their fathers but much earlier conflicts with their mothers. White (1961), Stoller (1973), and Chassaguet-Smirgel (1979) all suggest that the paranoid Schreber's repudiation of his femininity was based on his hatred of a mother who acted as the agent of his father's brutalities. Schreber's delusions united him not only with his father but "with the mother from whom he had been severed too early" (Chassaguet-Smirgel, p. 187). By implication Chassaguet-Smirgel also suggests that the "narcissistic cathexis of femininity" (p. 183) is a key factor in shaping the normal gender identity of both sexes.

SEX DIFFERENCES IN HOMOSEXUALITY AND PARANOIA

One line of explanation for these related problems may lie buried in the information, acquired since Freud's day, of a sex difference in incidence of homosexuality, paranoia, and depression. Specifically, men more often than women report homosexual behavior (Kinsey et al., 1948, 1953) and more often apply for psychiatric help for homosexual symptoms (Safer, personal communication). Men also more often than women fall ill of paranoid schizophrenia; women more often than men fall ill of depression (Lewis, 1978). Furthermore, the evidence on the relationship between homosexuality and paranoia is "impressive" in the case of men, while for women the evidence is, if anything, against such a connection (Fisher and Greenberg, 1977). Among paranoid women the persecutor is male more often than female.

It is possible that these pieces of evidence may be fitted together if we suppose that, for men, the confounding of power and masculinity makes it more difficult to "settle" for homosexuality. For men, therefore, the homosexual choice more often evokes shame, hatred, guilt, and a projection into paranoia. For women, in contrast, the solution of heightened tenderness toward the same sex not only coincides with their socially fostered nurturant role but can also express itself directly as a protest against the injustices of men's superior power. For women, therefore, a homosexual choice need not proceed into paranoid projection. Women's greater socialization into tenderness in general, however, brings them into greater risk of depression.

In Freud's clinical accounts of paranoia in men, particularly in the Schreber case (see below), the homosexual theme is clear: The chief sexual persecutor is a male. In his brief account of two sessions with a paranoid woman the chief persecutor is not same-sex but her male lover, and the evidence for the homosexual theme is derived from slight evidence in a labored way, to fit a preexisting theory. Thus, fitting both sexes into the same theoretical system led Freud astray. If we assume, however, that the affects of shame and guilt that accompany a same-sex choice are more unbearable for males, who have less developmental support for reaction-formations of heightened tenderness, we can account for men's greater proneness to paranoia and for the role of homosexuality in paranoia among men. Reaction-formations of heightened tenderness are, in general, more comfortably experienced by women. When they take the form of homosexual choice they need not develop into paranoia. These reaction-formations are also, however, the source of women's greater tendency to depression. In thus restating the problems that Freud raised in terms of shame and guilt — in terms of the affective conflicts with which people cope — rather than in terms of instinctual stages, we are at least converting the problems into more graspable forms.

Freud's theory that the genesis of homosexuality lies in a "narcissistic regression" has encountered considerable difficulty when it comes to applying it to the two sexes (Lewis, 1976). When a man makes a regressive narcissistic identification with his earliest object choice he thereby "chooses" his mother, and so changes his gender role. But when a woman makes such a narcissistic regression, she need not make a change in the gender role, since her first caretaker is the same sex as herself. Freud actually used the term "narcissistic" to refer to the adolescent's choice of same-sex lover, in the case of the man, a replica of himself in age and personality. But in the case of the woman, as we shall see, the same-sex love object is years older and a replica of *mother*, not of the self (Freud, 1920b).

Freud's hypothesis about narcissism was clearly derived from considerations governing the life of man (Lewis, 1979). These considerations led him to the prediction that men have an easier task in the assumption of their gender identity since they continue to love their first objects — their mothers. Since women shift from their first love to their fathers, Freud thought they should find it easier to become homosexuals, clinging to their first love (Freud, 1922). As is the case with many of Freud's insights, he was surely on the right track in supposing that having a same-sex or an opposite-sex first caretaker would make a difference in development. But the difference can be seen as favoring girls in the formation of their gender identity.

Margaret Mead (1949) suggested that men have a different and more difficult gender identity task than women. A man's "earliest experience of himself is one in which he is forced, in the relationship to his mother, to recognize himself as different, a creature unlike his mother" (p. 167). Lynn (1962) put this same idea somewhat differently: A woman has only to learn a lesson in mother-emulation; a man has to solve the problem of differentiating himself from his mother and identifying with his father.

The change in the pattern of "species-reproductive" behavior which accompanied the emergence of the human species may also cause men to have more trouble than women in sustaining their part in the reproductive process. The human species is the only primate species in which estrus in the female does not govern the reproductive cycle. With the loss of estrus in the female, human reproduction is less under biological and more under social control than it is among nonhuman primates. With "pink swellings" gone as a relatively no-fail stimulus to penile erections, men are no longer so certain of erections and ejaculations as their primate cousins. As Desmond Morris (1971) puts it (and Morris is no sentimentalist when it comes to animal behavior) ". . . the human animal 'makes love' to a complete and special individual . . . we now perform the mating act not so much to fertilize an egg as to fertilize a relationship" (p. 101).

For men, however, ejaculation and orgasm cannot occur unless there has been a prior event — the erection of the penis. Intercourse for men still involves the same three-stage process that it does in primates: arousal-erection, intromission, and ejaculation. A man's failure to have an erection or to maintain it prevents intercourse; no such burden of responsibility is carried by women. A woman has only to be there and willing to permit penetration. A man must be aroused — a state not necessarily under his conscious control. The act of intercourse is thus easier for the woman, and her orgasm plays no role in fertilization. Ford and Beach (1951), in their cross-cultural study, report that "love charms are much more often employed by men than by women" (pp. 108–109). As Horney (1932) puts it: "The man is actually obliged to go on proving his manhood to the woman. There is no analogous necessity for her. Even if she is frigid she can engage in sexual intercourse and conceive and bear a child. She performs her part by merely *being*, without any *doing* . . . . The man on the other hand has to do something in order to fulfill himself" (p. 350). Fromm (1943) also describes how the fear of impotence may increase a man's need for "mastery" and thus bring him into states of hostility that need "defense": reaction-formations or projections.

These conceptualizations lead to the prediction that men should not only have a harder time assuming their masculine gender identity than women, but a harder time maintaining their role in "species-reproduction." In consequence, disturbances of gender identity and deviant sexuality including homosexuality, should be more frequent among males than females. In fact, this prediction has considerable evidence to support it. Men are more prone to sexual deviations than women (Kinsey et al., 1948; Kinsey et al., 1953; Gebhard et al., 1965; Money and Ehrhardt, 1972; Stoller, 1968). This evidence should be considered against the background fact that women are much more likely than men to report and seek help for psychological troubles (Garai, 1970). The greater frequency of homosexuality among men in both normal and psychiatric populations is thus not an artifact of women being better able than men to hide their homosexuality as Socarides (1974) has suggested.

Along with sex differences, differences between people in cognitive style, as these reflect the outcome of affective struggles, have also emerged since Freud's time. These differences are a help in grasping the dynamics of paranoia, and depression. As might be predicted, there is evidence of a connection between paranoia and field-independence among male paranoid schizophrenics (Witkin, 1965; Johnson, 1980). As we shall see in Chapter 6, there is parallel evidence of a connection between field-dependence and depression, particularly in women. Studies of defensive styles among normal people show that turning aggression against the self is associated with field-dependence; while projection of hostility and blame outward more often occurs among field-independent people (Gleser and Ihilevich, 1969). That self-directed hostility is characteristic of depression is agreed by both Freudian and cognitive–behavioral theorists. Paranoia clearly involves the projection of hostility, in contrast to depression. Homosexuality, one factor

which Freud emphasized as itself a complicated end-result of affective struggles, is also a defense against hostility. Connecting homosexuality (in both
sexes) with differences in cognitive style is a step not yet taken but one which
may help to unravel the question of why the outcome of defenses against
hostility sometimes produces depression, sometimes homosexuality,
sometimes paranoia.

In the remainder of this chapter we shall first examine Freud's analysis of
the Schreber case, and the subsequent discoveries made by Baumeyer (1956)
and Niederland (1959a,b; 1960) from the records of Schreber's hospitalizations, and from reading the works of Schreber's famous physician-father.
We shall then examine the experimental and clinical work that has been done
on Freud's hypothesis of a special role of unconscious, projected homosexuality in paranoia. We shall touch on the evidence on the mechanism of projection. We shall then examine Freud's clinical writings on homosexuality,
but postpone reviewing the evidence that has accumulated on these
hypotheses over the past decades to Volume 2. In what follows, we have
been enormously helped by the literature reviews done by others, in particular, the work of Kline (1971) and Fisher and Greenberg (1977). As we
have seen in preceding chapters, reviewing Freud's clinical writings (here on
paranoia and on homosexuality) will highlight the affective states with
which he was actually dealing.

THE SCHREBER CASE

Before turning to Freud's analysis of the Schreber case, an analysis confirming Freud's already existing hypothesis that homosexuality plays a central role in paranoia, it will be helpful to review some of the history of the
celebrated memoirs that made Schreber the "most frequently quoted patient
in psychiatry" (MacAlpine and Hunter, 1955). Daniel Paul Schreber, a noted
jurist, fell ill with paranoid delusions soon after his transfer and promotion
in 1893 to the position of presiding judge of an appeals court in Dresden.
This was Schreber's second hospitalization, the first having occurred in 1884,
after he had run for the Reichstag in the Leipzig area. Schreber spent the
years from 1893 to 1902 in the Schloss Sonnenstein Asylum near Dresden.
By 1902 he felt himself completely recovered from his illness and applied to
the court for a judgment requiring his discharge from the sanitarium, a
discharge that the psychiatric authorities were not prepared to grant. The
judge, while deciding in favor of Schreber's claim, noted his still clearly delusional ideas that he had a mission to redeem the world and to restore it to its
lost state of bliss by being transformed into a woman. The court apparently
agreed with Schreber that such views cannot be proved or disproved.

Schreber's memoirs of his psychotic experiences were published in 1903, and excited considerable interest among psychiatrists. Freud's analysis of the memoir was published in 1911.

Schreber's autobiographical account of his family, contained in Chapter 3 of the memoirs, was deliberately withheld by Schreber as "unsuitable for publication" (Freud, 1911, p. 37). Freud was thus forced to rely on guesswork for an account of Schreber's childhood and his actual emotional circumstances at the time of his illness. Some forty years later, in 1951, Baumeyer (1956) discovered some records at Schloss Sonnenstein of Schreber's hospitalizations, including notations suggesting that Schreber's father was a severe obsessional with homicidal tendencies. Niederland (1959a,b; 1960) studied the published writings of Schreber's father, a prominent physician, whose recommendations on physical fitness are still enthusiastically followed by members of Schreber Vereine, "associations dedicated to the propagation of physical culture, calisthenics, gardening, fresh air activities and the like" (Niederland, 1960, p. 492). Schreber's father was an orthopedic physician, who had originally intended to manage a pediatric institution near Leipzig but was considered unsuitable by the local health authorities, who found him too strong-minded. Schreber père had the "missionary zeal of a reformer . . . and expanded originally limited orthopedic methods into a general system of physical culture . . . adding disciplinary, moral and religious ideas . . . into a regimented educational system for the use of parents and teachers . . ." (Niederland, 1960, p. 496). One of the biographers (Ritter) of Schreber père admires him as a spiritual precursor of Nazism. As we shall see when we look at Schreber fils' accounts of his delusions, each of them can be connected to childhood tortures inflicted by this zealous father on his "beloved" children for their own good.

Freud has been faulted by Schatzman (1973) for having made the probably incorrect guess that Schreber's post-childhood relations with his "excellent father" were good. But his criticism misses the point. Freud did guess, on the basis of the clinical material, that Schreber's relations with his father were characterized by enormous hostility which the child found too guilt-evoking to allow into awareness. It is the struggle to maintain the loving relationship in spite of hating that is the source of symptom formation. The discovery nearly half a century later that Schreber's father was indeed "homicidal" rather confirms that there was a kernel of "truth" in the content of his son's symptoms.

Reading Freud's analysis and interpretation of Schreber's symptoms leaves no doubt that homosexuality is prominent in the content of the delusions. But it is also apparent that if we follow Schreber's affective states as they are implied in the content, we find him mostly in the morally elevated position of the one who is unjustly persecuted and carnally abused by God, or else in the morally elevated position of the one performing the mission of copulating with God, bringing Him into a more sensitive appreciation of mankind, and producing a new human species attuned to the virtues of "voluptuousness." In his delusion Schreber himself is either not guilty, or else he is, even more positively, a champion of the Good. In this solution that he found to the problem of God's evil, Schreber feels sane even though he is aware that others may doubt his special mission.

Freud is emphatic on the point that Schreber's emasculation fantasy — that he was handed over to Flechsig (his former psychiatrist) for the purpose of carnal abuse, with God's connivance — came first in the order of events, and that his Redeemer fantasy was second.

> The Redeemer delusion is a phantasy that is familiar to us through the frequency with which it forms the nucleus of religious paranoia. The additional factor, which makes the redemption dependent upon the man being previously transformed into a woman, is unusual and bewildering, since it shows such a wide divergence from the historical myth which the patient's phantasy is setting out to reproduce. It is natural to follow the medical report in assuming that the motive force of this delusion complex was the patient's ambition to play the part of Redeemer, and that his *emasculation* was only entitled to be regarded as a means for achieving that end. Even though this may be true of his delusion in its final form, a study of the *Denkwürdigkeiten* compels us to take a very different view of the matter. For we learn that the idea of being transformed into a woman (that is, of being emasculated) was the primary delusion, that he began by regarding that act as constituting a serious injury and persecution and it only became related to his playing the part of Redeemer in a secondary way (p. 18).

But what is essential in the affective states being described by Freud is that the emasculation was first experienced as a persecution — as Schreber put it, *contrary to the "Order of Things"* — and only later on regarded as *in accordance with the Order of Things*, that is, a part of the Redeemer's mission to bring about the cultivation of voluptuousness (my italics). At first it is an unbearable humiliation; later on, it is a source of moral strength.

When he was being persecuted, Schreber was the (unjust) victim of every sort of jeering and humiliation on the subject of his emasculation. "'Rays of God' calling [him] 'Miss Schreber,'" mocked him. Or they would say: 'So *this* sets up to have been a Senatspräsident, this person who lets himself be f−d'" (p. 20). When he was being unjustly persecuted by emasculation — against the Order of Things — Schreber was full of (just) protest and righteous indignation, or else in a state of (understandable) humiliated fury. But when he was becoming a woman Redeemer, he was both proud and forgiving of his former persecutors.

Freud reviews in some detail Schreber's attitude toward God and his theological system that involves *"nerves, the state of bliss, the divine hierarchy and the attributes of God"* (p. 21). The nerves of God are infinite but limited to dealing only with the souls of the dead.

> It was only in exceptional instances that He would enter into relations with particular, highly gifted persons . . . . God does not have any regular communication with human souls, in accordance with the Order of Things, till after death . . . . Souls that have passed through a process of purification enter into the enjoyment of a *state of bliss* . . . . In the course of their purification, "souls learn the language which is spoken by God himself, the so-called 'basic language,' a vigorous though somewhat antiquated German, which is especially characterized by a great wealth of euphemisms . . . . On one occasion God uttered a very current word in 'basic language' — the word, 'Slut!'" (p. 23) (quotations verbatim from Schreber).

Because God communicates only with the dead He does not really understand the living human being.

> "The pen well-nigh shrinks from recording so monumental a piece of absurdity as that God, blinded by His ignorance of human nature, can positively go to such lengths as to suppose that there can exist a man too stupid to do what every animal can do — too stupid to be able to sh—. When upon the occasion of such an urge, I actually succeed in evacuating — and as a rule I nearly always find the lavatory engaged, I use a pail for the purpose — the process is always accompanied by the generation of an exceedingly strong feeling of spiritual voluptuousness" (p. 27).

In other words, God is not only an accomplice in the sexual abuse of Schreber's body, but he is stupid . . . "'God strikes me above all, in almost everything that happens to me, as being ridiculous or childish. As regards my own behavior, this often results in my being obliged in self-defence to play the part of a scoffer at God, and even, on occasion to scoff at Him aloud'" (p. 27).

Once again, if we follow the affects implied in Schreber's account, God is not only a homosexual, but a figure of ridicule. Freud specifically points to the "mixture of reverence and rebelliousness" (p. 29) in Schreber's attitude toward Him, but without especially emphasizing Schreber's scorn of God.

In discussing the "state of bliss," Schreber makes what Freud calls a "surprising" distinction between a male and a female state of bliss. "'The male state of bliss was superior to the female, which seems to have consisted chiefly in an uninterrupted feeling of voluptuousness'" (p. 29). Freud considers that the sexualization of the state of bliss is itself also surprising. He suggests the possibility that Schreber's concept is derived from a condensation of two principal meanings of the German word *"selig"* — namely, "dead," and "sensually happy." Schreber "had come to see that the cultivation of voluptuousness was incumbent upon him as a duty, and that it was only by discharging this duty that he could end the grave conflict which had broken out within him — or as he thought, about him. Voluptuousness, so the voices assured him, had become 'god-fearing' and he could only regret that he was not able to devote himself to its cultivation the whole day long" (p. 31). The content of the "state of bliss" is thus sexual, as Freud suggests. But the affect surrounding it (which Freud takes for granted) is righteous, so that Schreber need no longer be in a state of guilt over the enjoyment of the voluptuousness of his bodily functions.

Since it is Schreber who makes the connection between femininity and endless voluptuousness, one may hear in Schreber's delusions about becoming the wife of God not only a homosexual longing but a protest against the confounding of gender and voluptuousness (Lewis, 1976). We now know that Schreber's father had reared his children with inordinate harshness; the confound between masculinity and toughness and between femininity and tenderness must therefore have been particularly compelling for Schreber *fils*. For years, moreover, Schreber had been hoping that his wife might become pregnant, but she had had, instead, two miscarriages in the six years of their marriage. Some weeks before he fell ill he had thought one night, as he was falling asleep, "that after all it really might be very nice to be a woman submitting to the act of copulation" (p. 13). One may hear in this fantasy, again, not only a homosexual wish, but also a wish that a man might be able to bear children. That he would bear children impregnated in him by God was clearly implied in his paranoid delusions about becoming the founder of a new breed of humanity. In thus interpreting Schreber's hypnagogic fantasy and his subsequent delusions as an example of "womb envy" we catch more of Schreber's affects of helplessness and (unjust) fury at his wife's inability to bear children. This humiliation might even have been compounded by the fact that Schreber *père* was a noted expert on child-rearing; Schreber *fils* might well have felt the sting of not being able to emulate his distinguished pedagogue-father, who had sired five children. In any case, Horney's attempts to persuade Freud that men as well as women have sources of envious affects in the contemplation of the anatomy of their bodies ultimately brought the two psychoanalysts to a parting of the ways. Horney's emendation of Freud's male model of psychosexual development made it easier to separate gender and social role and thus prevent their easy confounding.

Some of the educational procedures to which Schreber was subjected during his childhood by his reformer–physician father are to be found in Schreber *père's* own writings. Each of the cruel child-rearing practices finds an echo in the "miracled-up" world of Schreber's delusional system in which he lived during his illness. Niederland's account (1959b) supplements Freud's analysis of Schreber's Memoir since it connects new passages of the memoir's text with additional information gathered from the writing of Schreber's father. There are, according to Niederland, literally hundreds of "divine miracles" occurring to Schreber's body and Chapter XI of his Memoir, entitled, "Bodily Integrity Damaged by Miracles," contains a detailed description of many of them. The reader will note the characteristic contradiction and absurdity in the idea that miracles "damage" rather than foster "bodily integrity." This is a message in which an observer can see the ridicule of his father's emphasis on bodily functions, but the patient presumably cannot. His paranoid ideation, however, expresses it. Niederland (p. 393) quotes the opening paragraph of this chapter, which is worth reproducing in full:

"From the first beginnings of my contact with God up to the present day my body has continuously been the object of divine miracles. If I wanted to describe all these miracles in detail I could fill a whole book with them alone. I may say that *hardly a single limb or organ in my body escaped being temporarily damaged by miracles, nor a single muscle being pulled by miracles*, either moving or paralyzing it according to the respective purpose. Even now the miracles which I experience hourly are still of a nature as to frighten every other human being to death . . . . In the first year of my stay at Sonnenstein sanatorium the miracles were of such a threatening nature that I thought I had to fear almost incessantly for my life, my health or my reason . . . ." [In a footnote Schreber adds: "This, as indeed the whole report about the miracles enacted on my body, will naturally sound extremely strange to all other human beings, and one may be inclined to see in it only the product of a pathologically vivid imagination. In reply I can only give the assurance that *hardly any memory from my life is more certain* than the miracles recounted in this Chapter. *What can be more definite for a human being than what he has lived through and felt on his own body?* Small mistakes may have occurred as my anatomical knowledge is *naturally only that of a layman"*] (my italics).

Niederland calls particular attention to this last sentence, in which Schreber uses the term "layman" for himself, in obvious contrast to his father's status as a physician.

Among the miracles performed on Schreber's body were not only his emasculation but also the removal of his inner organs, as well as damages inflicted on his head, chest, abdomen, and nerves, and finally miracles enacted on his muscles and skeleton. There are marked similarities between each of these and the physical manipulations that Schreber *père* invented for the successful upbringing of children. These child-rearing methods included "an orthopedic apparatus, the so-called *Schrebersche Geradehalter*, to secure a straight and upright body posture day or night. One of these contraptions consisted of a system of iron bars fastened to the chest of the child as well as to the table near which the child was sitting; the horizontal iron bar pressed against the chest and prevented any movement forward or sideward, giving only some freedom to move backward to an even more rigidly upright position . . . . Another heavy belt was used at bedtime to make sure that the child remained in a supine position all night long. This belt was fastened to the bed and ran tightly across the child's chest, thus keeping his body posture straight as well as supine through the night" (Niederland, 1959b, p. 395). In short, from head to foot, each portion of the child's anatomy was to be regulated for his better health and well-being.

Moreover, Schreber's father advocated that "no nonsense" be tolerated from infancy onward. In a *Book of Health,* published in 1839, and designed as a guide to parents on the care of infants, Schreber *père* details advice on how to combat crying during the first year of life.

"Crying and whimpering without reason express nothing but a whim, a mood, and the first emergence of stubbornness; they must be dealt with positively, through quick distraction of attention, serious words, knocking on the bed (actions which usually startle the child and make him stop crying), or if all this be to no avail, through the administration of comparatively mild, intermittently repeated, corporeal admonishments. It is essential that this treatment be continued until its purpose is attained . . . . Such a procedure is necessary only once or, at most, twice — and then one is master of the child forever. From then on one glance, one word, one single menacing gesture are sufficient to rule the child . . . .

"This is also the best time to train the young child in the art of renouncing. The mode of training here recommended is simple and effective: While the child sits in the lap of its nurse or nanny, the latter eats and drinks whatever she desires: however intense the child's oral needs may become under such circumstances, they must never be gratified. Not a morsel of food must be given the child besides its regular three meals a day. The father is particularly strict in this situation. He relates an episode in my own family when a nurse, with one of the Schreber children sitting in her lap, was eating pears and could not resist the impulse to give a small piece of the pear to the begging child, though this had been strictly verboten. The nurse was immediately fired, and since news about this drastic action spread quickly among the children's nurses then available in Leipzig, the father writes, from then on he had no further trouble with any other such erring maids or nurses" (Niederland, 1959b, pp. 387–388).

Schreber's confounding of harshness with masculinity and voluptuousness with femininity thus had ample encouragement in the atmosphere that prevailed in his own household of origin.

Freud's analysis of Schreber's Memoir was made without any of the information since collected about Schreber's father, as well as without firsthand acquaintance with Schreber himself. The information subsequently brought to light by Baumeyer (1956) suggests that Schreber had many more symptoms of depression than his Memoir recorded. He speaks, for example, of his first illness, the one in which Flechsig was helpful to him, as a case of "hypochondria." Records of his hospitalization show, however, that he had been taking "large quantities of morphine, chloral and bromide for several weeks" before his first admission; that he was suicidally depressed, showing "retardation of speech and emotional lability" (p. 61). It is interesting to observe, in passing, that these symptoms of depression, so apparent to an observer, were ignored by Schreber, while his delusions were articulated and fully detailed. A man raised not to be a "crybaby" does not record his depression.

Freud began his account of Schreber's Memoir with a justification for analyzing from a written document: It was that paranoiacs "possess the peculiarity of betraying (in distorted form it is true) precisely those things that other neurotics keep hidden as a secret" (p. 9). This was an observation similar to the one he made about obsessional neurosis, calling it a dialect of hysteria that should be even more comprehensible to us because of its ideational content. Reviewing the Schreber case with hindsight suggests that the ideational content is so articulate and translatable partly because the affects of shame and guilt are only implied. In depression, as we shall see, they are not only directly expressed — these affects *are* the symptom. Colby's (1977) suggestion that the shame–humiliation hypothesis is preferable because it is more inclusive of the phenomena of paranoia than any other formulation seems amply justified from our review. My own formulation (1971) that it is bypassed shame which takes the form of guilty ideation in paranoia also includes bypassed shame and guilty ideation about homosexual longings but it does not insist that these are the exclusive content evoking shame and guilt.

PARANOIA IN WOMEN

Some years after his publication on the Schreber case, Freud (1915) encountered a case of paranoia in a woman which seemed on the surface to run counter to his hypothesis about the central role of homosexuality in the illness. On closer examination, however, it seemed to him that the homosexuality thesis was, after all, correct. A reading of this paper suggests, however, that Freud was involved in the very process that his own writings insisted should be avoided — seeing what his theory demanded should be there. The entire account is based on two visits, in the first of which the woman was accompanied by her lawyer and only in the second of which Freud saw her alone. It is amusing that the editors of the *Standard Edition* cite it as an example of the dangers of "basing a hasty opinion of a case on a superficial knowledge of the facts" (p. 262) — a defense of Freud that might well be interpreted as a "projection" of what was happening in this case account.

The young woman was brought to Freud by her lawyer, who suspected paranoia. "A young woman had asked him [the lawyer] to protect her from the molestations of a man who had drawn her into a love affair. She declared that this man had abused her confidence by getting unseen witnesses to photograph them while they were making love, and that by exhibiting these pictures it was now in his power to bring disgrace on her and force her to resign the post she occupied" (p. 263). In this account, contrary to expectation, the chief persecutor is not same-sex but an opposite-sex figure whom the patient loves or has loved: "There was no sign of the influence of a woman, no trace of a struggle against homosexual attachment" (p. 265). Freud is very articulate about his dilemma: He was faced with either giving up his theory about homosexuality in paranoia, or concluding that the woman was not paranoiac but had had "an actual experience which had been correctly interpreted" (p. 266). Still another possibility which he apparently did not contemplate was that the woman was paranoid but not so in defense of her homosexuality. In any case, he "saw another way out" (p. 266), which was to ask to see her again, alone, and obtain a fuller account of her actual experiences. The woman reluctantly agreed to a second visit, in the course of which additional details emerged that Freud found confirmatory of his thesis that she was paranoid because she was homosexual.

Freud already knew, from the patient's first visit, that she held a responsible post in a big business concern in which her lover was a fellow-employee. This man, "highly cultivated and attractive," had paid her attentions and "in turn she was drawn towards him. For external reasons, however, marriage was out of the question, but the man would not hear of giving up their relationship on that account. He had pleaded with her that it was senseless to sacrifice to social convention all that both longed for and had an indisputable right to enjoy, something that could enrich their life as nothing else could. As he had promised not to expose her to any risk, she had at last consented to visit him in his bachelor rooms" (p. 264). The additional material that Freud elicited on her second visit was as follows: The visit to her lover's rooms during which she heard the noise that made her suspicious of a camera-click, was actually the second rather than the first visit. The day after her first visit to his rooms he appeared in the office of her supervisor, an elderly lady with "white hair like my mother's," to discuss some business matter. "While they were talking in low voices the patient suddenly felt convinced that he was telling her about their adventure of the previous day — indeed that the two of them had been having a love affair, which had hitherto been overlooked. The white-haired, motherly old lady now knew everything, and her speech and conduct in the course of the day confirmed the patient's suspicion. At the first opportunity, she took her lover to task about his betrayal. He naturally protested vigorously against what he called a senseless accusation. For the time being, he succeeded in freeing her from her delusion, and she regained enough confidence in him to repay her visit to his rooms" (pp. 266–267). It was on this second visit that she heard the camera-click and later encountered the people she thought had been paid to photograph her for purposes of blackmail.

From the fact that the elderly woman supervisor was involved in the woman's dread of exposure, Freud deduces that "it was the strength of her mother-complex" that drove her to paranoia. "The *original* persecutor [Freud's italics] . . . is here again not a man but a woman . . . . Her love for her mother had become the spokesman of all those tendencies which, playing the part of a 'conscience,' seek to arrest a girl's first step along the new road to normal sexual satisfaction" (p. 267).

Once again, as in the case of Dora (Chapter 2), Freud's sympathies are clearly on the side of the woman's lover, whose letters to the patient made a "very favorable impression" (p. 265). That the risks of exposure were far greater to her than to her lover was not considered by Freud. It is still the case today, and it was surely much more the case in Freud's time, that the woman employee caught in a love-affair "at the office" is more heavily censured than the man, if only because men are in more powerful positions. Freud did not inquire into the "external reasons" that made marriage an impossibility, so we do not know what they were, but they appear to have rested on grounds that would protect him rather than her. Whatever they were, the emotional posture in which both parties were placed in the absence of marriage was one requiring perfect mutual trust. This is clearly harder to achieve for the person — the woman — who is risking greater reprisals. The humiliating idea that he might be seducing her was overcome by the time she first visited his rooms. What actually happened during their lovemaking to revive it we do not know, but it was revived the next day in the form of the "conviction" that he was betraying her to her supervisor. Freud's idea was that the patient's homosexual longings created her conviction. But it could just as well have been evoked by states of shame–humiliation which were bypassed during their lovemaking and then issued in a conviction of *his* guilt (cf. p. 126). Freud did, in fact, consider that the patient might have experienced a "lack of satisfaction" in her lovemaking and that this along with her "conscience" (p. 271) might have played a part in her subsequent rejection of the man.

In any case, the patient did not develop persecutory ideas specifically involving her woman supervisor, as Freud's theory requires. The main persecutor, against whom she sought legal help, was her male lover. Toward the end of his brief paper, Freud writes that the "patient protected herself against the *love of a man* by means of a paranoiac delusion" (p. 271) (my italics). He, however, seeks to rectify the implied contradiction to his homosexual thesis by supposing that the patient had made "an advance from a female to a male object" by means of the paranoid delusion. Such an advance is labeled "unusual" in paranoia and Freud then shifts the ground of his speculations to questions of "psychic inertia" (Jung's term) or "fixation" as hindering appropriate instinctual development which in this case would have resulted in a successful love affair with the man. But this was, of course, not the main issue, which was the question of the persecutor's gender.

As we shall see a little later on in this chapter, the evidence accumulated since Freud's time offers support for the thesis that the chief persecutor is of the same sex among male paranoid patients but not among females. Since the Schreber Memoir, another remarkable document, this one written by a woman paranoid schizophrenic, has also appeared (O'Brien, 1958). In this document, entitled *Operators and Things*, O'Brien details a six-month-long episode, largely self-cured, in which her persecutors were all male. Her case also involves feelings generated at the office where she worked. Each of her persecutors, who appeared one morning at the foot of her bed, has a name that implies his evil function. O'Brien, in fact, supplied a "glossary" of terms at the back of her book, which might easily be labeled a glossary of different forms of guilt, betrayal, treachery, character assassination, and the like. For example, a chief persecutor was named "hook-operator." His function was to plunge hooks into people's backs. O'Brien's account is reminiscent of Schreber's in its articulate formulation of the evils with which she was coping, and like Schreber's, her persecutors were powerful men, who were guilty of mistreating her.

In his 1922 paper on jealousy, paranoia, and homosexuality, Freud describes jealousy as "one of those affective states, like grief, that may be described as normal" (p. 223). Freud also distinguishes three layers or grades of jealousy: (1) *competitive* or normal, (2) *projected*, and (3) *delusional* jealousy. In what is really a kind of naive or common-sense psychology of the affects involved, he thinks of normal jealousy as a compound of grief at losing the loved object, of narcissistic wound, "in so far as this is distinguishable" from the pain of loss, of enmity against the successful rival and a "greater or lesser amount of self-criticism which tries to hold the subject's own ego accountable for his loss" (p. 223). Normal jealousy is experienced bisexually: the man will feel not only pain for the loss of the woman he loves but also grief at the loss of the man and hatred of the woman as his rival. One man, for example, "went through unendurable torments by consciously imagining himself in the position of the faithless woman. The sensation of helplessness which then came over him and the images he used to describe his condition — exposed to a vulture's beak like Prometheus or thrown into a nest of serpents — were referred by him to several homosexual acts of aggression to which he had been subjected as a boy" (pp. 223–224). Freud is referring without specifically naming it, to the experience of humiliated as well as helpless fury in his account of these "homosexual" aggressions. Jealousy, by implication, involves both humiliation and humiliated fury.

Projected jealousy "is derived in both men and women *from their own actual unfaithfulness in real life* or from impulses toward it which have succumbed to repression" (p. 224) (my italics). It is a means of obtaining "acquittal by his conscience — if he projects his impulses to faithlessness . . . . [he] can justify himself with the reflection that the other is probably not much better than himself." Clearly, projection is a mechanism that can and does occur in response to *conscious* as well as unconscious guilt. We shall return to this point shortly.

In Freud's view, it is only jealousy belonging to the third layer — delusional jealousy — that has its origin in unconscious homosexuality and "rightly takes its position among the classical forms of paranoia" (p. 225). Yet immediately upon making this apparently clear distinction Freud tells us that projected jealousy also has an "almost delusional character" (p. 225) and that "one cannot dispute with the content" of projected jealousy. It is thus apparent that from his descriptions of the affects involved there is no intrinsic reason why "projected" or "delusional" (paranoid) jealousy needs to be exclusively homosexual in its content.

Among the major areas of investigation that have followed Freud's writings on paranoia have been researches into the phenomena of projection itself, apart from paranoia. Freud's term "projection" has become a household word. The phenomena described by the term — "rational" ways of attributing one's guilt to others — have, of course, long been part of folk wisdom.

Investigations into the phenomena of projection and other "defenses" have been much aided by the work of Anna Freud (1946) and Madison (1961), who showed clearly that Freud's early concept of repression was an overall concept, covering a wide variety of defensive processes, and that many defenses are normal. A clear division has emerged, for example, between defenses of "vigilance" that can actually lower perceptual thresholds and defenses of "denial" that involve some kind of perceptual loss or at least a heightening of perceptual thresholds.

Much of the work on the phenomena of projection has been done by experimental psychologists. As might be expected, the cognitive processes in projection have been of particularly compelling interest, since projection involves articulated content rather than perceptual "blackout." During the thirties, for example, the Gestalt psychologist, Schulte (1938) (not a Gestalt *therapist* — these had not yet emerged — but a student of the Gestalt laws of perception), became interested in the reorganization of the perceptual field that can take place, making the self the center of attributions. In more recent years, "attribution theory" has become a flourishing field of research (e.g., Kelley, 1971, and others), following some of the ideas of Heider (1958), also in the Gestalt tradition.

In attribution theory, however, the ideas attributed to others are ideas one is *aware* of having. The experimental variation of conditions under which attribution of traits to others occurs has shown that emotional factors do play a large part. But these results are not represented as relevant to the Freudian theory of projection in which the ideas "attributed" are presumably unconscious. What is usually disregarded is the fact that projection, as Freud described it, was not *only about unconscious ideas, as we have just seen. Rather, projection involves both* heightened awareness of "sensitive" or guilty content *and* a process that somehow refers or attributes that material away from the self.

It is interesting to note further in this connection that Freud did not regard projection *only* as a defensive process, but also as a normal perceptual function. "Projection was not created for the purpose of defence; it also occurs where there is no conflict" (Freud, 1913a, p. 64). Freud had earlier written:

> We should feel tempted to regard this remarkable process [projection] as the most important element in paranoia and as being pathognomonic for it, if we were not opportunely reminded of two things. In the first place, projection does not play the same part in all forms of paranoia; and in the second place, it makes its appearance not only in paranoia but under other psychological conditions as well, and in fact it has a regular share assigned to it in our attitude towards the external world (Freud, 1911, p. 66).

Freud's promised work on projection may be a missing paper. As I have suggested (Lewis, 1958), in a review of the meanings of the term "self," localization of percepts as "out there" is a function of the self as an organization of stimuli, and can involve the "phantom limb," still experienced as a part of the self when the limb has been amputated. "Mislocalizations," in other words, are not exclusively the result of emotional conflict. The controversy between Freudian and more recent cognitive theorists may thus not be so sharp as is often supposed.

The controversy within experimental psychology has been over whether Freud's concept of projection can be put into experimentally verifiable terms, and if so, whether the experiments based on these formulations offer evidence for the existence of what has come to be termed "classical projection." One review of this experimental literature (Holmes, 1968) offers the conclusion that there is no experimental evidence whatever for classical projection. Both Kline (1971) and Fisher and Greenberg (1977), who do find some evidence for it, fail to cite Holmes.

In an approach once more to the problem, Halpern (1977) formulates "classical projection" as operating "when a threatening sexual or aggressive impulse is repressed and then attributed to a suitable other" (p. 537). Halpern arranged an ingenious experiment, using normal subjects, but dividing them according to "higher" and "lower" defensiveness on the Crowne–Marlowe (1964) Social Desirability Scale. He predicted that more defensive subjects who said they had no sexual dreams or fantasies would also respond to pornographic materials by subsequently rating photographs of faces they did not like as more "lustful" than less defensive subjects would. His predictions were confirmed; moreover, the effects obtained were significantly increased when the disliked other (in the photograph) was a male, and still further increased when women rated male targets. Halpern regards his findings as evidence confirming Freud's theory of projection. In addition, his findings speak against attribution theory, since his higher-defensive subjects were not *conscious* of the lust they attributed to others.

Halpern's experiment and conclusions are a sample of the lively research still growing out of Freud's formulations of projection. Most of the experimental work done in this area is with normal persons, and implicates such fundamental questions in normal personality as cognitive and other personality types. Volume 2 will therefore deal more fully with these issues.

We come back, now, to the question of the role of homosexuality in the genesis of paranoia.

EVIDENCE ON THE ROLE OF HOMOSEXUALITY IN PARANOIA

Fisher and Greenberg (1977), reviewing the experimental studies of homosexuality in paranoia, comment on the "valiant attempts to objectify and quantify an exceedingly complex variable" (p. 268). Experiments comparing paranoid and nonparanoid schizophrenics have made use of the tachistoscope, the stereoscope, measures of attention, Rorschach, and TAT's, and have been carefully controlled for such extraneous factors as age, chronicity, socioeconomic status, and the like. They write: "One cannot fail to be impressed with the convergence that has emerged from this diversity. In numerous ways it has been shown that paranoids and nonparanoids respond differently to stimuli with homosexual connotations" (p. 268).

Fisher and Greenberg are careful to point out that the experimental confirmation of a consistent connection between homosexuality and paranoia does not by itself confirm Freud's hypothesis about the etiology of paranoia. Homosexuality could still be a "minor etiological variable, with some other variable being of much greater importance" (p. 269). At the same time they emphasize that "there is no other theoretical model that would logically predict the existence of a difference in response to homosexual themes in paranoid as compared to nonparanoid schizophrenics" (p. 269). They do also remind us that the experimental work on homosexuality in paranoia has been done on men, and so cannot be generalized to women.

As an example of "one of the earliest and most successful experiments" (Fisher and Greenberg, 1977, p. 260) on the role of homosexuality in paranoia, let us look at the work of Zamansky (1958). Zamansky's experiment is also cited by Kline (1971) as offering powerful support for a connection between homosexuality and paranoia. Zamansky hypothesized that, if Freud is right, "men with paranoid delusions when compared to men without these delusions will manifest a greater attraction to males than to females" (p. 412). Further, he predicted that paranoid men would especially avoid homosexually threatening stimuli, and would defensively express a preference for women in a setting where it was obvious that their attitudes toward men and women lovers were being evaluated. The experimental arrangements involved measuring the time spent looking at pictures of men and women in various combinations; this assessment was successfully camouflaged as a task of defining which picture had the greater surface area. As predicted, the paranoid schizophrenics looked at pictures of males longer than at pictures of females, while the nonparanoics looked at the females longer. When asked to indicate which sex they preferred, the two groups did not differ. Zamansky, while concluding that his findings offer support for Freud's hypothesis, also cautions that homosexuality may not be the main etiological factor in paranoia, but only a manifest of some other more central factor. As I have suggested, this more central factor may turn out to be the affective states of shame and guilt, to which homosexuality would be expected to contribute, moreover, in different ways for the two sexes.

As for Freud's hypothesis that the persecutor in paranoia is of the same sex as the patient, the evidence is inconsistent, but stronger for men than for women. For example, Klein and Horwitz (1949) found that *both* male and female patients had male persecutors; Klaf and Davis (1960) similarly found 85% of their male paranoids with a male persecutor and 61% of their females also with a male persecutor. As we saw earlier, in Freud's brief case account (1915) of a woman paranoid patient, a man was the "blackmailer." That the persecutor for both sexes tends to be male suggests that homosexuality may have a different affective meaning for the two sexes, as well as a different origin in the way gender identity is assumed. We shall return to this question shortly.

The Origins of Homosexuality

As we saw earlier, Freud's description of the genesis of homosexuality was that it is a product of exaggerated affects developed in response to the Oedipal triangle. The forbidden affects of hatred of the opposite sex parent are managed by an "identification" with the loved–hated parent and an adoption of the opposite-sex gender. Freud's theory also assumed that bisexual attraction was a normal part of psychosexual development, so that the opposite-sex identification and congruent same-sex choice of lover were within easy reach as solutions of the love–hate conflict.

One consequence of this view of homosexuality was that it contributed strongly to the general sexual enlightenment that accompanied the dissemination of Freud's writings. Since the choice of a lover's gender is nearly as complicated and difficult a process in the heterosexual outcome as it is in the homosexual, there is nothing necessarily neurotic in homosexuality. Freud was also remarkably clear about the lack of intrinsic correspondence between the assumption of gender identity and the choice of lover's gender. Thus he writes that:

> A man with predominantly male characteristics and also masculine in his erotic life may still be inverted in respect to his object, loving only men instead of women. A man in whose character feminine attributes obviously predominate, who may, indeed, behave in love like a woman, might be expected to choose a man for his love-object; but he may nevertheless be heterosexual, and show no more inversion in respect to his object than an average normal man. The same is true of women (Freud, 1922, p. 170).

In this passage Freud is clearly anticipating the modern work of Money and Ehrhardt (1972), Green (1973), and their associates.

Freud's clinical writings on homosexuality are very sparse; there is only one case account of his brief treatment of an eighteen-year-old girl (Freud, 1920b). This was a case, moreover, in which he deemed it necessary to transfer the patient to a same-sex therapist, since he thought the girl's transference to himself would be too hostile for any progress to be made. The young woman was brought by her father, having evoked his fury by her "devoted adoration" of a certain "society lady" about ten years older than herself. (This woman was, in the father's opinion, nothing but a *cocotte*, who had promiscuous affairs with persons of both sexes who would pay her.) The girl's parents were both concerned that she paid no attention whatever to her own reputation, openly courting and pursuing her beloved; at the same time she had no scruples whatever about deceiving her parents. One day, by something close to design on her part (as it later became clear), the father met his daughter in the company of the notorious lady, and gave her "an angry glance," at which point she abruptly flung herself over a wall, narrowly escaping serious injury. After her recovery, the parents were less angry than frightened; her "lady," instead of treating her with indifference, took her more seriously, but strongly advised her to give up her passion. Even this persuasion did not work, and the father, in desperation, brought her to Freud.

Freud, as indicated earlier, by no means acceded to the parents' wish that their daughter be "cured." It is "not a matter of indifference whether someone comes to analysis of his own accord or because he is brought to it — whether it is he himself who desires the change, or only his relatives, who love him (or might be expected to love him)" (p. 150). Freud clearly was of the opinion that it is up to the person to "choose whether he wished to abandon the path that is banned by society . . . . One must remember that normal sexuality too depends upon a restriction in the choice of object. In general, to undertake to convert a fully developed homosexual into a heterosexual does not offer much more prospect of success than the reverse, except that for good practical reasons the latter is never attempted" (p. 121).

Freud's interpretation of her falling in love with an older, sexually experienced woman (not for the first time) was that the older woman represented her mother. The mother had always treated her only daughter with great harshness, favoring her other children who were sons. Furthermore, a new baby son was born only two years before the open homosexual episode, when the "patient" was sixteen years old. In this combination of circumstances — an unloving mother and a father who betrayed her by fathering a child with the mother — the young woman turned her back upon men; moreover, she "changed into a man and took her mother in place of her father as a love-object" (p. 158). Moreover, in doing so, she retired from competition with the mother, and at the same time obtained revenge upon her father who was clearly devastated by her homosexuality. This analysis also fit the rather different attitudes of the two parents toward their daughter's homosexuality; the mother was tolerant, as if glad she no longer had a rival; the father was furious as "though he realized the deliberate revenge being directed upon himself" (p. 160).

The young woman participated in the analysis without any attempt to deceive Freud into thinking that she was there because she was dissatisfied with her sexual preference. She told him that she would marry, in order to be free of her parents' control and to pursue her own aims. Her attitude toward the analyst was apparently reminiscent to Freud of the Wolf-Man's: "She participated actively with her intellect, although absolutely tranquil emotionally. Once when I expounded to her a specially important part of the theory, one touching her nearly, she replied in an inimitable tone, 'How very interesting,' as though she were a *grande dame* being taken over a museum and glancing through her lorgnon at objects to which she was completely indifferent" (p. 163). Freud calls these "Russian tactics."

The transference and counter-transference complexities Freud faced are glimpsed in his account of what he called her "hypocritical dreams." At the same time that she was telling him she had no intention of changing, she produced dreams that were unmistakably heterosexual, and also expressed her joy at the prospect of a new life with her own children. Freud interpreted these dreams only as having the intention to deceive him — but he also speaks of her desire to please him (and her father). Freud seems to have been struck only by the hostile transference implied by hypocritical dreams. That she might have sensed how pleased he would be if she did change her sexual preference (even though his professional attitude was correctly neutral) is likely. It is also likely that, since she was consciously proud of her choice, there would be humiliation for her in what might be experienced as his triumph in her "accommodation," even if the accommodation was in accord with her wishes. The affects of pride and shame remain unspoken in this situation, but are nevertheless quite potent.

Freud's description of his young patient's personality is quite consonant with affects of pride (and shame). There is, for example, his account of her *"grande dame"* treatment of him which clearly nettled him. She is described by him not only as "beautiful and clever" but "spirited; not at all prepared to be a 'second to her slightly older brother' . . . she was in fact a feminist; she felt it to be unjust that girls should not enjoy the same freedom as boys and rebelled against the lot of women in general" (p. 169). In such a politicized context, her heterosexual feelings would necessarily have a hard time making themselves heard, and it is likely that they were actually more important in her "hypocritical" dreams than Freud allowed.

In any case, it is after he describes his reaction to these dreams that he digresses to remark on how astonishing it is that "human beings can go through such great and important moments of their erotic life without noticing them much, sometimes without having the faintest suspicion of their existence . . . . It must be admitted that poets are right in liking to portray people who are in love without knowing it, or uncertain whether they do love, or who think that they hate when in reality they love. It would seem that the information received by our consciousness about our erotic life is especially liable to be incomplete, full of gaps, or falsified" (pp. 166–167). One can speculate that it is particularly the affects of shame at the threat of unrequited love that are warded off by such blindness. Freud seems to have been somehow sensing as he wrote this passage, that both he and the young woman were afflicted with blindness to their own affects. It is worth noting that the kind of case Freud was describing is a most familiar phenomenon in clinical practice today. But with the development of political movements in support of a lesbian choice — these movements themselves a product of Freudian enlightenment — fewer of these cases eventuate in "forced" psychiatric treatment.

In summary, Freud's observations about the role of homosexuality in paranoia brought him into difficult problems of explaining the "choice" of paranoia, depression, or homosexuality as the outcome of affective struggles in the Oedipal situation. Information accumulated since his time suggests that sex differences in both species-reproductive behavior and social role are important variables in these problems. Freud's model of paranoia was derived from his study of men and applied less successfully to women. Accumulated evidence about paranoia among men supports Freud's observation without necessarily supporting his concept of etiology. Accumulated evidence also strongly supports Freud's description of the defense of "projection." It seems likely that a model of paranoid processes that focuses more directly on the affects involved may be more useful in explaining "choice" of paranoia than was Freud's hypothesis of a structural regression. Differences between the sexes in characteristic affective conflicts would also help to explain the "choice" of paranoia versus depression.

CHAPTER 6

Depression
The Problem of Grief and Mourning

Depression is the term both for a normal mood, universally experienced in relation to loss, and for a pathological state in which no appropriate stimulus for such distress is apparent. In this respect of spanning normalcy and pathology, depression is similar to anxiety; the two states are, moreover, often concomitant. Both states are, above all else, affective states, unlike paranoia, obsessional neurosis, and hysteria in which the affects can play hide-and-seek and "strange" symptoms can prevail. A depressed or anxious person may not be able to account for his or her affective state, but the experience is eminently understandable to everyone since everyone has "been there."

Freud's (1917) contribution to the understanding of depression consists of a relatively brief fifteen-page paper which focuses on the difference between normal mourning, as in bereavement, and melancholia.[1] In that paper there is no case material in which we might follow the course of emotional events in depression. Depression was mentioned as an additional feature in the cases of Lucy R. and Dora, and in connection with the Rat-Man's confession of his obsessional ideas. But there exists no clinical case account devoted specifically to a depressed patient in Freud's voluminous writings.

This fact reflects the contrast between Freud's discovery of the affects as the source of mental illness and his relative neglect of them in his formal

[1]Melancholia and pathological depression have since become interchangeable terms.

presentations. The affect of depression, in particular, is so universal and so relatively wordless (or, at best, so monotonously banal both to the sufferer and to an observer) that it does not readily invite "scientific" consideration in its own right.

The reason for this neglect is also historical (Bowlby, 1973). Freud first discovered the importance of repression, that is, of the defenses against affects. Although he was aware very early — as evidenced by a note to Fliess in 1897 (Freud, 1917) — of the role of grief and mourning in hysteria, obsessional neurosis, melancholia, and paranoia, Freud did not give grief and mourning his systematic attention until nearly two decades later. It is interesting to note, in passing, that in this very early note to Fliess, Freud spoke of "identification" with the mourned parent's illness as a phenomenon in hysterical illness. By the time Freud had turned his attention to the problem of grief, moreover, his theoretical views had been set in the mold of a "secondary drive" theory of human attachment, that is, a theory in which the only primary needs are the physiological needs of the body. Attachment is derived only secondarily from the fulfillment of these needs. In such a system the foundations of human attachment are inevitably "narcissistic."

Freud's views on mental illness as a regression to childhood experience were solidified by the time he wrote *Mourning and Melancholia*. In the symptoms of depression he saw evidence of a regression to the oral or narcissistic stage of development, that is, to an even earlier stage than the anal-sadism central to obsessional neurosis. This view perpetuates, by implication, a denigration of the affects. The quintessentially affective state, depression, reflects an even graver developmental deficiency than the "crazy ideas" of the obsessional neurosis or paranoia.

Controversy over how to conceptualize the depression that accompanies loss of loved persons rests, in part, on the controversy over a "narcissistic" or a "social" conception of the infant self. On this question, psychoanalysis itself is deeply divided. For example, Bowlby's views (1969) of the mother–infant "attachment" as a biologically given system, necessary for species survival, are closer to a social than to a narcissistic concept of infant behavior. Bowlby's views are of particular importance since they are based on observations about the mother–infant interaction in human beings as well as in other mammalian species. The Harlows' work (Harlow and Mears, 1979) on the "affectional systems" developed by monkeys likewise grew out of attempts to test Freudian hypotheses about the role of sex and love in psychological development. Psychoanalysts have also contributed to this line of animal research started by the Harlows. Kaufman (1973) and Rosenblum (1971), for example, traced a difference in the extent of monkey infants' depressive reactions to separation to species differences in sociability and in the quality of mothering. Other studies of monkeys have discovered the analog of Bowlby's "protest" and "despair" on separation (McKinney, Suomi, and Harlow, 1973). These animal studies are essentially about the nature of social behavior as well as the nature of depression and they will be discussed more fully in Volume 2.

At this point it will be useful to sketch a very brief overview of the implications of radically differing theoretical formulations about infancy for conceptualizing depression. In the Freudian view of the earliest self as narcissistic, the pain of loss of separation is attributable to the absence of the mother as the source of "narcissistic supply" and if physical deprivations occur too often, the "transformation from a greedy stomach-love to a truly constant love-attachment is slow to come" (A. Freud, 1953, p. 17). The Harlows' work and the work of Bowlby cast doubt on the notion of a "greedy stomach-love." Monkey infants reared with a mother-surrogate supplying major physiological needs were still damaged in their social behavior.

The development of "object-love," moreover, is no proof against depression as a reaction to loss. In the Freudian view, persons who in later life react with depression to loss of loved persons must, by implication, be suffering from a narcissistic regression in which the capacity for object-love must be (if only temporarily) deficient. In this view depression is inherently a pathological process, or at the very least the sign of one. Bowlby (1963) and Jacobson (1971) have also pointed to this difficulty inherent in Freud's views.

In Bowlby's view, depression on loss of attachment-figures is inevitable in adulthood as in infancy, since attachment is a biologically given system which includes depression on loss. As Bowlby (1973) points out, failure to conceptualize grief as a given of the attachment system has made it seem "childish, even babyish to yearn for the presence of a loved figure or to be distressed during her (or his) absence" (p. 80). Bowlby's framework for depression thus decreases the burden of pathology even in depressions already acknowledged as pathological.

But pathological depression, in Bowlby's system, rests on *actual* bereavement in childhood. While Bowlby does leave room in his clinical descriptions for the importance of noxious affective interactions, his theory explicitly requires that pathological depression be the outcome of actual childhood bereavement. On the other hand, the traditional secondary drive theory of infants' attachments to their mothers does not necessarily preclude an emphasis on the *feeling-states* induced in the infant by the mother's presence or absence. Even so radical a view as Melanie Klein's — namely, that the death instinct as expressed by destructive rageful feelings is each infant's primary endowment — insists that the development of affective states is an interaction between these aggressive affects and the mother's loving or aggressive feelings (Klein, 1957). So, Sandler and Joffe (1965), from an orthodox standpoint, describe the mother as a "vehicle" for the attainment of an "ideal state" of well-being: The loss of the mother signifies the loss of an aspect of the *self*. Object-loss may thus bring about acute mental pain through creating a wound in the self. In this formulation, the (narcissistic) self becomes a social product in an interaction between its feeling-states and the feeling-states of its mother (or caretaker). Since it is an interaction of *feeling-states* that is significant rather than the mother's actual presence or absence, there is a considerable increase in the variety of interaction patterns that can create depression, even in the actual presence of the mother. Depressions in adulthood may thus be linked not only to actual parent losses, as Bowlby's hypothesis and as empirical studies tend to confirm (see Beck, 1967; Heinecke, 1973; Lewis, 1976 for reviews on this point), but to "narcissistic" injuries incurred in an interaction between the child's feelings and its caretaker's. These are more subtle phenomena which so far have been only studied clinically (for example, Cohen et al., 1954; Jacobson, 1971).

Thus, Bowlby's theoretical system encounters difficulties which it solves by assuming that pathological depression in adulthood rests on a biological flaw in human equipment to deal with bereavement. Freud's theory bases pathological depression on a narcissistic regression to pre-oral identifications. As we shall see, the difficulties in both systems may be reduced, however, if the affects involved in depression are more accurately specified.

Mourning and Melancholia

Let us turn now to an examination of the central ideas in Freud's seminal paper. A word should be said, first of all, about the translation of the German word, *"Trauer"* as "mourning." Another meaning is equally appropriate to *"Trauer"* — namely, "grief." The editors of the *Standard Edition* call this fact to our attention. They tell us also that they chose "mourning" which is the "outward manifestation of grief" (Vol. XIV, p. 243, footnote 1). Whether this was with Freud's consent or not they do not say; the question is hardly material. What is important is that, once again, although in a small detail, we see an emphasis away from the affects.

As usual, Freud opens his paper with a modest disclaimer. In this instance it is a reminder that his observations apply only to those cases in which the psychogenesis of the illness is certain, as contrasted with cases which may be somatic in origin. It is worth noting that this distinction between somatic and psychological factors in depression is still very much in use. It forms part of standard measuring instruments for depression such as Beck's (1967). The concept of a somatic base for depression, including the possibility of some genetic predisposing factors, is also very much alive as a research question (e.g., Winokur, 1973), as is the search for biochemical agents in both the illness and the depressed mood (e.g., Schildkraut, 1965).

In his first observations about mourning or grief at loss Freud (1917) clearly regards the state as normal. "We rely on its being overcome after a certain lapse of time, and we look upon any interference with it as useless or even harmful" (p. 244). The work of mourning consists in withdrawing attachment or "cathexis" from the lost person. "Each single one of the memories and expectations in which the libido is bound to the object is brought up and hypercathected and detachment of the libido is accomplished in respect of it" (p. 245). The question that puzzles Freud is why this process should be so "extraordinarily painful," and specifically how to explain its painfulness in terms of "economics." It is also remarkable, he thinks, that "this painful unpleasure is taken as a matter of course by us" (p. 245). The problem to which Freud refers is, of course, contained in the controversy over the nature of the child's tie to its mother that we have just briefly sketched. In Freud's theoretical structure, moreover, "economics" are based on the tendency of the nervous system to get rid of stimulation as quickly as possible. Overstimulation is the greatest threat to the organism. Why, then, decathecting should be so painful when energy is being reduced is puzzling; in addition, it is puzzling why the organism undertakes decathecting by first hypercathecting its lost "object." Once again it is clear that Freud's metapsychology brought him into difficulties that a simpler description of the power of affects might have avoided.

On the other hand, Freud's observation that we take grief or mourning as a matter of course raised the fundamental question of whether or not these affects are universal, as folk wisdom seems to suggest. This is a reminder, once again, that Freud was writing at a time when the science of anthropology was first beginning. The cross-cultural studies which have undertaken to answer this question systematically have only recently been performed by anthropologists (e.g., Rosenblatt, Walsh, and Jackson, 1976), with an essentially positive answer.

The principal feature distinguishing mourning from melancholia is the "disturbance of self-regard" which is exaggeratedly present in melancholia. It is important to note that Freud does not speak of guilt as the affect present in melancholia, but very carefully, of a disturbance in "self-regard." This distinction is important because guilt is often a basis for loss of self-regard, but by no means the only stimulus. At the time *Mourning and Melancholia* was written the superego concept had not yet been formulated. Freud was speaking, more descriptively, of a "critical agency" which could criticize either the *self* or its more "objective" actions. In subsequent years, the superego became a virtual synonym for conscience or guilt, thus blurring the many ways in which self-regard may fall.

As Freud made clear, his student Abraham had been the first to suggest that a comparison between mourning and melancholia would be fruitful. Abraham (1911) had actually undertaken a study of the processes leading to depression and his paper includes a case account. In Abraham's formulation, a person falls into depression when "he feels himself unloved and incapable of loving" (p. 138). Abraham's patient fell ill with depression for the first time at puberty in apparent response to a teacher's "brutality [in calling] him a physical and mental cripple in front of the whole class" (p. 140). This humiliation struck the patient "like a blow" (p. 143). A loss of self-regard which follows upon "loss of love" is thus fundamental in Abraham's formulation which Freud was following. The distinction between guilt and "self-regard" has since been reestablished by Bibring (1953) and others including myself (Lewis, 1971), and as we shall see later on in this chapter, has formed the basis for hypothesizing different kinds of depression, for example, anaclitic as contrasted with introjective depression (Blatt, 1974), or shame versus guilt depressions (Gibson, 1967).

Continuing his account of the fall in self-regard as the distinguishing phenomenon in melancholia, Freud tells us that "in mourning it is the world which has become poor and empty; in melancholia it is the ego itself. The patient represents his ego to us as worthless, incapable of any achievement and morally despicable; he reproaches himself, vilifies himself and expects to be cast out and punished. He abases himself before everyone and commiserates with his own relatives for being connected to anyone so unworthy. He is not of the opinion that a change has taken place in him, but extends his self-criticism back over the past; he declares that he never was any better" (p. 246). Once again, as in the case of obsessional neurosis, Freud insists that it would be "fruitless from a scientific and therapeutic point of view to contradict" the patient, since the patient "must surely be right in some way" (p. 246).

It is fascinating to follow Freud's views of the "reality" behind the patient's self-abased view of himself. On the one hand, the patient's estimation of himself is only keener than other people's and by implication more accurate. On the other hand, Freud "wonders why a man has to be ill before he can be accessible to a truth of this kind [namely, that he is] . . . petty, egoistic, dishonest, lacking in independence, one whose sole aim has been to hide the weakness of his own nature" (p. 246). The "truth" to which Freud is referring here seems to be the priority of hate in human nature, or as he would still later put it, the death instinct as represented by anal-sadism.

One can understand these views partly as a reflection of problems arising from the secularization of guilt. On the one hand, excessive guilt is an illness; on the other it might just be an appropriate description of what was formerly regarded as the sinfulness of mankind in relation to God. It was Fromm (1951) who was particularly active in articulating sharp differences with Freud on this issue of human nature, as we shall see in Chapter 7, and again in Volume 2. Fromm's work along these lines was also influential in the development of "interpersonal" as contrasted to "classical" psychoanalysis.

On the very next page of *Mourning and Melancholia*, Freud resumes the secular view that there is "no correspondence, so far as we can judge, between the degree of self-abasement and its real justification. A good, capable, conscientious woman will speak no better of herself after she develops melancholia than one who is in fact worthless; indeed, the former is perhaps more likely to fall ill of the disease than the latter, of whom we too should have nothing good to say" (p. 247).

Freud notes, also, that the normal affective attitude of a person "crushed" by remorse and self-reproach is not apparent in melancholia. "Feelings of shame in front of other people, which would more than anything characterize this latter condition, are lacking in the melancholic, or at least they are not prominent in him. One might emphasize the presence in him of an opposite trait of *insistent communicativeness* which finds *satisfaction in self-exposure*" (p. 247) (my italics).

This passage has often been quoted to show that Freud observed an absence of shame in melancholia (depression), and this interpretation is readily understandable since it is literally what he said in the first sentence quoted. Yet the next sentence catches something of the paradoxical quality of the shame experience — that it can express itself as "satisfaction in self-exposure." The "insistent communicativeness" of what would ordinarily be too shameful to expose implies that it *is* shameful as well as guilty content that the melancholic is experiencing.

It is when Freud comes to the problem of explaining the abased self-regard of the melancholic that he first makes a clinical observation of which he is very sure, and which has since been confirmed in everyday practice. He then attempts to reconstruct the process behind the clinical observation. The observation is this: The self-reproaches are unconsciously meant for "someone whom the patient loves or has loved or should love. Every time one examines the facts this conjecture is confirmed" (p. 248).

Freud's reconstruction of the process by which the reproaches meant for the loved person are transferred onto the self is also introduced confidently, but is much less convincing than its terse wording might suggest. It is worth quoting in full, so that one can see how often it begs the question.

> An object-choice, an attachment of the libido to a particular person, had at one time existed; then, owing to a real slight or disappointment coming from this loved person, the object-relationship was shattered. The result was not a normal one of a withdrawal of the libido from this object and a displacement of it on to a new one, but something different, for whose coming about various conditions seem to be necessary. The object-cathexis proved to have little power of resistance

and was brought to an end. But the free libido was not displaced onto another object; it was withdrawn into the ego. There, however, it was not employed in any unspecified way, but served to establish an *identification* of the ego with the abandoned object. Thus the shadow of the object fell upon the ego, and the latter could henceforth be judged by a special agency, as though it were an object, the forsaken object. In this way an object-loss was transformed into an ego-loss and the conflict between the ego and the loved person into a cleavage between the critical activity and the ego as altered by identification.

One or two things may be directly inferred with regard to the preconditions and effects of a process such as this. On the one hand, a strong fixation to the loved object must be present; on the other hand, in contradiction to this, the object-cathexes must have had little power of resistance. As Otto Rank aptly remarks, this contradiction seems to imply that the object-choice had been effected on a narcissistic basis, so that the object-cathexis, when obstacles came in its way can regress to narcissism. The narcissistic identification with the object then becomes a substitute for the erotic cathexism, the result of which is that in spite of the conflict with the loved person the love-relation need not be given up (p. 249).

The first difficulty in this much-quoted passage is picked up by Freud himself. It is the contradiction between a strong object-cathexis and a weak one hypothesized simultaneously. The solution, offered by Rank and accepted by Freud, that a simultaneously strong and weak object-cathexis is "narcissistic" begs the question. It is circular reasoning to say that a (strong) object-choice that was effected on a narcissistic basis becomes weak because it was effected on a narcissistic basis. Labeling the object-choice as narcissistic cannot solve the contradiction since by definition narcissistic cathexes are not object-cathexes at all.

What Freud is really describing is the phenomenon that when one loves someone, "real slights and disappointments coming from this loved person" (p. 249) are very powerful sources of humiliated fury — the shame of unrequited love. That rejected love can turn into hate is a commonplace observation. This affective sequence is as much taken for granted as the phenomenon of bereavement. Freud does, in fact, accept it as descriptively accurate that melancholia is instituted by "all those situations of being slighted, neglected or disappointed which can import opposed feelings of love and hate into the relationship or reinforce an already existing ambivalence" (p. 251). Invoking a regression to narcissistic — that is, essentially nonexistent — object-choice does not solve the problem of why rejected love turns into hate. If anything, it creates a pejorative atmosphere around such affective sequences so that the process underlying them is harder to discern.

There is a second difficulty in Freud's reconstruction of the process by which reproaches meant for the loved person are unconsciously transferred to the self; it comes from Freud's notion that the withdrawn libido establishes an identification with the person. This makes it sound as if identification is established only under conditions of disrupted object-relations. In fact, it is likely that identification plays a part in any love relationship. Fantasizing what the loved person is doing or thinking, including vicarious participation in his or her experience, involves imagery of what the loved person is feeling about the self; this is not ipso facto an indication of "narcissism." On the contrary, it is the profoundly social nature of the self that determines — in fact, guarantees — its frequent peregrinations into the position of the "other." There it can also vicariously experience the other's hatred or scorn of the self in the form of shame. Once again, underlying assumptions about human nature are clearly at issue.

This criticism, of course, is possible only with hindsight. Freud's concept that an identification with parental figures takes place in earliest infancy, however it comes about, was one of his most significant ideas. Talcott Parsons (1958), for example, has traced the influence of this idea on the development of an integration between psychology and sociology. In *Mourning and Melancholia*, Freud regarded identification as taking place even earlier than "object-choice," but after the analogy of the first "oral or cannibalistic phase" (p. 249), the ego identifies with the object by "devouring" it. In his later writings Freud (1921, 1923) reiterated that identification occurs prior to object-cathexis: "It is a direct and immediate identification and takes place earlier than any object-cathexis" (1923a, p. 31). One can interpret this later emphasis on the primal nature of identification (together with the absence of cannibalistic imagery), as an implicit statement of the social nature of the human beast. In any case, the evidence accumulated since Freud's time suggests that this is a viable hypothesis.

The idea that depression is the experience of self-directed hostility without necessarily implying that it is turned around from a loved person onto the self, has been enormously influential in psychiatry. As we shall see later on in this chapter, it is an idea that is common to widely disparate views: psychoanalysis, behavior modification, assertiveness training, Gestalt therapy, and primal scream therapy; it is probably safe to say that it is one concept on which all therapies are likely to agree. In *Mourning and Melancholia*, Freud has expanded this concept of aggression turned inward to include obsessional neurosis and hysteria as well. It is worth noting just how he puts it in *Mourning and Melancholia*, especially since the concept is often simplified and distorted, particularly in "expressive" therapies, to mean that it is hostility *in general* rather than hostility resulting from the threat of "loss of love" which must be uncovered and expressed.

> If the love for the object — a love which cannot be given up though the object itself is given up[2] — takes refuge in narcissistic identification, then the hate comes

[2]The distinction between a "love which cannot be given up" and an "object itself [which is] given up" seems a particularly slippery one.

into operation on this substitute object, abusing it, debasing it, making it suffer and deriving sadistic satisfaction from its suffering. The self-tormenting in melancholia, which is without doubt enjoyable, signifies, just like the corresponding phenomenon in obsessional neurosis, a satisfaction of trends of sadism and hate which relate to an object, and which have been turned round upon the subject's self in ways in which we have been discussing. In both disorders the patients usually succeed, by the circuitous path of self-punishment, in taking revenge upon their loved one through their illness, *having resorted to it in order to avoid the need to express their hostility to him openly* [my italics]. After all, the person who has occasioned the patient's emotional disorder, and on whom his illness is centered, is usually to be found in his immediate environment (p. 251).

This phenomenon of aggression turned back from a loved person onto the self is also Freud's formulation of the dynamics of suicide, and here again his concept has been the stimulus for a wealth of research. Freud was enormously puzzled about how to "conceive that the ego can consent to its own destruction" (p. 252). The source of his puzzlement is really the same as in his quandary over why the work of grief and mourning should be so painful; how does a "narcissistic" ego come to care so much about what does not directly threaten its own *physical* existence that it will kill itself?

The analysis of melancholia now shows that the ego can kill itself only if, owing to the return of the object-cathexis, *it can treat itself as an object* — if it is able to direct against itself the hostility which relates to an object *and which represents the ego's original relation to objects in the external world* [my italics]. Thus in regression from narcissistic object-choice the object has, it is true, been got rid of, but it has nevertheless proved more powerful than the ego itself. In the two opposed situations of being most intensely in love and of suicide the ego is overwhelmed by the object, though in totally different ways (p. 252).

In this passage we see, again, that the "original relation" between ego and the object is narcissistic. But we see also that Freud has failed to distinguish between a concept of the ego and a concept of the self. The awkwardness of a formulation that speaks of the ego treating itself as an object reflects this deficiency. It is the *self* and the "other" that have been fused or confused in melancholia and suicide. As I have pointed out elsewhere (Lewis, 1958, 1978) this failure to conceptualize the self as distinct from the ego was a grievous error. It led Freud to the position he took in *Beyond the Pleasure Principle* (1920a) in which he postulated a death instinct. Freud failed to see that it is the *self* that is the target of hostility in masochism, not the ego. Even in suicide, which culminates in the ego's total destruction, the main target is the *self* (as, for example, in Binswanger's case of Ellen West, 1958). This distinction does not carry us too much further into an explanation of the *dynamics* of suicide, but at least it does not require the postulation of a death instinct to "explain" *why* people kill themselves.

The last part of *Mourning and Melancholia* is devoted to a discussion of the mysterious occasions when melancholia turns around into mania. Such cases, he says, cannot be regarded only as somatic or nonpsychogenic, although it is tempting to do so, because, for one thing, some good therapeutic results with psychoanalysis have been reported. (Freud does not cite specifics, but he is here undoubtedly referring to Abraham's account (1911) of his success with a cyclothymic patient.) The explanation Freud tentatively offers for the turnaround in affective state is that "the ego had got over the loss of the object (or its mourning over the loss, or perhaps the object itself) and thereupon the whole quota of anticathexis which the painful suffering of melancholia has drawn to itself from the ego and 'bound' will have become available" (p. 255). But, says Freud, while this explanation sounds plausible, it entails difficulties, mainly in the economics of the change. Freud nevertheless returns to this explanation, adding that melancholia is like an "open wound," calling for a particularly high anticathexis to combat it, and so permitting a "triumphant" release when the ego has got over its loss. In this explanation of mania Freud is adumbrating the sequence from humiliation to triumph which he often described elsewhere. Once again, the formulation of events in terms of economics and energetics tends to obscure the affective states that are at play.

In distinguishing between obsessional neurosis and melancholia, Freud, as we saw in Chapter 4, suggested that the "object" has not been given up in obsessional neurosis, while in melancholia it has. It was on this basis that he explained an observed difference between the two illnesses in the frequency of suicide. Obsessional neurotics commit suicide less often than melancholics because the boundaries between the self and the "other" are still clear. This distinction has also been the source for predictions that obsessional neurotics and depressives should differ from each other in cognitive style. As we shall see, this suggestion has received some confirming evidence (Witkin, 1965; Lewis, 1978).

At least five problems in the psychology of depression thus emerge from a reading of *Mourning and Melancholia:* (1) the somatic basis of depression; (2) the role of guilt and shame in depression; (3) turning of reproaches meant for the loved person back upon the self via (4) the process of identification; and (5) differences in self-boundaries between the depressive and the obsessional neurotic, including the question of suicide prediction. This last theme is really the question of cognitive style in more modern terminology.

Let us consider the developments since Freud's time under each heading.

(1) The Somatic Basis of Depression

There is a consensus among many viewpoints, including the psychoanalytic, that at least some cases of depression are of somatic origin, although no organic basis is apparent. Freud's views in this regard were consonant with general psychiatric opinion, as is psychoanalytic thinking today. Jacobson (1971), for example, distinguishes between endogenous and reactive depression, the former being without apparent psychological causation, and therefore presumed to be somatic in origin. Bipolar depression, that is, cases which involve mania, are also considered to be of somatic origin. Similarly, psychotic depressions have been distinguished from neurotic depressions, with the hypothesis that the former are organically based.

It is interesting to observe that the question of whether it is legitimate to distinguish between endogenous and reactive depression has been the subject of considerable debate, in which psychoanalysts are not in their familiar position on the side of the psychological factors. It is nonanalytic psychiatrists who have objected to the distinction between "internal" and "external" causes, the latter being equated with the psychological side of life. Beck (1967) has summarized the debate which, as he remarks, has served to refine the concept of depression. For example, Beck quotes Mapother as refusing to acknowledge the distinction between purely psychogenic and purely structural causes of depression. Mapother's description of the phenomenon of depression is worth quoting: "The essence of the attack is the clinical fact that the emotions for the time being have lost enduring relation to current experience and whatever their origin and intensity they have achieved a sort of autonomy" (quoted in Beck, 1967, p. 66). This conception of depression has surely been influenced by Freud's notions of a displaced or perseverating mourning.

When we examine the specifics of depressive symptoms it is apparent that some of them have a distinctly physiological aspect, a phenomenological characteristic that suggests the operation of somatic factors. Beck's widely used scale for measuring depression makes use of these somatic or vegetative signs: insomnia, fatigability, loss of appetite, weight loss, body worries, and loss of libido (sex interest). Each of these vegetative signs can, of course, equally well be the physiological result as well as the cause of depression.

In any case, if a somatic factor is involved, it might be expected that somatic symptoms should be more prominent in more severely depressed patients than in less depressed and nondepressed patients. Contrary to expectation, however, Beck reports not only that the inter-correlation of physical and vegetative symptoms with each other is low, but that these symptoms have only a slight relation to depth of depression. The somatic signs of depression thus remain descriptive only. They allow us still to maintain Freud's circumspect handling of the problem of organic origin: there are *some* cases which may be of this kind.

(2) The Role of Shame and Guilt in Depression

In a fascinating historical review, Murphy (1978) points out the neglected fact that the advent of guilt feelings in textbook descriptions of depression occurred in Europe only after the sixteenth century. In Asia and Africa today, moreover, guilt feelings as symptoms in depression are rare, except among the Westernized part of the population. In contrast to findings from the United States that exaggerated guilt feelings are associated with greater severity of illness and poorer prognosis in depression, Murphy, Wittkower, and Chance (1964), in a survey of six sub-Saharan peoples, found guilt feelings rarely reported in severe depression.

In an effort to throw light on this Western phenomenon, Murphy reviewed the economic, political, and social situation in seventeenth-century England, studying the change from a "guilt-free to a guilt-rich depression" (p. 230). In Robert Burton's *Anatomy of Melancholy*, published in 1621, the whole literature on the subject is summarized, including the view of writers of the preceding centuries. Although Burton was an Oxford don and clergyman, not a physician, he had studied all the relevant writers and presents us with what Murphy regards as a balanced view of melancholia as it was understood in his time. Murphy's synopsis of Burton's principal symptoms of melancholia contains three points: "The first is that fear, sorrow and anxiety feature prominently . . . so that this is clearly an affective disorder. The second is that somatic symptoms are as numerous as mental ones, so that this could better be called a psychosomatic disorder rather than a mental one. Third, self-accusations and delusions of sin and guilt are not listed" (p. 230). Moreover, Murphy tells us: "Burton is clearly of the opinion that when a melancholic patient feels troubled by his conscience, there is usually good reason for this, so that the disease is not causing the feelings of guilt but merely disposing the patient to recognize them" (p. 230).

By 1669, another extremely popular book had been published, written by Richard Baxter, in which reference to self-reproach, despair, and delusions of guilt were a prominent part of the syndrome of melancholy. Somatic symptoms, in contrast, were less prominent. Between 1620 and 1670, in other words, "English melancholia acquired its 'modern' characteristics" (p. 233).

Murphy traces this development to changes in religious belief, economics, and child-rearing practices which were overtaking sixteenth- and seventeenth-century England. The prominence of guilt in depression is congruent with an individual's conscience being directly known by God rather than through the intervention of priests. It also parallels the development of economic entrepreneurialism, with its freeing of individuals to be their own masters but with concomitant loss of community. Finally, it parallels the marked increase in affection and respect with which children were treated as contrasted with their status during the Middle Ages. Adults who are thus treated as children are more likely to attribute their unhappiness to their own guilt. In support of this view, Murphy cites his own study of student mental health in three cultural groups in which he found that students who had the most comfortable upbringing tended to develop psychosomatic symptoms under stress while students who had more disturbed upbringings, or were on poorer terms with their parents, tended to attribute their problems to others.

The absence of guilt in Burton's account of melancholy may, of course, have been the result of great risk of acknowledging it in a world not yet secularized. It is of interest, in this connection, that Johannes Weyer, a sixteenth-century physician, had attempted to defend accused witches on the ground that their conscience was exaggerated but had been forced to withdraw this defense. Characterizing guilt as a mental illness rather than as a "reality" is a dangerous crack in Church control.

In any case, Murphy's historical record is a confirmation that along with the greater secularization of life came the appearance of guilt in accounts of depression. Why depression should be especially distinguished in this respect and whether it is the only mental illness involved are unanswered questions. What is particularly significant is that the affects of loss and sorrow remain constant throughout the changes in the description of depression that Murphy recounts. The presence or absence of guilt and somatic symptoms may be moot, but loss and sorrow are not.

It is actually the pursuit of the affects in depression, especially disentangling shame from guilt, that has led to the most fruitful developments within psychoanalytic thinking. It is my own opinion that this differentiation is vital to the understanding of depression. Specifically, an understanding of the phenomenology of shame can help us to grasp the mediating process by which reproaches unconsciously meant for the other are experienced as self-reproaches. The vicarious experience of the other's negative view of the self is a hallmark of shame; this phenomenology makes it easier to comprehend how reproaches may swing back and forth in their target.

Perhaps the most important clarification of the affects in depression since Freud's work is the work of Bibring (1953). Bibring's main thesis is that depression is an affective reaction to what is perceived as a state of helplessness. Bibring bases his formulation on clinical observations, summarized by Fenichel (1945), that lowered self-esteem is common to all forms of depression. As we saw earlier, Freud was careful to use the term "self-regard" in describing depressive affect, but his metapsychological statements about a cannibalistic introjection of the loved person such that the "critical agency" or superego blames the self rather than the introject led to the notion that depressives suffer from guilt. Bibring explicitly disagrees with what had become the classical view, that depression is the result of aggression turned back upon the self by the superego or guilt. In fact, he regards depression as "essentially independent of the vicissitudes of aggression" (p. 40). Further he hypothesizes that the observed "turning of aggressive impulses against the self is secondary to the breakdown of self-esteem" (p. 45).

Bibring does not abandon the notion of fixation, but he suggests an entirely different description of one; instead of the oral–narcissistic regression that Freud postulated, Bibring speaks more simply of the central predisposing factor in depression as a "fixation of the ego to the state of helplessness" (p. 39). Just as Freud (1926a) formulated anxiety as a given ego-signal of danger, so Bibring postulated depression as a (presumably given) affective state of the ego faced with helplessness.

As to the specifics of what the ego is helpless to do, Bibring emphasizes its helplessness to maintain "narcissistic" goals or aspirations: these may date from any psychosexual phase, from the oral wish to be loved and cared for, through the anal wish for mastery of self and other persons, to the phallic wish to be sexually admired and powerful. In short, as I translate Bibring's meaning, the ego is helpless to maintain its position as the loved person in its own and the "other's" eyes. It has thus fallen victim to a loss of *self*-esteem, or shame. Aggression or protest is a normal response to this loss, as it was in infancy (cf. Bowlby's later demonstrations). But it is not the *cause* of depression, rather the result of it. As Rapaport (1967 [1959]) remarked, commenting on Bibring's paper, depression is viewed as a structured affective state, reactivating a past structured affective state. Once again, it is to be noted that psychoanalytic theory rejoices in the occasions when its thinkers talk about affects. Mendelson (1974) has noted the fact that prior to Bibring, no major psychoanalytic theorist referred to depression as an affective state.

As Fliegel (1979) has suggested, the reactivation of a structured affective state is an idea shared by Melanie Klein and Bibring, and very different from the idea of id regression to a pathological fixation point. Even though the two theorists have very different theoretical orientations, Klein's being based on a death instinct, they come to the same terms when struggling to put depressive affects into words.

Sandler and Joffe (1965), in an attempt to bridge the gap between Bibring's description and classical formulations about the role of aggression, suggest that depression is the "mental pain" occurring in response to a loss of an "ideal state" of the self. This ideal state is itself the product of an interaction with its earliest caretakers and, later on, with other beloved persons. Sandler and Joffe suggest, however, that mental pain occurs only if the aggressive response to loss of love is blocked by superego prohibitions or guilt. The aggressive response is then turned against the self, resulting in depression.

It is clear that this formulation rests on blocked aggression (turned against the self) as a primary cause of depression since mental pain occurs only secondarily in the absence of aggression. It thus leaves Bibring's formulation essentially unchanged, and the difference between the two viewpoints unresolved. It seems to me that the difference may be resolved if we assume that *aggressive* attempts to restore the ideal state of the self in one's own and the other's eyes are intrinsically doomed. Countering shame by raging at the shaming unloving one *is* the loss of the ideal state of the self. The point is that one *is* actually helpless to restore a loved one's good feelings about the self, and the perception of this state of affairs is intrinsically painful, that is, shaming or humiliating. It is this affect of shame that is the most central one in the depressive state. Aggression against the shaming other may indeed also evoke guilt for the pain inflicted; guilt is also a depressing affect. But it is not the primary base of depression; that is an experience of distressing or painful loss.

Blatt (1974) attempted to integrate diverse observations about depression by proposing a phenomenological study of two major types of depression: (1) anaclitic depression, characterized by feelings of helplessness, weakness, fears of being abandoned, and by wishes to be cared for, loved, fed, and protected; and (2) introjective depression, which is developmentally more advanced and characterized by "intense feelings of inferiority, worthlessness, guilt and a wish for atonement." Blatt's purpose was not only to integrate varying descriptions of depression, but to develop a "depression experience questionnaire" (DEQ) by means of which depressive phenomena may be studied among normal persons as well as among patients. In this assessment "symptom-oriented" items such as depressed affect, sadness, lethargy, fatigue, and somatic–vegetative disturbances, such as sleep loss, decline in appetite or sexual interest, were omitted. The goal was rather to study the "object-relations" or interpersonal world of depressive experience.

Based on a review of clinical literature, 66 items were winnowed from 150 statements describing different aspects of depressive experience, and administered to a large number of men and women undergraduates, together with such other indicators of mood and self-concept as the Wessman–Ricks Mood Scale and the Osgood Semantic Differential (Blatt, D'Afflitti, and Quinlan, 1976). Among the principal findings of this probe was the appearance of a significant sex difference in the experience of depression, so that the data for males and females had to be treated separately. In a factor analysis of the DEQ, Blatt et al. also found evidence for their prediction of a difference between anaclitic and introjective depression. Three stable factors were found: (1) "dependency," (2) "self-criticism," and (3) "efficacy." An inspection of the items in their DEQ suggests, moreover, that there is considerable overlap between the "items labeled dependency/anaclitic and shame, and a corresponding overlap between self-critical/introjective items and guilt."

A follow-up study by Chevron, Quinlan, and Blatt (1978) yielded significant gender differences in depressive experience. As one would expect on the basis of sex-role stereotypes, women have higher levels of depression associated with "self-criticism." Moreover, women who described themselves as less warm and expressive on the Broverman scale of sex-role stereotypes, also rated themselves as more depressed on the Zung depression scale. Men who described themselves as less competent than other men, were also more depressed on the Zung scale. Thus, women and men who describe themselves in terms that have them failing in their stereotypical sex-role are also more depressed. We shall return to the question of sex differences in depression shortly.

Izard (1972) specifically includes shame in his differential emotions theory of depression. He found shame or shyness elevated in the emotional profiles of hospitalized depressive patients and in depressed outpatients in psychotherapy. An empirical comparison of the emotion profiles of depressed patients and high school students recalling and imaging an experience of depression showed that the greatest difference between the two groups was on shyness, with depressed patients having significantly higher scores. Izard interprets these findings as support for the importance of shame in depression.

Smith (1972) offers some empirical evidence for the connection between shame and depression. Seventy persons, forty men and thirty women, with a mean age of 31 years, all patients at a pastoral counseling center, were studied. Shame and guilt proneness were assessed by using an early-memories test and a shame–guilt test. As predicted, patients who were relatively shame-prone were more likely to be suffering from depression. This result held for both sexes and was stronger for women. In addition, as predicted, shame-prone patients showed significantly more self-directed hostility.

Nonanalytic authors have also fathered evidence which suggests that shame plays a major role in depression, although shame is not explicitly identified by them. Beck (1967) studied the content of depressed patients' dreams, with the hypothesis that they should be distinguishable from both normal and other psychiatrically ill persons by their "masochistic" content. As predicted, depressed patients' dreams portrayed them as "recipients of rejection, disappointment, [and] humiliation" (p. 217). Among the items scored as masochistic in content were "negative representations of the self" as deficient or unattractive, being thwarted by external factors, being deprived, excluded, superseded, or abandoned, being punished, and being a failure. There is, in other words, a heavy complement of shame items in the masochism scale.

Beck (1967) also reports that depressed patients rate themselves low on traits which are socially desirable. A significant negative correlation was obtained between self-acceptance and depression; Beck concludes that self-concept is low in depressed as compared with nondepressed patients.

Perhaps the most important development among nonpsychoanalytic workers has been the attempt to describe depression in terms of a cognitive deficit rather than as an affective disturbance. Particularly prominent in this attempt has been the work of Beck (1967) who argues that cognitive distortions of depressive self-perceptions are more important than their affective experiences, and may, in fact be the cause rather than the result of their illness. In more recent years, another model of cognitive distortion has been proposed by Seligman (1975). These developments will be only briefly discussed since they both follow the essential pattern already discerned in cognitive–behavioral versions of phobia and obsessional neurosis: the "dynamic" or affective basis of the illness is deemphasized, and the symptoms are attacked directly in "programs" for behavioral change.

In the case of depression, the affective triad of helplessness, self-denigration, and hopelessness in the depressives' perception of themselves is ascribed by Beck to a cognitive deficit. Cognitive tuition is therefore instituted to change the depressives' perception of themselves. In Beck's model of cognitive deficit we may discern a connection to psychoanalytic thinking. Beck assumes that loss of love or being thwarted causes the "hyperactivation" of primitive, rigid cognitive schemas, which then perseverate to make the individual depression-prone. Beck's model of the cognitive deficit specifies that the depressed individuals have learned to exaggerate their causal responsibility for negative (bad) events and to underplay their responsibility for positive (good) events.

Seligman's model is phrased more explicitly in the language of contingencies and reinforcements, and suggests that depressed individuals underestimate their causal responsibility to control important events in general, attributing their fate to external factors and thus perceiving themselves as "helpless." A recent issue of the *Journal of American Psychology* devoted to a review of the many experimental studies that have developed in response to Seligman's formulations suggests that experimental support for the formulation is by no means unequivocal. Among the criticisms that have been offered is that Seligman's and his colleagues' experiments were done with normal college students, whose depression scores were within the normal range. One critic (Costello, 1978) suggests that we should beware of making a fetish of the simplicity and testability of proposi-

tions. In fact, psychoanalytic formulations have been ignored as complicated and fanciful even though their predictions came (much earlier) to
the same point as learning theorists: namely, that depressives suffer from a
perception of their helplessness. As we have seen, this is precisely the
descriptive point at which Bibring arrived in 1953. Bibring, moreover,
specified what he thought depressives were helpless to do — recapture an
ideal state of the self, the loss of which brings with it the affect of lowered
self-esteem or shame. This is as testable an hypothesis as predictions about
attributions of success and failure in the relatively trivial tasks ordinarily
used in experiments on learned helplessness.

With the attention paid by cognitive theorists to the "cognitive deficit"
in depression had come the realization that depressive symptoms involve a
paradox (Abramson and Sackeim, 1977; Rizley, 1978). Depressed people
feel helpless to affect their destiny at the same time that their (helpless) self
seems to them to be the appropriate target of hostility. If they are, indeed, as
helpless as they feel, logic dictates that they should *not* feel responsible (guilty) for what they are incapable of doing. This paradox in depression seems to
me to make sense if one realizes that depressed people are experiencing
simultaneously two characteristics of shame: hatred of the deficient self
(which is focal in awareness), and the helplessness of the self to change its
vicarious experience of the "other's" negative feeling.

In summary, then, an important trend since Freud's 1917 paper has been
the rediscovery of shame as well as guilt in the phenomenology of depression. As we shall see in the next section of this chapter, this revival of interest
in shame may be particularly helpful in illuminating the process by which
self-directed hostility becomes so prominent in depression.

(3 and 4) Turning Reproaches Meant for the Loved Person Back upon the Self via Identification

As indicated earlier, this is perhaps the most influential of all of Freud's
concepts, not only in depression to which it was originally specific, but as a
general process common to all mental illness. In any case, this formulation of
Freud's was so influential that it found its way into the official description of
psychoneurotic depressive reaction as it was given in the American
Psychiatric Association 1952 diagnostic manual: "The reaction is
precipitated by a current situation, frequently by some loss sustained by the
patient, and is often associated with a feeling of guilt for past failures and
misdeeds." As we have seen, Freud's concept was formulated before the
development of the superego concept; with the advent of the superego concept, itself a process of "internalized aggression," there developed a short-

hand designation of the superego as a synonym for guilt. There was thus an easy transition into the concept that depressives (along with other mentally ill persons) suffer from the excessive or "archaic" guilt over transgressions.

As we have just seen, however, the distinction between guilt and other forms of sorrow has been clearly maintained in clinical descriptions of depression over the centuries (Murphy, 1978) as well as in current empirical work on depression (Blatt, 1974; Izard, 1972). I have suggested (Lewis, 1971, 1978) further, that the phenomenology of shame involves an "identification" between the self and the significant "other" such that the self experiences vicariously the other's rejection of the self. In this vicarious experience, the other's rejection is verbalized as self-reproach and experienced as the affective state of depression.

As we have also seen, there also occurred within the psychoanalytic movement a controversy over retroflected hostility in depression (for example, Bibring, 1953; Sandler and Joffe, 1965).

The major empirical work within the psychoanalytic movement that has implications for the issue of retroflected hostility in depression is that of Bowlby (1960, 1963, 1969, 1973). Freud's reconstructions of depression had led him into the earliest period of life. Bowlby translated these speculative reconstructions into testable propositions founded on ethological theory. It should be noted, further, that Bowlby acknowledges his debt to Melanie Klein, by whom he was trained, although explicitly disavowing her theoretical framework.

Bowlby's empirical work leads him to the same prediction that Freud makes, namely, that people who become pathologically depressed in adulthood are suffering the remnants of pathological mourning in childhood. But the process by which pathological mourning leads to adult depression is very differently described in Bowlby's version. Specifically, Bowlby's account does not focus on the turning of hostility meant for the other back upon the self as a particularly central or difficult problem. Rather, his account more or less takes for granted that reproaches against the self as well as the "other" are a normal component of separation. In fact, Bowlby explicitly suggests that healthy mourning, as well as pathological, involves "anger with the lost object, with others and with the self" (1963, p. 509).

Some detail of Bowlby's (1963) formulation is necessary at this point. It is in this paper that Bowlby explicitly discusses his differences with his psychoanalytic colleagues; it is thus the best basis I could find for a discussion of these differences. Bowlby's thesis is that "first, . . . once the child has formed a tie to its mother figure, which has ordinarily occurred during the middle of the first year, its rupture leads to separation anxiety and grief and sets in train processes of mourning; secondly, that in the early years of life these mourning processes not infrequently take a course unfavorable to future personality development and thereby predispose to psychiatric illness" (p. 500). During the early phases of life, when the "instinctual response systems . . . remain focused on the object . . . yearning and an angry effort to recover the lost object seem to be the rule" (pp. 500–501).

Two separate issues are contained in this formulation. One is the issue of predisposition to depression based on childhood mourning; the other is the issue of aggression both as a normal part of the childhood experience of separation and as a part of the adult experience of depression. Let us consider the two issues separately.

The Predisposition to Depression. The assumption of a biologically given species-adaptive attachment system between infant and caretakers brings with it a caretaker-retrieval mechanism which includes aggression. The appearance of these same retrieval mechanisms "after bereavement in a way that seems maladaptive is due . . . *to irretrievable loss of object being so statistically rare that it has not been taken into account in the design of our biological equipment"* (p. 510) (my italics).

It seems apparent that, just as Freud's formulation begged the question of why narcissistic regression occurs in depression, so Bowlby's formulation that depression rests on a flaw in our biological equipment also begs the question. Bowlby's hypothesis, strictly interpreted, requires that people who fall ill of depression in adulthood should have suffered bereavement in childhood. As I have shown in a review of this literature (Lewis, 1976) there is indeed evidence of an extra frequency of childhood bereavement in adult depression but the evidence is by no means overwhelming. The evidence for an excess of childhood bereavement in *all* psychiatric illnesses is stronger, and where there is such evidence it is even stronger for women than for men. Bowlby does not suggest, moreover, although his thesis requires it, that *all* instances of childhood bereavement are fated to result in adult depression, and in this respect, his explanation of a fault in biological system for dealing with childhood bereavement still leaves other kinds of dynamics wide open. In his 1973 publication, Bowlby explicitly cites parental *threats* of abandonment — through *threats* of either suicide or desertion — as childhood experiences increasing adult proneness to pathological depression and anxiety.

It is interesting to note, in passing, that Bowlby's emphasis on real childhood bereavement as a factor in adult depression is something akin to Freud's first emphasis on real childhood seductions in hysteria. Both sets of events do occur, and they do leave painful psychological scars, but they cannot account for instances of depression or hysteria where such *actual* events have not taken place.

The Role of Aggression in Separation: Appropriate and Inappropriate Protest. Bowlby's hypothesis is that "so far from being pathological, an open

expression of . . . angry strivings to recover the object is a sign of health and
. . . it enables the bereaved gradually to relinquish the object. What seems to
characterize pathological mourning is an inability to accept and express this
striving; instead, it becomes repressed and unconscious, and so, insulated
from change, persists" (p. 501). Bowlby here seems to be on common ground
with Freud in supposing that the element in pathological mourning is that the
affects of protest and yearning are unconscious. As Freud puts it, the identification with the lost object is unconscious. But the question for both formulations is why the angry protest and reproach to the lost object should
become unavailable — or, in Freud's terms, why the identification with the
hated object is unavailable to awareness.

Freud's answer was the essentially circular one, that there was a regression to earliest "narcissistic" identification. Bowlby's answer is that when
separations are temporary, yearning and protest are effective in maintaining
the mother–child tie; when separations are permanent, as is the case in
childhood bereavement, yearning and protest are not effective, and "should
be expected to diminish and disappear" (p. 505). But instead, for reasons of a
defect in biological endowment of the species, they sometimes persist even
when they can no longer be effective. But this explanation does not directly
address the question of why yearning and protest should become unconscious because they have persisted beyond their effectiveness. Bowlby
does, however, suggest that it is the inappropriateness of the anger that
makes it unavailable: "turning of anger and reproach away from an appropriate object and toward an inappropriate one, so that one of their main
components becomes unconscious" (p. 512).

As I have suggested (Lewis, 1971), it is a characteristic of the
shame–humiliation experience that it is regarded as an "inappropriate" state.
There is, in fact, good reason why shame comes to be regarded as an inappropriate affect. For one thing, each of us learns before we are very old that
protest is *not* an effective mode of retrieving the lost *good opinion* of the
beloved other. In fact, a long and arduous program of tuition is instituted
early in each person's life, by means of which the caretaker seeks to teach the
child to differentiate between appropriate and inappropriate protest at
separation. A very early lesson is that inappropriate protest is both shameful
and punishable, that is, blameworthy. It is, furthermore, a characteristic of
the shame state that it tends to be wordless or hidden; in other words,
shameful protest over lost love is characteristically suffered in silence and experienced as depression.

Bowlby is critical of classical psychoanalysis for too much emphasis on
the affects rather than on motivation. As a result, the "unconscious effort to
recover the lost object" has not had sufficient consideration in
psychoanalytic thinking. Bowlby also sees as one reason for this the over-

whelming emphasis that Freud gave to identification with the lost object as the key to pathological mourning rather than the unconscious striving to recover it and the unconscious reproach designed to discourage repetition of the loss.

The identification that Freud postulated as the means by which reproaches meant for the other are transferred onto the self can, however, easily be understood as a "retrieval" of the lost person. If, moreover, we shift the scene of operations from the adult level to infancy, we find considerable evidence that the attachment system Bowlby postulates does indeed involve something like an "identification" which can be witnessed very early in the "secure" or "insecure" self of the infant. This quality of the infant's self often betrays the "security" of the mother's self.

If we assume that the attachment system Bowlby has described as a motivational one actually develops within a system of affect-exchange, it seems possible to reconcile views that emphasize motivation with views that emphasize the power of affects. "Identification" is an inadequate term that attempts to capture the process of affective *exchange* by which a self responds to the emotions of another person through a vicarious experience of the other's affective state.

It is significant in this connection that Bowlby describes the use of vicarious figures in children's efforts to master separation. Laura, the two-year-old whose reactions to separation were filmed, was very much concerned when other children cried, although she cried only a little herself. "On one occasion a small boy was screaming piteously. Laura's immediate response was to become solicitous and to demand that the boy's mother be brought. A little self-righteously she exclaimed, 'I'm not crying, see!' and then, emphatically, 'Fetch that boy's Mummy!'" Laura's "self-righteous" comment that she was not crying suggests that the affect she was mastering was the shame of crying. Her vicarious concern for the little boy's cries suggests that one mechanism by which humiliation may be relieved is by turning it into a vicarious experience of the other's state and into the gratifying experience of being *able* to help the other. Laura also insisted, on another occasion, that "My Mummy is crying for me — go fetch her." Here Laura's grieving was vicariously experienced as her mother's grieving, in a relieving exchange of affects between her mother's and her own self.

Evidence which has mounted rapidly in response to the impetus of Bowlby's formulations has shown us that children who are able to tolerate separation better than others are those who have "incorporated" mother as a "secure base" from which to operate. They have developed what Benedek (1938) called "self-confidence" in the expectation that their needs will ultimately be met. The psychic situation of such children can be generalized as one in which they are secure of mother's love and of their own love of her.

The contrasting psychic situation is one in which the children are insecure in the loving relation of the self to the mother; this means that they are prone to interpret separation as *rejection*, to which the emotional response is a particular kind of protest — humiliated fury.

Bowlby suggests that "reproaches leveled against the object may be expected to insure that the object becomes less prone to go away again. For example, there is many a mother who has vowed never again to leave her young child in strange surroundings after she has been exposed to the reproaches he levels against her following her return home" (p. 509). Moreover, Bowlby terms the reproaches "more or less bitter." I think it is likely that the reproaches are not only designed to prevent a repetition of desertion, that is to alter mother's feeling and behavior, but they function to communicate to her that the child experiences her desertion as some kind of loss to the *self*. This loss to the self has variously been called a "narcissistic" injury, a loss of "ideal state," or an "open wound," in Freud's terminology. More recent attempts to put it in words have evoked the analogy to being burned (Engel, 1961), a comparison that reminds one of the "burning" rage that is experienced in humiliated fury. Bowlby's emphasis on the bitterness of the feeling seems to me to be reaching for the same point, namely, that *humiliated* fury is evoked by separation.

The special quality of the affective communication in humiliated fury is that it is a self-to-other message about how rageful the self feels at its inferior place "in the eyes of" the other. I suggest, in other words, that a special form of aggressive affect is normally elicited in both separation and depression, namely shame-rage, or humiliated fury. In this affective state, the message of rage easily includes both the separated parties as targets. Bowlby's observations that aggressive feeling includes the self as well as the other seem to confirm this suggestion.

I am assuming, in other words, that the medium in which the mother–infant attachment system develops is an exchange of affects. It is an exchange, moreover, in which the mother's affects of pride, joy, anger, shame, humiliated fury, and guilt are inevitably involved. This exchange of affects involves the repeated exercise by each party of attempts at vicarious experience of the other's affective states. Bowlby has taught us that crying, smiling, sucking, clinging, and following are innate releasers of mothers' caretaking behavior; eye-to-eye contact is another possible releaser (Robson, 1967). These nonverbal messages evoking maternal behavior are received, however, within the context of the mother's existing system of affects. Angry protests evoke her anger, shame, and guilt; the infant's happiness and contentment evoke her joy and pride. The infant's vicarious experience of the caretaker's affects is the process by which "identification" takes place. It is this "identification" with the prideful, joyous "secure" mother that is expressed in a "secure" sense of self and the "identification" with the "rejecting" mother that brings depression.

It should be noted that we now know, as Freud did not, that very young infants are biologically equipped to participate in affective social interactions much more complicated than had been imagined. For example, two- to three-day-old infants respond with crying to the sounds of other neonates crying; girl infants are even more sensitive in this respect than boy infants (Simner, 1971). A pattern of neonate movement has been shown to be in synchrony with patterns of adult speech (Condon and Sander, 1974). As still another example of the recent evidence for the infant's biological endowment for vicarious experience or identification with its caretaker, twelve-day-old infants have been shown to "imitate" adult mouth, hand, and tongue gestures (Meltzoff and Moore, 1977). Freud's idea that identification precedes "object-choice" seems to have been one of his really inspired guesses.

In the exchange of affects, shame and guilt are of particular importance in shaping the developing identification. Specifically, the infant's coming to appreciate that yearning and protest are "inappropriate" responses to his "real situation" is a function not only of structural and cognitive development but of some necessary shaming and guilt induction on mother's part. However gently spoken, the cognitive message that some protest is inappropriate must be conveyed. This message is a double one: at the same time that it accepts the validity of the infant's distress feeling it reduces the painfulness of separation by emphasizing that it does not mean "rejection." In so doing it begins a long process of differentiation between appropriate and "inappropriate" anger — that is, ultimately between righteous indignation and humiliated fury. If the infant recognizes that his protests are "inappropriate" and protests nonetheless, his behavior evokes the caretaker's righteous indignation and punishment, that is, the inculcation of guilt. Both shame and guilt are necessary for the balanced development of autonomy of the self and the affectionate relatedness of the self to others.

Let us follow, as an example, the interaction between the infant's "releaser" of crying and the caretaker's emotional responses, with particular reference to the operation of the affects of shame and guilt. Mothers' responses to crying are very early geared to a distinction between protests that are "only" about the absence of mother's cuddling and protests which are "realistically" based on physical discomfort. Woolf (1969) in his study of infants' crying observes that mothers very early distinguish between their infants' "mad" cries and those that signify "real" pain or physical distress. Soothing these "unrealistic" angry protests is gratifying up to a point; it is necessarily soon accompanied by the mother's communication that they are "inappropriate" to the child's "real" state of physical discomfort. In other words, a system is early established in which the infant's crying over what he appears to perceive as "rejection" is countered by mother's message (which may be very tenderly conveyed) that such protests are inappropriate and therefore shameful. This message fosters the autonomy of the infant's self; failure of his autonomy in future evokes a shame signal. It is a characteristic of the shame experience in adulthood that it is experienced as "inappropriate."

Along with shame messages over crying there are also nonverbal messages that are precursors of guilt. The message that crying is "inappropriate" implies that the child *can* wait for or do without mother's cuddling. It thus implies that the self is *able* but unwilling to accept separation. Such protest behavior is thus not only "inappropriate" and shameful, but "wrong" or "bad," requiring punishment for the child's guilt. The punishment may be the threat of the caretaker's "rejection"; this threat is often added to the message of guilt, in the form of threats of abandonment, in turn, evoking humiliation. In another combination, guilt induction or punishment may take the form of evoking the infant's vicarious experience of the mother's suffering.

That both shame and guilt messages are necessary to the successful development of healthy attachment and a secure self is suggested by the evidence, now available, that the most competent nursery school children have been treated with a combination of sympathy for their humiliated protests at separation and firmness of discipline (Sroufe, 1979).

When we consider, further, the complicated interaction between mother's proneness to the affects of shame and guilt and her reception of infant's protests, we glimpse that there are a large number of permutations and combinations that can govern these affective exchanges. A mother, for example, who is ashamed of her own incompetence may interpret her infant's protests as indicators of her own inadequacy. If her humiliated fury is evoked, she may readily "jump" her infant into a premature message that separation is "inappropriate" thus confounding his separation and "rejection" experiences. Or she may "rationalize" her own proneness to shame as guilt over what she regards as her failure to supply endless tenderness. Thus she will fail to transmit the message that separation protest is "inappropriate," and so herself foster a sense of her infant's inadequacy. A mother rather more prone to guilt than shame may also prematurely interpret the child's crying as "wrong," thus simultaneously evoking the infant's humiliated fury at her rejection of him and short-circuiting the infant's experience of distinguishing between humiliated fury and more "rational" anger.

In summary, the problem of "explaining" the turning of aggression from the other onto the self may be eased by combining the evidence from Bowlby's work that separation protest is normal with the suggestion that the affective quality of that protest is *shame*-rage or *humiliated* fury. It is this affective state that has been variously called "narcissistic injury," "open wound," or loss of "ideal state." In this affective state, aggression against the "other" is vicariously experienced as the "other's" rejection of the self. The aggression, moreover, is regarded as "inappropriate," or "unjust," thus evoking guilt along with shame in an affective experience of depression.

(5) Sex Differences and Cognitive Style Differences in Depression

The fact that women are more prone to depression than men has been known in psychiatry ever since statistics began to be collected. Data from New York State Hospitals as early as 1910, for example, showed that although the incidence of mental illness in general was greater for men than women, women were more prone to depression than men (Malzberg, 1940). But there has been very little attempt to interpret this difference in proneness to depression, either in analytic or nonanalytic circles.

As we have seen, Freud's brief suggestion that there is a difference between obsessional neurotics and melancholics in the permeability of their self-boundaries was, in effect, a suggestion about a difference in cognitive style. In developments since Freud's time, the viability of a concept of cognitive style has been empirically demonstrated (Witkin, Lewis, Hertzman, Machover, Meissner, and Wapner, 1954; Witkin, Dyk, Faterson, Goodenough, and Karp, 1962), and there is ample evidence that, at least in Western cultures, women are more field-dependent than men. There is evidence, also, of a connection between patients' cognitive style and proneness to shame or guilt (Witkin, Lewis, and Weil, 1968; Crouppen, 1977). I have suggested that this network of evidence can be interpreted to mean that women's greater proneness to depression is mediated by their greater proneness to shame. There is, as we have seen, some direct empirical evidence of a connection between shame and depression (Beck, 1967; Smith, 1972; Blatt, D'Afflitti, and Quinlan, 1976; Izard, 1972; Crouppen, 1977).

Let us now look briefly at the evidence for the separate parts of this package of evidence.

Sex Differences in Proneness to Depression. The evidence is strong and unequivocal that women are more prone to depression than men (Lewis, 1976, 1978), whether the data are obtained from state hospitals, private hospitals, outpatient clinics, or rural or urban areas, and whether they relate to "the feeling of depression, neurotic depression, or depressive psychosis" (Silverman, 1968, p. 73). The severity of depression also seems to be greater in women (Lewis, 1976, 1978).

Depression cuts across class lines (Silverman, 1968), and women's greater proneness to depression than men's also cuts across class lines

(Weissman and Paykel, 1974). This finding is in sharp contrast to those for schizophrenia and to the rates for male psychotics, which are strongly associated with poverty and social disorganization (Faris and Dunham, 1939; Hollingshead and Redlich, 1958; Dohrenwend and Dohrenwend, 1969; Levy and Rowitz, 1973). This contrast between depression and schizophrenia can be understood as reflecting men's direct participation in competitive economic struggles, as compared with women's relative exclusion from the world of work (Cohen, 1961).

There is some relationship between depression and high social class; that is, more cases of depression have sometimes (not always) been reported from the more affluent classes (Silverman, 1968). This may be because more affluent women have the leisure in which to cultivate ideals of devotion to others. Ethnic groups among whom women's devotion to the family is an ideal might be expected to show more depression than ethnic groups with a less strong tradition for women. On the basis of a strong Jewish tradition of women's devotion to the family, Bart (1971) predicted and confirmed that depression in middle-aged women is more frequent among "Jewish mothers" than among other women. Along with their exclusion from economic independence, women's biocultural role involves them more directly than men in nurturant roles within the family, at the greater risk of the shame of "loss of love" when the "nest is empty."

Sex Differences in Proneness to Shame. That women are more prone to shame than men is a long-standing and widespread observation. Darwin (1872), for example, observed that "women blush much more than men" (p. 311). Two major factors join in fostering women's greater shame-proneness. First, the anaclitic identifications made by girls growing up in the nuclear family remain central in women's personality (Sears, Rau, and Alpert, 1965); these loving identifications continue the threat of "loss of love" or shame into women's adulthood. Women, for example, show more anxiety over "loss of love," while there is a tendency for men to show more "castration anxiety" (Bradford, 1968). Even in their symbolic conceptions of the Deity, as reflected in Rorschach responses, fear of God is more characteristic of men, while more benevolent representations of the Deity are more characteristic of women (Larson and Knapp, 1964).

Second, the widespread exclusion of women from positions of power in work fosters a culturally sanctioned adjustment in women's position of economic dependency and devotion to the family. Men, in contrast, are pressed into aggressive, independent behavior in order to meet their responsibility for a livelihood within a competitive economic system. Women's position of economic and social inferiority provides an objective basis for feelings of inferiority that induce shame; men's greater aggressiveness involves them more in guilt.

Evidence is strong and conclusive that men are more aggressive than women (Maccoby, 1966; Maccoby and Jacklin, 1974). Women's lesser aggressivity in itself is a predictor of their greater proneness to self-directed hostility and shame. The direct evidence for women's greater sociability than men is less clear-cut, but on balance it appears that women are more "nurturant" and "positive" in their attitudes toward "others" than men. In a total of 47 studies (Maccoby, 1966) of "interest in and positive feeling for others," "need for affiliation," and "nurturance," women and girls were reported as showing more positive attitudes than men and boys in all but five studies. (In these five, there was no sex difference.) In their recent survey, Maccoby and Jacklin (1974) label as myth the idea that girls have a greater capacity for social behavior than boys. But the evidence they present that girls and women are more sociable than men and boys is still strong. For example, girls are more motivated by "social goals," while boys are more motivated when the circumstances are competitive; girls' friendships are more intimate, boys' are more gregarious and aggressive, involving gangs; women's ego-investment is more affiliative, men's more involved with status and power. Leaving aside the question of whether women's greater sociability is more the result of biological role than of cultural expectations, positive feelings for "others" find a more significant role in the life experience of women than of men. If women "care more" about "others," it follows that the "others" are for this reason alone more able to make women ashamed (in their own and others' eyes). The empirical studies which have addressed the question of sex differences in proneness to shame have been few, but their evidence is mainly in the predicted direction (Lewis, 1978).

Field-Dependence and Depression. Depressives have long been described as being "overinvolved" with others (Freud, 1917; Fromm-Reichmann, 1959; Lewis, 1958; Weissman and Paykel, 1974). In addition to this general clinical description, there is empirical evidence of a connection between depression and field-dependence (Witkin, 1965; Levenson and Neuringer, 1974). Of particular interest is the finding (Levenson and Neuringer, 1974) that male psychiatric patients ($N = 84$) who committed suicide were more field-dependent than a matched group of nonsuicidal patients. Scores on the picture-completion, object-assembly, and block-design subtest of the WAIS (which correlates highly with the rod-and-frame and embedded-figures tests) were used as the measure of field-dependence. The patients who committed suicide had significantly lower scores on these WAIS subtests (although they actually had somewhat higher IQs and had achieved a slightly higher level of education). Levenson and Neuringer interpret their findings as indicating that a person who commits suicide has a cognitive style that lacks the "problem-solving processes to re-orient his relationship to his environment" (p. 184). This formulation, which is similar to

Beck's formulation of the cognitive deficit in depression, is also congruent with the idea that depression reflects the helplessness of the (attached) person to change what he perceives as the negative feelings of the "other" (shame).

Thus, it is possible to assemble a network of evidence that field-dependent people are more prone to depression; that women are more field-dependent than men; that field-dependent people are more prone to shame; and that women are more prone to shame. This network, taken together, suggests that women's greater proneness to depression is mediated by their greater proneness to shame.

As a clinical illustration of the role of shame-rage in depression, one sequence from the experience of a field-dependent, shame-prone woman patient in psychotherapy may be cited (Lewis, 1971). The incident involves the failure of the (male) therapist to keep his appointment with her without notifying her. As we follow the sequence of events in the transcript of the sessions following, we see that humiliated feeling is described by the patient as "so upset[ting] [she] is on the verge of tears," that is, depressed. We can see, also, that two sessions later, at a moment when the therapist is rather sharply criticizing her for what she perceives as her righteous indignation at him, she rather suddenly begins to analyze her own propensity to "forget appointments" without any apparent awareness of a connection to the previous incident in which the therapist "stood her up." In one later excerpt she is also clearly depressed as she describes her own shortcomings.

> P: . . . because I had called your secretary 'cause it was a holiday, and I was wondering whether you would be in. She said, "Yes." You know so, actually, I wasn't prepared for your not coming. Uh . . . but it just seems, you know, I say, "well just my luck." These things are always happening to me, and, . . . , I just felt a little helpless.
>
> T: Always happening to you?
>
> 1. *(Feeling of helplessness, "no control" over things evokes anger)*
>
> P: Yeah, these things, these, these — you know — situations (inaudible) situations you're completely helpless. I mean there is nothing I can do about it. You weren't there, and you weren't coming, and, uh . . . , and the time was gone. And really there was nothing that I could do about it. And I get angry when I'm so helpless. When, when things around me go wrong and, uh, and I just have no control over it, you know? It makes me angry and, uh, and that's what I was — I was angry (slight laugh), I, you know —
>
> T: At me?
>
> P: Uh, no at your secretary (laugh). Because she had taken my phone number, and, uh, she said in case anything goes wrong at any time we wanna get in touch with you, can I please have your phone number, and you know I figured, well she had my phone number, and, uh, and "oo" I was ripping you know (slight laugh). And, uh . . . , I was, I was, I was very upset (inaudible).
>
> T: But angry at her rather than angry at me.

2. *(Anger (humiliated) feels "upset"; on the verge of tears)*

P: Yeah, because I thought she, uh, well she did call the next day, and she said that she couldn't, uh, she wasn't there, she didn't know about it. Well, she spoke to my mother, I wasn't home. I don't know exactly what she said. But just waiting for the bus — oh . . . (laugh). You know I really, uh . . . , upset (slight laugh) (inaudible) because I . . . I was very, I was upset at the time; I was on the verge of tears I was so upset because I had this test. I just hate wasting time. I generally am a great time-waster anyway, but, uh, I can blame no one but myself. But here I have no control over the situation. You know I hate that feeling. I hate the feeling of being helpless, and not being able to do anything about it. I guess everyone hates that feeling. But, uh . . . , it just wore off, you know — given a few days it generally wears off. It was at the moment —

T: But how come you think you were anxious — you were angry at my secretary rather than me?

P: (laugh) Well I was, I, I sort of got angry at you later on (laugh). At first, uh . . . I well. Well, I thought, you know, uh, but when she said that she wasn't there, you know, it's not her fault, so I have to be angry at someone of course. So you know I was sort of — not really angry, just a little annoyed, that, you know, you hadn't gotten in touch with me, that's all. You know some — but, you know, I, I didn't know the situation or anything, you know. Uh, it's just a matter of I had to be angry at someone. I had to get the anger out of my system so — my first thing was just getting angry at her because I thought — I didn't know the situation, and I felt she should have gotten in touch with me, and, uh —

T: But at the time you felt that more she should have gotten in touch with you, even that I should have been here.

3. *(Humiliated anger is "at the situation" — the whole world's against me)*

P: Well, that's just it, you couldn't of been here. Uh, through no fault of mine. But the point, the point is, uh . . . , I, I knew that you couldn't be here, you know? I, I just, just angry at the situation in general, that you weren't here and I had wasted the day . . . And, uh, things like this, uh, often happen and I, I just hate, I just hate the feeling of not being able to do anything. I, I don't know, it's sort of, um . . . like the whole world's against me (slight laugh). You know, that feeling . . .

T: The whole world, instead of me.

4. *(Humiliated anger issues into guilt)*

P: Yeah, you know, just things are in general — just things like that happen, and there's no one really you can blame, um . . . , rationally, you know and really feel right about blaming the person. In fact if I had blamed you I would have felt downright guilty, because I, I feel I had no grounds, I would have no grounds to be angry at you because you couldn't help it. And yet probably you know unconsciously I, uh, I probably was angry at you for not coming. So, uh, I had to blame it on somebody, so I blamed it on your secretary, and I guess that's the whole thing . . . I feel guilty — if I am angry, um, at someone who I, I feel rationally I feel I had no grounds to be angry at, uh, I feel guilty, and I'll try to talk myself out of the anger, and (inaudible) you know (inaudible) reason to be angry at him. But still it doesn't take away the feeling of, uh, uh, of the anger, or, or of, or of I guess the frustration . . . I, I guess you know that's it.

Let us begin by observing in the material under the heading 1 that although the patient's reaction is variously described as a "feeling of helplessness" or "no control," the component of humiliation which this feeling implies is not explicitly identified. The patient is angry at herself, not for moral transgression, but for an incapacity or failure to make things go right. This is shame-anger. Anger is a feeling which can mobilize the self. Shame- or humiliation-anger is eroded in intensity by the fact that the anger is at her own helplessness. The self is mobilized, but it is the target of the evoked hostility. No wonder the combination can feel like "tension." The moment the anger is directed outside the self — at the therapist's secretary or at the therapist — it is deflected back upon the self by a feeling of guilt at *unjust* anger (heading 2). The source of anger is a feeling of her own incapacity to begin with, and its target is likewise the inadequate self.

The material under the next heading (3) reminds us that humiliation-anger feels like diffuse anxiety or tension. The patient feels upset and "on the verge of tears," i.e., depressed. In particular, the depressed feeling can be understood as a product of the self-directed hostility.

The material under the last heading (4) illustrates the fate of the hostility arising from inadequacies and directed against the self. The image which forms is of the self — little, helpless, as the patient says, "like the whole world's against me."

This latter feeling is a self-pitying one. The patient's slight laugh at this point may indicate her awareness that she is indulging herself. The patient is herself aware that her reaction is disproportionate. Her use of a simile "like" the whole world's against her indicates her awareness that her feeling is excessive. She labels her reaction as "not rational" also because there really is no one to blame, "just things like that happen . . . in general." It was no one's fault, she reasoned, "but it doesn't take away the feeling of . . . frustration." The patient is thus indicating her awareness that no one intended to slight her: "it happens in general." Nevertheless, she did not escape her humiliated feelings which were evoked when she arrived to find the therapist absent, i.e., to find herself "stood up."

The patient is also aware that the feeling passes, i.e., that this was a trivial event. "Given a few days it generally wears off." It is interesting that this observation occurs immediately after she is prepared to forgive herself for her furious reaction. "I guess everyone hates that feeling of not being able to do anything about it."

As the material under headings 3 and 4 indicates, the patient feels guilty for irrational or unjust anger. She is here describing the bind which is intrinsic in humiliated fury. The anger pushes toward discharge; but it is anger which results from her own feeling of helplessness, i.e., anger of impotence or shame-anger which is directed against the self. Its source in a feeling about the self is recognized as "not rational." Anger which is "not rational" evokes guilt; if she should discharge her anger on others, she would feel guilty. This is a very different situation from righteous indignation at one's own or other's moral transgressions. Then, in contrast, the expression of anger at one's self or at others seems right, and a way of rectifying or changing the situation which evoked guilt in the first place.

Two sessions later, in a moment of battle with the therapist, she can be found blaming herself for "missing appointments" — a reproach clearly applicable to the therapist, but now applied to herself.

P: . . . another thing that you know I find — like when I have a lot of things to do not even in school, just in gen — well I should say, not tests, but going you know but making appointments to see people, and, um, but to see more than one person, and doing little things, buying little things that — unless I make a long list of things that I have to do, I'm constantly rehashing it in my mind. And I go crazy. I just — I get so nervous, and I do it over, and over, and over again and I leave out one and then I have to go back and do it all over again. And I say I know there is supposed to be ten things but I only count nine. You know I really can't take it. I really get very, uh, upset when I have a lot of things to think about. I just can't handle it (pause). And that's what I have now I'm very — that's what happens to me (inaudible) things pile up. And papers to do, and tests, and all sorts of things that I've stuck — and I'm always afraid I'm gonna forget to do them. Even forget to go to an appointment or, uh, you know, something like that.

T: You sort of have to keep telling yourself over, and over and over again about the appointments.

P: Yeah. Because I'll forget. I mean if I don't keep on reminding myself I'm gonna forget completely. I have a terrible memory. I know it . . . ever since this therapy has been going on.

A few moments later, after a sympathetic remark by the therapist, a saner view of "forgetting appointments" is apparent in the patient's thoughts:

T: But you seem to have some sort of feeling of tremendous battle going on inside.

P: Battle?

T: Yeah, fighting against yourself.

P: You mean I'm trying to destroy myself? (slight laugh).

T: I don't know. Making yourself forget things that you shouldn't forget —

P: Yeah, and you know I find — you know a lot of people forget to go to appointments. You know? I mean, you know, they sort of joke about what a terrible memory they have, and, uh . . . they always, you know, forget to meet people and things. There are people who always do that, you know. So it seems like a pretty common thing (inaudible) to forget these little appointments and everything. Especially when you have a lot of them. But the thing is I worry about it so much. This is what gets me down. So perhaps if I'd miss some appointments it wouldn't be so terrible, but just the fact that all the strain I go

through worrying about whether I'm going to remember or no. You know?
That's — this is — I mean, I don't like having a bad memory but if I have to
have one, why do I have to worry about it too. This is my complaint. Not so
much the memory.

The patient can now view lapses in memory as the sort of thing one can
"joke about," i.e., less humiliating.

SUMMARY

In summary, Freud emphasized the depressive's close emotional involvement with significant others. He also emphasized the influence of guilt
as a force turning hostility evoked by feeling unloved back upon the self. An
important development since Freud's time has been the rediscovery of shame
as well as guilt in depression. Bowlby's demonstration that separation normally evokes protest, coupled with the observation that the protest takes the
form of humiliated fury, or shame-rage, helps to clarify the role of
retroflected hostility in depression. Women's greater proneness to depression
may be a function of their greater proneness to shame.

CHAPTER 7

Psychoanalysis as Therapy Today
The Problem of Abreacting Shame and Guilt

As has become apparent in each of the preceding chapters, psychoanalysis as a model of psychotherapy invented by Freud shifted its focus away from symptom relief after catharsis of guilt and shame toward character reorganization. Today, symptom relief is not an important criterion for termination of analysis (Firestein, 1978). Intrinsic in this shift has been a change of emphasis away from unraveling the patient's states of shame and guilt over forbidden longings (as these resonated with childhood longings) toward locating the patient's psychosexual (instinctual) regression or childhood ego-impairment (as this forecast the present illness). As Freud made these shifts in emphasis he also became less enthusiastic about therapeutic success and more interested in the implications of psychoanalysis for general psychology and the social sciences. As I have suggested in previous chapters, Freud's diminution of interest in therapeutic success paralleled and may have been influenced by the relatively quick successes he achieved with the ready affects of hysterical women patients as contrasted with slow progress and fluctuating outcome of the work with the obsessional Wolf-Man, that champion representative of the affect of indifference. Whether or not there was a causal connection, Freud's own (self-fulfilling) prophecy (1926b) was that psychoanalysis would ultimately be more influential in general science than as a mode of therapy. He wrote: "The use of analysis for the treatment of neurosis is only one of its applications; the future will perhaps show that it is not the most important one" (p. 248). Moreover, Freud justified the lengthened time of analysis on the ground that it had higher aims than other therapies — and in the name of psychoanalysis as a research tool.

At the end of his career Freud had come to the view, expressed in *Analysis Terminable and Interminable* (1937), that analysis was of limited therapeutic power in the face of the intransigent instincts of the human being. Mental health achieved through analysis was only a precariously maintained balance dependent more on the kindness of fate in keeping instincts quiescent than on the new-found strength of the ego. He wrote:

> One has the impression that one ought not to be surprised if it turns out in the end that the difference between a person who has not been analysed and the behaviour of a person after he has been analysed is not so thoroughgoing as we aim it and as we expect and maintain it to be. If this is so, it would mean that analysis sometimes succeeds in eliminating the influence of an increase in instinct, but not invariably, or that the effect of analysis is limited to increasing the power of resistance of the inhibitions so that they are equal to much greater demands than before the analysis or if no analysis had taken place. I really cannot commit myself to a decision on this point, nor do I know whether a decision is possible at the present time (p. 228).

Attempting to specify the forces that work against recovery by means of psychoanalysis, Freud identified the "sense of guilt and need for punishment." Freud, however, conceptualized the sense of guilt as an unmistakable indication of the "presence of a power in mental life which we call the instinct of aggression or of destruction according to its aims, and which we trace back to the original death instinct of living matter" (p. 243).

Clearly, then, in his overview of this part of his life's work, Freud himself was not enthusiastic about psychoanalysis as a method of therapy, and he justified his disappointment by the notion that his therapeutic instrument was pitted against powerful destructive forces at work in every human being. Freud's prophecy that psychoanalysis would ultimately be better known for its contributions to the sciences than as a therapy was thus based on his own experience that the therapeutic method he developed and taught was less efficacious than it had at first appeared to be.

As I have tried to show in the preceding chapters, the decline in the efficacy of psychoanalysis as a treatment may have been the result of a shift in Freud's formulations away from the discharge of affects, specifically the affects of shame and guilt. The history of the development of Freud's thought is conventionally described as involving an increase in understanding beyond the first case of hysteria. And while in many respects this is, of course, true, there was no increase in understanding of or even familiarity with the powerful affective states of shame and guilt that were most immediately producing patients' conflicts and resulting symptoms.

I think it can be demonstrated that the proliferation of widely differing therapies — the veritable Tower of Babel of therapeutic languages — that have followed in the wake of Freud's work are in part the result of Freud's own shift in emphasis away from affective states as symptom producers, most particularly his formulation of the "forbidding" affects, shame and guilt, as structural institutions reflecting instinctual forces. The controversy that developed early within the ranks of Freud's students over what is repressed also ignored, or rather took for granted, the existence of the affective states of shame and guilt without directly addressing them as experiences. Adler (1931), for example, challenged Freud's view that repressed sexual longings are at issue in neurotic symptoms, positing instead that people are defending against unconscious "feelings of inferiority." Jung (1953) posited that more global longings for transcendence of self are at the root of neurotic symptoms. Although both these disputes were about what affects are forbidden, both schools took for granted the nature of the forbidding affects. By implication in Adler's system one is *ashamed* of feelings of inferiority and *guilty* for the aggression thereby evoked. In Jung's one is *guilty* and *ashamed* for the pursuit of mundane activities that dull one's soul. But the focus of therapy in these analytic schools is not on the affective and cognitive states of shame and guilt any more than it is in Freud's.

A central thesis in this chapter is that Freud's technique of investigation, that is, his opening up of the patient's free associations, is his most unique and lasting contribution to psychotherapy. It has influenced all succeeding psychotherapies, including even the behavioral ones since these clearly rely on at least a portion of the patient's own associative symptom context for a symptom-removal program, as well as on the atmosphere of relaxed personal acceptance that the accompanying muscular or hypnotic "relaxation" implies (see Chapter 3).

Freud's technique of free association was so revolutionary an insight because the centrality of the affective states of shame and guilt is intuitively recognizable in the stream of associations and fantasies; Freud's therapy was therefore always centered on the moral conflicts in his patients' lives. Although Freud recognized the tremendous power of the "sense of guilt" in each of us, his technique did not focus on the affective states involved and so lost its potential sharpness. So, for example, the recent work on "borderline" or "narcissistic" personalities (Kohut, 1971; Kernberg, 1975) suggesting that these patients are unable to profit from ordinary transference-analysis, may represent a failure to analyze bypassed shame in the patient–therapist in-

teraction (Lewis, 1980a). Specifically, unanalyzed shame in the patient–therapist interaction fosters the sudden development of negative
therapeutic reactions which have been reported for these patients.

As I try to find my way also among the conflicting and diverse
statements about the newer as opposed to conventional modes of
psychotherapy, the hypothesis I find most useful is that each mode of
therapy is trying to help in the abreaction of shame and guilt, just as I felt
compelled to focus on these states in my own work (Lewis, 1971). As we
shall see later on in this chapter, the concept of a focus also appears to be central in the recently developing short-term dynamic psychotherapies (for example, Malan, 1976b). A focus on self-acceptance — the "opposite" of shame
and guilt — is central, for example, to Rogerian therapy, both in its client-
centered and in its encounter-group forms. It is also central in the newer
techniques of primal scream (Janov, 1970) and emotional flooding (Olsen,
1977).

FREUD'S PAPERS ON THE TECHNIQUE OF PSYCHOANALYSIS

It is useful to review the few prescriptions for the actual technique of
psychoanalysis that Freud published (1911–1915). These were purposefully
vague as to the specific details of treatment procedure. There were a number
of reasons why Freud was purposefully vague. According to Strachey
(Freud, 1911–1915), Freud was unwilling to have patients become too
familiar with his technique lest it interfere with the spontaneity of their own
productions in treatment. An even more important reason was his awareness
of the complexity of interaction between therapists of varying personality
and patients whose personalities also varied widely. In such a complicated
interpersonal situation, formulating exact rules for what the therapist should
say is clearly a foolish undertaking. More important than any single detail of
procedure was the implied injunction to listen to the patient — with curiosity
and respect for his or her feelings.

It is this openness or acceptance implicit in Freud's technique that has
had a most profound influence on all present-day modes of therapy. Listen-
ing sensitively to the patient's unique modes of communication and provi-
sionally interpreting possible buried meanings in what is said is the art that
Freud invented and that all therapies respect even though they may disagree
about how the therapist should respond. Freud, moreover, insisted that one
could learn to do analysis best from experience, rather than from books,
likening the course of an analysis to the "noble game of chess . . . [in which]
only the openings and end-game admit of an exhaustive systematic presentation and the infinite variety of moves which develop after the opening defy
any such descriptions" (1911–1915, p. 123). Freud thus came to believe that

understanding the complexities of people's defenses against their own affects was immeasurably aided by "practicum" experience in which one undertook to investigate one's own emotional conflicts. Freud had developed psychoanalysis as a result of a painstaking self-analysis; he recommended to others that they undertake an analysis of themselves with a listener as an aid in facing painful affects and as a prophylactic against personal "blind-spots" in emotional response (Freud, 1911–1915, p. 116).

The resulting development of psychoanalytic training institutions in which didactic analysis is an essential of the required curriculum has had an enormous impact in the direction of humanizing psychiatry, specifically encouraging the notion that patient and therapist are not too different in their emotional conflicts and most particularly tending to democratize the relationship between patient and therapist. It has also had the inevitable effect of encouraging the formation of closed "guilds" and rigidifying the content of what is taught to prospective therapists as the fundamentals of their craft. The few cautious "recommendations" that Freud made — such as no note-taking, patient on the couch at least four or five times a week, paying for all sessions whether he or she attends them or not — have been reified into a set of prescriptions for correct technique of "classical" psychoanalysis. Deviations from this set of rules have been classified as something "lower-order," that is, suitable for "superficial" undertakings such as psychotherapy or for the treatment of psychotics who cannot "take" classical procedures. This reification of techniques is perpetuated through the indoctrination of psychoanalytic trainees. For example, one classically trained psychoanalyst in treatment with me found it a painful source of shame to admit that he occasionally took notes during sessions!

The principal aim of Freud's prescriptions for technique was to avoid interfering with the patient's natural flow of free associations. So, for example, in assessing the contradictory aims of research interests and of therapeutic aims, he cautioned against letting curiosity about dreams get the better of analytic sessions. He advised letting dream interpretation go unfinished if the dream could not be unraveled. He counseled against the therapist's bringing up an unfinished dream in the next session. The guiding thought in this counsel was that the therapist should "always be aware of the surface of the patient's mind at any given moment" (1911–1915, p. 92). The "rule [is] that the first thing that comes into the patient's head is the first thing to be dealt with" (p. 92). Freud was quite scornful of a "scientific" attitude that assumes the need to "write down every dream immediately" (p. 95) and to protect its text from distortion by systematic recording. For purposes of therapy, he urged allowing the patient's unconscious to take the lead in pointing to the nub of his conflicted feelings; the unconscious would make itself known through the spontaneous flow of the patient's associations.

Freud assumed that the patient's spontaneous attitude toward the therapist would be positive — a positive non-erotic transference (based on erotic needs) — and that this attitude toward the therapist involved the cure by "suggestion" common to all therapies, including his. "In analogous real situations [of affectionate and devoted dependence] people will usually say: 'I feel no shame in front of you; I can say anything to you'" (p. 105). He thus assumed that free associations would be facilitated by the "rapport" established between therapist and patient (p. 139). Although he called rapport a "transference" phenomenon, there is no question that he also meant to describe the actual present relationship between patient and therapist, rather than just remnants of past love.

> It remains the first aim of the treatment to attach him [the patient] to it and to the person of the doctor. To ensure this, nothing need be done but to give him time. If one exhibits a serious interest in him, carefully clears away the resistances that crop up at the beginning and avoids making certain mistakes, he will of himself form such an attachment and link the doctor up with one of the images of the people by whom he was accustomed to be treated with affection. It is certainly possible to forfeit this first success if from the start one takes up any standpoint other than one of sympathetic understanding, such as a moralizing one, or if one behaves like a representative of some contending party — of the other member of a married couple, for instance (pp. 139–140).

Freud also counseled against triumphantly flinging interpretations at patients: against "complacency and thoughtlessness" (p. 140). Clearly, he was describing the touchiness of patients' sources of guilt and shame — without using these terms — and counseling the therapist not to evoke them by the therapist's own behavior. How insistently these affective states are regularly evoked in spite of analytic benevolence, however, remained unnoticed.

It was from the unimpeded flow that the transference and resistance would emerge, pointing the way to the retrieval of the childhood fixations still operative in the "timeless unconscious." Since in this scheme interventions were thought to be maximally useful only if they stimulated the flow of associations, analysts were inevitably encouraged to keep silent and discouraged from offering reassurance or emotional support. Freud was emphatically against the therapist's "affording the patient a glimpse of his own mental defects . . . [in order to] enable him to put himself on an equal footing" (pp. 117–118). "The doctor should be opaque to his patients and, like a mirror, should show them nothing but what is shown to him" (p. 118).

Most particularly, Freud discouraged psychoanalysts from taking their patients' feelings toward the therapist as anything more than transferences of feelings actually meant for some significant figure in the patients' own lives. That shameful, hostile and therefore guilty feelings were being generated by the immediate therapeutic relationship was, however, a contingency with which he did not reckon. The result was that patients felt their very real feelings were being treated as trivial. It is fascinating that Freud was aware of the painfulness of this experience when it arose over erotic feelings toward the therapist. As we shall see in a moment, in the erotic version of the therapist–patient relationship he did not regard either the patient's or the therapist's feelings as unreal, even though he still regarded the patient's erotic feelings as transferences: "originally we knew only sexual objects" (p. 105).

Freud was well aware of the "emotional coldness" that was being recommended to the analyst:

> I cannot advise my colleagues too urgently to model themselves during the psychoanalytic treatment on the surgeon, who puts aside all his feelings, *even his human sympathy, and concentrates his mental forces on the single aim of performing the operation as skilfully as possible.* Under present-day conditions the feeling that is most dangerous to a psychoanalyst is the therapeutic ambition to achieve by this novel and much-disputed method something that will produce a convincing effect upon other people. This will not only put him into a state of mind which is unfavorable for his work, but will make him helpless against certain resistances of the patient, whose recovery, as we know, *primarily depends on the interplay of forces in him.* The justification for requiring this emotional coldness in the analyst is that it creates the most advantageous conditions for both parties: for the doctor a desirable protection for his own emotional life and for the patient the largest amount of help we can give him today (p. 115) (my italics).

It is significant that in this passage Freud makes an equation between putting aside human sympathy and putting aside therapeutic ambition. He seems to be implying that the latter feeling will evoke a need to be kinder (or more hostile) to the patient than is useful. Buried in this connection between the therapist's sympathy and ambition is the existential situation of emotional inequality between the two persons. That this was a trouble spot for technique that needed remedy was very early recognized by Alexander (1950), who suggested that the therapist role-play the attitudes ascribed to him by his patients. Alexander had found this technique useful and recommended it as a means of shortening the total time of analysis. Alexander and French (1946) thus early on tried to use the transference in a radical technique of brief therapy. Malan's (1976b, p. 352) account of the vituperative review accorded this work by Jones is most instructive; Jones simply distinguished their work from "real psychoanalysis," an attitude toward innovation still prevalent today among analysts.

In any case, Freud's technical recommendations, which were designed to foster the expression of the stream of consciousness, became the basis for a concept of the analyst in a state of emotional neutrality, and as a "blank screen." (It is this concept that has been widely caricatured, in the joke for example about the analyst who starts the session on time whether his patient is there or not.)

Another of Freud's counsels to the analyst was that he be as honest and truthful with his patient as the patient had obligated himself to be with the analyst. On the subject of money, for example, he spoke out against false shame in the analyst's acknowledging that he wants it. He counseled against free treatment, recounting his own experience that gratuitous treatment did not work. It complicated the transference — "in young women . . . the temptation that is inherent in their transference-relationship, and in young men their opposition to an obligation to feel grateful." Freud was aware of the social-class restrictions in accessibility to his treatment that were inherent in this prescription against free treatment. Immediately after commenting that "little can be done to remedy this" (p. 132), he suggested that perhaps the poor do not become neurotic and also suggested that they achieve secondary gain from their illness. It does not take much interpretation to suspect that Freud was in a state of guilt toward the poor, so that he denied that they suffer and then blamed them for exploiting their sufferings. It should be noted in passing that a recent study (Pope, Geller, and Wilkinson, 1975) of paying and nonpaying clients in a mental health clinic dispensing psychoanalytically oriented psychotherapy revealed no difference between the two groups of clients in any substantive indicator of progress.

Freud's adherence to strict honesty compelled him to recognize that simply interpreting erotic transference as "unreal" repetitions of the past was not the "whole truth" (p. 168). That such love is "less sensible, less concerned about consequences and more blind in its evaluation of the loved person than we are prepared to admit in the case of normal love . . . constitutes precisely what is essential about being in love" (p. 169). That a youngish analyst would have a hard time resisting the erotic feelings of his women patients was simply a fact of life from which there was no answer but to struggle against the "highly explosive forces" with which he is working both in his patients and in himself. Freud's prescription in this matter was strict and unequivocal: The analyst who has a love affair with his patient offers her only a "surrogate" and makes it harder for her to overcome her "condition [which] is such that until her repressions are removed, she is incapable of getting real satisfaction" (p. 165). That patient, it is true, will have a "great triumph . . . she would have succeeded in acting out, in repeating in real life, what she ought only to have remembered, to have produced as psychical material and to have kept within the sphere of psychical events" (p. 166). Freud is here implying that gratifying the patient's erotic feelings would offer her triumphant relief of her feelings of shame or humiliation vis-à-vis the analyst. He counsels, moreover, that the analyst be careful not to "steer away from the transference-love or to repulse it or to make it distasteful to the patient; but he must just as resolutely withhold any response to it" (p. 166). Freud is thus clearly advising the analyst not to make the patient ashamed of her erotic feelings. Yet confronted with the prospect of "bringing down on oneself the full enmity of the woman scorned" (p. 167), he appears to find this problem insoluble. It is likely that the difficulty might be mitigated if there were a full "analysis" of the affective states of shame, fury, and guilt, as these govern the patient's experience.

Perhaps the clearest indication of Freud's commitment to the rule of reason over affect comes from his warning to prospective analysts on the evils of patients' "acting out" or "repeating," as opposed to remembering, the past. It is to this problem that Freud devotes a whole paper on technique. And it is in this connection that Freud specifically evaluates as progress his shift from

> . . . Breuer's catharsis — which consisted of bringing directly into focus the moment at which the symptom was formed and . . . persistently endeavoring to reproduce the mental processes involved in that situation, in order to direct their discharge along the path of conscious activity. Remembering and abreacting, with the help of the hypnotic state, were what was at that time aimed at. Next, when hypnosis had been given up, the task became one of discovering from the patient's free associations what he failed to remember . . . The situations which had given rise to the formation of the symptoms . . . retained their place as the focus of interest; but the element of abreaction receded into the background and seemed to be replaced by the expenditure of work which the patient had to make in being obliged to overcome his criticism of his free associations, in accordance with the fundamental rule of psychoanalysis. Finally, there was evolved the consistent technique used today, in which the analyst gives up the attempt to bring a particular moment or problem into *focus* [my italics]. He contents himself with studying whatever is present for the time being on the surface of the patient's mind, and he employs the art of interpretation mainly for the purpose of recognizing the resistances which appear there, and making them conscious to the patient (p. 147).

Clearly, a focus on symptoms and the element of abreaction had receded into the background as Freud's approach to psychoanalysis changed. And it is precisely in these two areas that Freud's approach has been challenged by present-day psychotherapies, including my own focus on undischarged shame and guilt as the movers of neurotic symptom formation.

The examples that Freud cites in describing "acting out" are themselves illuminating. He writes:

> For instance, the patient does not say that he remembers that he used to be defiant and critical towards his parents' authority, instead he behaves in that way to the doctor. He does not remember how he came to a helpless and hopeless deadlock in his infantile sexual researches; but he produces a mass of confused dreams and associations, complains that he cannot succeed in anything and asserts that he is fated never to carry through what he undertakes. He does not remember having been intensely ashamed of certain sexual activities and afraid of their being found out; but he makes it clear that he is ashamed of the treatment on which he is now embarked and tries to keep it a secret from everyone (p. 150).

In these illustrations it is implied that these powerful affects are not only to be reconnected to the past from the present, but tamed in the interpretation.

Their specific connection to symptom formation is no longer a focus of the analytic work. Even more important, their evocation by the therapist–patient relationship is not understood as inevitable, so that new symptom formation within the patient–therapist relationship is to be expected as an ataraxic phenomenon.

It was Freud's emphasis on remembering rather than repeating, and on remembering instead of acting out that has given classical psychoanalysis its reputation as an overintellectual enterprise, relying too much on "insight" and too little on emotional abreaction. As I suggested earlier, Freud was working in a tradition of a hierarchical relationship of reason over emotions. Shakow and Rapaport (1964) suggest that Freud's philosophical orientation involved an "integration of intellect and affect, rather than adhering to either the Romantic Period's overemphasis on affect or to the later nineteenth century heavy emphasis on intellect alone. It was inevitable that some vestigial aspects of the Romantic Period in which he grew up remained. However, these aspects were not intrinsic" (p. 192). While such an integration is desirable in principle, Freud's shift in emphasis away from the affective states gave the emphasis to "reason."

Freud's ideas about the qualifications for becoming a psychoanalyst must also be considered as part of his statements about technique. As Strachey observes, in the paper on technique there is no mention of medical qualification as a necessity. By the time of *The Question of Lay Analysis* (1926b), Freud was emphatically of the opinion that medical training was not only not necessary, but in fact a hindrance to mastering the art. His opinion rested on the "axiomatic" assumption that "psychoanalysis is a part of psychology; not of medical psychology in the old sense, not of psychology of morbid processes, but simply of psychology" (p. 252).

With considerable bitterness Freud insisted that "doctors have no historical claim to the sole possession of analysis. On the contrary, until recently they have met it with everything possible that could damage it, from the shallowest ridicule to the gravest calumny . . . doctors form a preponderating contingent of quacks in analysis. They very frequently practise analytic treatment without having learnt it and without understanding it" (p. 230).

Freud was very specific about the reasons why medical training is a hindrance. He wrote:

> In his medical school a doctor receives training which is more or less the opposite of what he would need as a preparation for psychoanalysis. His attention has been diverted to objectively discernible facts of anatomy, physics and chemistry . . .
> His interest is not aroused in the mental side of vital phenomena; medicine is not

concerned with the study of the higher intellectual functions, which lies in the sphere of another faculty. Only psychiatry is supposed to deal with the disturbances of mental functions; but we know in what manner and with what aims it does so. It looks for the somatic determinants of mental disorders and treats them like other causes of illness (p. 230).

Freud's comments were especially directed to the American psychoanalytic movement which had taken (and maintains) the strongest stand against training nonmedical people. He warned the medical psychoanalysts that their ban was "more or less equivalent to an attempt at repression" (p. 258) and that it would solve none of the practical difficulties toward which it was presumably directed. As we shall see in a moment, the issue of medical versus nonmedical qualifications for psychoanalysts still vexes the field; the American ban on nonmedical training has undoubtedly contributed to the narrowed range of intellectual freedom among classically trained psychoanalysts in this country.

Freud's own suggested term for an analyst, whether medical or nonmedical, was "secular pastoral worker" (p. 255), a *"Seelsorger"* in his relation to the public. Freud's use of the term *"Seelsorger,"* literally "curer of souls," is a reminder of how relatively recent is the secularization of knowledge.

Our friends among the protestant clergy, and more recently among the catholic clergy as well, are often able to relieve their parishioners of the inhibitions of their daily life by confirming their faith — after having first offered them a little analytic information about the nature of their conflict. Our opponents the Adlerian "individual psychologists" endeavor to produce a similar result in people who have become unstable and inefficient by arousing their interest in the social community — after first having thrown some light upon a single corner of their mental life and shown them the part played in illness by their egoistic and distrustful impulses. Both of these procedures which derive their power from being based on analysis, have their place in psychotherapy. We who are analysts set before us as our aim the most complete and profoundest possible analysis of whoever may be our patient. We do not seek to bring him relief by bringing him into the protestant, catholic or socialist community. We seek rather to enrich him for his own internal sources by putting at the disposal of his ego those energies which, owing to repression, are inaccessibly confined to his unconscious, as well as those which his ego is obliged to squander on this fruitless task of maintaining these repressions. Such activity as this is pastoral work in the best sense of the words (p. 256).

Freud's use of the term "secular pastoral" is also an obvious allusion to the role of shame and guilt in neurotic disturbance. His attitude on the question of medical training as a hindrance to becoming a psychoanalyst was a clear result of the understanding that neurotic symptoms can be cleared by "pastoral" work, that is, by relief of shame and guilt.

CLASSICAL ANALYSIS IN THE LAST HALF-CENTURY

What has become of Freud's concept of psychoanalysis as a therapeutic technique in the fifty years since his last comments on it? The answer to this question involves the paradoxes with which this book opened. On the one hand, the opening up of people's emotional life to self-scrutiny with the expectation of self-improvement has had an enormous impact on psychiatry in the Western World. The impact has made itself felt as the central theme of the great variety of competing psychotherapeutic techniques that have come into being in the twentieth century. In contrast to this central, lasting impact of psychoanalysis, the proliferation of techniques, which differ on the question of what emotional content is to be emphasized in the opening-up and on what are to be the goals of the self-improvement, has tended to obscure the central theme of Freud's work. Freud's own dogmatic attitudes and the resulting acrimony of the debate about what emotions and what goals are best to pursue left classical psychoanalysis a heritage of timidity in pursuing new ideas. So, for example, the idea that the transference might better be analyzed in the context of the "therapeutic alliance" (Greenson, 1965) rather than the "blank screen" found expression within orthodox psychoanalysis long after it had been understood and accepted in neo-Freudian "interpersonal" psychoanalysis. Nevertheless, as suggested earlier, the narrowed range of classical psychoanalysis has been defended within its ranks by what must surely be the mechanism of "splitting": Classical psychoanalysis has placed itself at the apex of a hierarchy of therapeutic techniques. It regards the techniques suitable to the less healthy (and less wealthy) as of a lower order, because they are not classical psychoanalysis but at best "extensions" of it! One consequence is that the percentage of medical students who want to become psychoanalysts has dropped during the past ten years. And, although many medically trained psychoanalysts themselves are treating fewer patients than they used to by long-term classical methods and are using shorter-term methods instead, some of them see these trends as unjust developments reflecting attacks against a therapeutic method that is beleaguered only because it is so difficult and time-consuming to learn!

The narrowed range of intellectual freedom within medically dominated training institutes is also a heritage of the unsolved question of lay analysis. By implication, refusing to train nonmedical persons is a denial of the tenet that psychoanalysis is a branch of psychology. As one consequence, classically trained psychoanalysts, especially in this country, must receive new information, much of which comes from the field of psychology, as if it were from foreign territory. Erikson's revisions of Freud's developmental stages are still a bit suspect as to their orthodoxy. Special treatises are needed to help psychoanalysts absorb Piaget's work (Woolf, 1960). Developments such as the work on cognitive style, done by (psychoanalytically oriented) psychologists such as Klein, Witkin, and myself, are more difficult to integrate and absorb than they would be in an atmosphere in which psychoanalysis was recognized as a branch of psychology rather than of medicine.

In contrast, psychoanalytically oriented training schools for nonmedical people, whether university-based or free-standing, have suffered no decline in enrollments. Their curricula are much more wide-ranging, offering students first-hand experience with a wide variety of techniques of psychotherapy. For example, one university-based postdoctoral training center for psychologists that I know offers a prospective student three options: a Freudian, an Interpersonal–Humanistic, and a third (or Nonaligned) track of study.

Although classical psychoanalysis became the domain of the medical profession in our country, Freud's themes of emotional openness and resulting self-correction found a particularly early and sympathetic reception in the United States (Burnham, 1967). Burnham tells us that in the first two decades of this century, for example, "psychoanalysis received more attention in the United States than anywhere else in the world" (p. 46). Burnham suggests that psychoanalysis coincided with the ideals of self-improvement through self-knowledge that were traditional virtues in this country, virtues grounded in both democratic and religious traditions. He cites the fact that as early as 1907, an eminent American internist, Lewellys Barker, advocated using Freud's methods in a program for the patient's "autoperfectibility" (p. 50). Psychoanalysis also joined the strong, existing currents in American culture of progressivism and reformism, especially with respect to the conspiracy of silence about sex. Burnham remarks that "it may come as a surprise to many to learn that the profound alterations in this sphere [attitudes toward sex] which have been attributed to Freud were well under way" (p. 52) *before* his influence was felt. Burnham also documents, of course, the extent to which existing puritan attitudes toward sex hindered (and still hinder) the unprejudiced consideration of Freudian psychoanalysis. He cites Woodworth, one of this country's most eminent experimental psychologists, who honestly admitted that he "greedily devoured" case histories for the sexual gratification they gave him. Woodworth also warned that both opponents and proponents of psychoanalysis were governed by this attraction (Burnham, 1967, p. 110).

In Burnham's view, psychoanalysis was so readily absorbed into American medicine and psychiatry because Freud's teachings were watered down and not really understood. It is also possible that the essentials of Freud's message, emotional openness as a key to self-correction (or improvement), struck a responsive chord in American psychiatry, as it did everywhere it was heard.

Psychoanalysis made its influence most particularly felt in the field of psychiatric diagnosis in which, for the first time, such disorders as hysteria, phobia, obsessional neurosis, paranoia, and depression were specifically traced to emotional conflicts. One roundabout but nevertheless revealing indication of the importance of psychoanalysis in psychiatry comes from the historical study of changing patterns of diagnosis. In one study (Blum, 1978) of changing patterns in a VA hospital over the twenty-year period from 1954 to 1974 significant trends were discovered that could not be explained by shifts in patient population or actual symptomatology but involved changing modes of diagnosis. Specifically, at the start of the interval studied, 1954, a year which coincides with the peak of psychoanalytic influence, patients were diagnosed as "neurotic" significantly more often than in 1974. In contrast, the category of "affective disorder" was used significantly less often in 1954 than in 1974, and the frequency of the category "schizophrenia" also rose significantly over the same twenty-year period. As one factor accounting for these results, Blum suggests that a change in treatment emphasis from a "psychoanalytic–psychological perspective" to a "pharmacological–medical" perspective may account for his findings. The change in treatment perspective itself would be a result of the increasing availability of drug therapies. This interpretation implies, of course, that diagnostic categories are formulated pragmatically in terms of available therapeutic modes. As suggested earlier, the discovery of mood elevators for depression (affective disorders) and mood tranquilizers for schizophrenia need not be interpreted as evidence against the usefulness of Freud's discoveries but only against the lack of specificity in diagnosis that was fostered by Freud's emphasis on character reorganization as the therapeutic aim. On the contrary, the reduced use of the category of neurosis over the twenty-year interval from the 1950's to the 1970's suggests that the pinpointing of patients' affective states is, in fact, a more useful way of approaching the patients' psychiatric condition than is the more global assessment of neurosis.

PSYCHOANALYTIC REVISIONISTS: HOMOGENIZATION

What has become of the psychoanalytic revisionists with whom Freud fought so bitterly? History seems to have judged their heresies to be relatively less devastating to the fabric of psychoanalytic thinking than did Freud. The term "psychoanalyst" today can appropriately refer to institutionalized schools of Freudians, whether of the "object-relations" or "ego-psychology" variety, and to Adlerians, Jungians, Sullivanians, and Existentialists. One is reminded rather sadly of a joke that made the rounds during the Cold War: A policeman is about to wield a nightstick against a demonstrator, who shouts: "Not me, I'm an anticommunist." "I don't care what kind of a communist you are," the cop replies as he swings his stick, "you're all alike."

Bitterness today is more likely to arise between behavior therapists and psychoanalytically oriented therapists (of all persuasions), with the behaviorists often adopting the view that there is nothing to be learned from psychoanalysis. For example, one university-based predoctoral program for clinical psychologists is so committed to behaviorism that it specifically refuses permission to its students to intern in any facility that is psychodynamically oriented. Journals exclusively reporting research in behavioral modification techniques have sprung up with the same fervor that accompanied the psychoanalytic journals in the early days of this century.

The specifics of the revisionists' disagreements with Freud have been reviewed by many scholars, most recently by Dieter Wyss (1973). Wyss's analysis of the problems inherent in Freudian theory has many resemblances to my own independently developed formulations, even though Wyss's antipositivist philosophical foundations are very different from mine. Specifically, Wyss pinpoints the difficulty Freud's theory had in finding a place for the meaning of "anti-logical" or "a-logical" behavior. This seems to me to be another way of saying that Freudian theory suffered from the absence of an adequate theory of human emotions and their origin in human sociability. Although I do not agree with Wyss's premise that "the nature of life and the essence of the soul are quite simply *irrational*" (p. 515), it is clear that he believes that affects move human behavior and that Freud in his metapsychology tended to confound them with the irrational.

Wyss criticizes Freud for having an arbitrary and mechanistic concept of the separability of affect and idea. In Wyss's theoretical system, only the will is able to make such a separation, and human nature is understandable only to a "limited extent in the purposive terms appropriate to acts of will" (p. 511). Wyss's concept of the "will" is quite similar to Freud's concept of the superego as conscience. Actually Freud had observed clinically that particular affective states, namely shame and guilt, often − but not always − fostered the separation of affect and idea. To the separation of ideation and affect Freud gave the name "isolation of affect," carefully distinguishing between this defense and the total repression of ideas which leaves anxiety behind as a residue. But when Freud's theoretical formulation of the superego gradually became synonymous with guilt as a drive regulator, and his attention turned from the hysterias to obsessional neurosis and paranoia, psychoanalysis became increasingly geared to the intellectualized pursuit of unraveling or interpreting distorted cognitive content in terms of childhood fixations. The concept of neurotic symptoms as above all rooted in the affective base of forbidden longings for human relatedness was further eroded, moreover, when psychoanalysis came to regard symptoms as less significant than primary narcissism or character deficiencies. Wyss's review of Freud's followers and deviationists focuses on the need to keep the person from getting lost either to trauma or to instincts or to the unconscious or to archetypes or to introjects. As he summarizes his view, the "basic factors involved in psychotherapy, no matter what its origins, are perception and love" (p. 561). By perception Wyss means the necessity of seeing through the person; by love he refers to the therapist's attitude of loving acceptance. These two attitudes "meet in the *Gestaltkreis* which each therapist and patient pass through in the course of treatment" (p. 561). As I have suggested in each of the previous chapters, following the patient's own course of experience as he or she falls into the affective states of shame and guilt involves both perceiving and conveying the patient's dilemma and responding with acceptance of his or her need to maintain affectional bonds.

It should thus come as no surprise that the various schools of psychoanalysis have become, if anything, more homogeneous than different from each other over the past fifty years. There are remarkable uniformities today at least in the appearance of psychoanalysis (Fisher and Greenberg, 1977). These uniformities rest on a common adherence to humanistic values. This basis of agreement, while fundamental, is so broad that it can lead to a number of apparent contradictions. Psychoanalysts, for example, have differing opinions when it comes to such questions as the relation of their theory to the details of therapeutic practice, or even on the question of whether there is an explicit relation between psychoanalytic theory and therapeutic practice (Glover, 1958). At the same time, psychotherapists who regard themselves as nonanalytic but humanistic in outlook are in excellent agreement with psychoanalysts when it comes to describing the ideal therapeutic relationship (Fiedler, 1950). Analytic, client-centered, and eclectic psychotherapists are also in agreement about the characteristics of the ideal therapist (Raskin, 1965). Freud's discovery of the transference — that is, his clinical description of the fundamental affectional bonds that were governing his patients' symptoms — thus still remains a central core around which all schools of therapy operate, including even behavioral therapies, as we saw in Chapter 3. It is this basic affectional bond which is, in turn, explicitly acknowledged as the fundamental premise of humanistic values. One important study (Sloane, Staples, Whipple, and Cristol, 1977) of patients' experience in therapy found that patients in short-term dynamic psychotherapy and in behavior therapy were alike in placing a high value on insight, on the patient–therapist relationship, on catharsis and on trust. All these are staple ingredients of psychoanalytic psychotherapy rather than of behavior therapy, which officially ignores the emotional components of therapeutic success. Sloane et al. suggest that behavior-therapy patients place much more emphasis on the therapeutic relationship than do their therapists and that behavior therapists may be underutilizing a powerful, unacknowledged force in their treatment procedure.

It is worth looking in more detail at the many ways in which psychoanalysis presents a uniform appearance. In the first place, a survey of psychoanalysts, psychiatrists, clinical psychologists, and practicing social workers practicing in Chicago, Los Angeles, and New York (Henry, Sims, and Spray, 1968), found that while a strong majority of the psychoanalysts and half of the psychiatrists labeled their therapeutic orientation as "psychoanalytic," they did not differentiate as to whether it was "Adlerian," "Jungian," "Freudian," or "Bettelheim" in inspiration. Only a very small percentage of practicing psychoanalysts in this sample (5%) found it necessary to differentiate themselves as "neo-Freudian," "Ego-psychology," "Fromm," "Horney," "Transactional," or "Kleinian" in persuasion. Practicing mental health professionals who are psychoanalysts clearly regard the "school" to which they belong as less important than their major designation as psychoanalysts.

Second, Henry et al. found that the psychoanalysts in their sample were a particularly homogeneous group of people. They were predominantly Jewish by "cultural affinity," politically liberal, and came from families of East European origin. Henry (1971) interprets this finding as reflecting an affinity between psychoanalysis and Eastern European cultural tradition; specifically, an emphasis on ritual, a strong investment in intellectual functioning, and a positivist approach to human behavior. Whether or not these are the connecting links between psychoanalysis and the cultural background of its adherents, they were essential parts of Freud's own heritage.

Third, present-day analysands are a relatively homogeneous group, similar to their analysts in background and humanistic attitude (Aronson and Weintraub, 1968; Weintraub and Aronson, 1968; Kadushin, 1969). The analysands in these studies are predominantly Jewish, like their therapists, but even more significantly, analysands are themselves practitioners in the mental health field. This finding is consonant with an earlier one by Knapp, Levin, McCarter, Wermer, and Zetzel (1960) that more than half of patients applying for analysis are mental health workers themselves. Aronson and Weintraub (1968) found, moreover, that the more senior the analyst, the more likely his (or her) practice was to be taken up with analyzing colleagues. This is, of course, an outgrowth of Freud's fervent belief that analysis cannot be taught except by personal experience, and the corollary notion that the more experienced and senior therapist is the better (as well as the more prestigious) one to have (Roazen, 1974). Training of the young by the old, however, does increase the tendency to rigidify psychoanalytic thinking, as we have already noted.

Fourth, psychoanalysts saw themselves as treating their patients for either "psychoneurosis" or "character disorder," without particularly specifying any particular symptom or symptoms. The nonanalytic psychiatrists, clinical psychologists, and psychiatric social workers were also partial to these same two categories of patient designation. Their behavior is congruent with a finding by Aronson and Weintraub (1969) that the psychoanalysts in their survey thought of the majority of their patients as having "character problems," even though the majority of their patients actually had at least one specific neurotic symptom. As we saw earlier in this chapter, the trend in inpatient hospital diagnosis has been changing away from such global categories (Blum, 1978) as character problem or neurosis. Their continued use by psychoanalysts tends to reflect Freud's emphasis away from specific symptoms; the more recent change in diagnostic trends suggests that affective *symptoms* (including the symptoms involving shutdown of affect) are reasserting themselves as central in treatment.

In the light of Freud's refusal to specify more than the opening and closing moves of the process, it is not surprising that it is notoriously difficult today to pin psychoanalysts down to uniform details of their therapeutic procedures. This statement reflects evidence accumulated within the psychoanalytic movement itself (Oberndorf, Greenacre, and Kubie, 1949; Rangell, 1954). (See Fisher and Greenberg, 1977, for a review of additional evidence on this point.) Oberndorf et al. put their findings this way: "There was nothing on which they [psychoanalysts] agreed, not on the type of case best suited for analysis, nor the method of approach, nor the method of termination, nor results, nor how many patients were helped through analysis to avoid serious mental illnesses" (p. 11). This state of affairs is in sharp contrast to the rigorously specified "programs" sponsored by behavior-modification therapists, and the difference has been interpreted to mean that psychoanalysis is "unscientific" in contrast to behavior therapy. As I have tried to show, particularly in Chapter 3, behavior-modification therapists, like psychoanalysts, also still confront the difficulty of fitting their patients' emotional states — in my view, particularly their states of shame and guilt — into a theoretical framework for understanding symptoms. Psychoanalysts' difficulty in specifying their own operations may, in fact, derive precisely from the fact that their attention is not focused directly on their patients' symptoms. Another aspect of the same point is that psychoanalytic thinking is phrased in metapsychological terms that are often far removed from their patients' actual emotional states and symptoms. A focus on symptoms was, as we know, counter-indicated by Freud both on the ground that therapy for symptoms was too trivial a task and on the ground that exploration of the human personality (and evolving theory) was a more important part of the psychoanalytic endeavor.

It is instructive in this connection to read a comment made more than 25 years ago by Anna Freud (1954): "If all the skill, knowledge and pioneering effort which was spent on widening the scope of application of psychoanalysis had been employed instead on intensifying and improving our technique in the original field [hysteria, phobic, and compulsive disorders], I cannot help but feel that, by now, we would find the treatment of the common neuroses child's play, instead of struggling with their technical problems as we have continued to do" (p. 610). One can only agree with Anna Freud's guess, particularly in the light of the way our review of hysteria, phobia, compulsive disorders, paranoia, and depression insistently suggests that these disorders are connected to undischarged states of shame and guilt.

Studies of the psychoanalytic enterprise which observe psychoanalysts in action tend to show much more agreement and specificity about the process of treating patients than do studies relying on self-reports of their ideational processes. An important study by Bellak and Smith (1956), for example, tape-recorded continuous analytic sessions of two patients and offered the transcripts of sessions to independent analysts for predictions about the nature of immediately succeeding sessions. Another group of judges assessed what actually had happened in these succeeding sessions. Those analysts who had been predictors next served as judges of what had happened, while the judges took a turn at predicting. The raw data forms for this study are themselves excellent examples of the metapsychological categories within which judgments and predictions were embedded: the patients' "transference (positive and negative); acting-out; insight; working through; resistance; anxiety; aggression (extra and intra); passivity; guilt; depression; elation; oral strivings; anal strivings; phallic strivings; oedipal strivings; genital strivings; homosexuality; scoptophilia" (p. 396) were the categories of prediction and judgment. Similarly, the patients' defenses were predicted and judged: "repression; projection; regression; reversal; identification with the aggressor" (p. 396). As is readily apparent, of this entire series only four categories are directly affective, and there is no mention whatever of specific symptoms observed. Yet in spite of the fact that judgments were required to be made in metapsychological terms, there was considerable agreement among the analysts; reliability coefficients ranged from .11 to .78 with correlations more often in the middle range than at the low end. When it came to predicting the course of events, however, the success of the predictors in matching the judgments of what had happened was random. Bellak and Smith summarize their findings by pointing to the relative agreement among analysts on the structure of a case, and by suggesting also that the "basic vocabulary" of psychoanalysis is deficient. They report that their participating analysts referred "to the same thing by different names — for example, 'resistance' or 'repression'" (p. 412).

Strupp's studies of psychoanalysts in action have also revealed that they are, as a group, clearly distinguishable as to what they do, especially in comparison to a group of Rogerians. Psychoanalysts use exploratory questions, passive acceptance, passive rejection, reassurance and interpretation much more often than Rogerians, who rely heavily on the technique of reflecting feelings. Since psychoanalysts' conception of their task is so much less focused than that of other therapies, it is not surprising that studies of what they do in sessions reveal a much greater diversity of operations than in more focused therapeutic undertakings.

PSYCHOANALYSIS' THERAPEUTIC SUCCESS?

How has psychoanalysis fared as a method of therapy since Freud's day? It is hard to arrive at an answer to this question in an unprejudiced atmosphere. On the one hand, there is Freud's increasing disdain for therapeutic advantage; on the other hand there is the openly scornful attitude of behaviorists like Eysenck (1952), who cite statistics condemning psychoanalytic therapy as a total waste of time, if not actually harmful. Also obscuring the question of its actual therapeutic potency are the manifold variables that make comparative outcome studies so difficult to conduct in the first place, let alone on so global an enterprise as classical psychoanalysis. Comparing the results of a four- or five-year personal involvement in almost daily therapeutic sessions, for example, with the results of a short course in behavioral management of phobia is like comparing elephants and oranges. Nor can one readily compare even a shorter course of psychoanalysis undertaken by people seeking self-fulfillment with a "control" group that did not undertake such an enterprise. Because psychoanalysis is an undertaking which promises to release energies otherwise wastefully employed in "repression" (Freud) — or as I now phrase it, in undischarged shame and guilt (Lewis, 1971) — subjective accounts by patients of its effects on their well-being are really the only outcome measures that directly apply. When a "subjective" criterion of a patient's felt improvement is used, there is considerable evidence that psychoanalysis is effective. One argument sometimes employed against this kind of reasoning is that patients have a need to "justify" their investment in psychoanalysis and so exaggerate its positive effects. But by the same token, patients also have the retrospective need, as Freud experienced quite often, to minimize the effects of analysis upon themselves, especially if unanalyzed shame in the patient–therapist relationship is still pushing the patient to a retaliatory downgrading of the analyst and the analytic enterprise. Schjelderup (1955) has evidence that patients tend to minimize changes retrospectively. In short, a subjective criterion is flawed by its nature, but psychoanalysis is a uniquely subjective undertaking. This characteristic of it has pushed many, from its founder to Eysenck, to confound the subjectivity of experiences with a lack of "scientific" validity.

Let us look briefly at Eysenck's (1952) blast at psychoanalysis, to get some sense of the bitterness with which it has been attacked. His methodological point is itself sound: a control group of untreated patients with symptoms is needed in order to compare treatment effects with possible spontaneous remission. In order to construct such a control group Eysenck utilized figures collected by colleagues on so-called untreated patients. But one group of these patients had actually been hospitalized, which surely constitutes an attempted therapeutic intervention. The other group of patients had also actually been treated by their own physicians. There were thus in fact no untreated patients in Eysenck's control group. Moreover, Eysenck used as an indicator of improvement in his control group the frequency with which the patients withdrew their compensation insurance claims. Not only is this a dubious indicator on which to base a supposed 70% "spontaneous remission" rate, but one of Eysenck's critics (Bergin, 1971) has challenged the accuracy of the actual calculations. It has also been shown that the improvement rates as presented for the psychoanalytic side were also apparently shortchanged (Kline, 1971). For example, Eysenck assembled data from five psychoanalytic sources, totaling 706 cases, out of which 44% had been designated by their analysts as improved. But this figure counted as "failures" patients who broke off treatment before agreed-upon termination. If this category had been excluded, the success rate would have been 66%, a not inconsiderable difference. In short, Eysenck's demolition of psychoanalytic therapy on the grounds that its successes were even less frequent than "spontaneous remissions" has not withstood its critics' scrutiny, and is generally regarded as an example of antianalytic bias.

On the question of whether psychoanalysis produces results better than no treatment, Fisher and Greenberg (1977) were able to locate six studies which, in spite of varying methodological flaws, yielded a positive answer. One most impressive study (Orgel, 1958) of 15 ulcer patients found that 10 of them who completed their analyses were symptom-free at termination and remained so for from 11 to 22 years afterwards, requiring no medications or special diets. These patients had been bothered by ulcer symptoms for from 5 to 15 years before psychoanalytic treatment began. Similar positive findings on the effects of psychoanalytic treatment were obtained on patients with chronic psychogenic symptoms (Dührssen and Jorswieck, 1965) and by O'Connor, Daniels, Karush, Moses, Flood, and Stern (1964) on patients with ulcerative colitis. Improvement in the health of patients chronically afflicted with psychosomatic symptoms cannot be attributed only to their subjective need to magnify the outcome of their treatment.

One of the most significant developments since Freud's time has been the blurring of the distinction between psychoanalysis and psychoanalytically based or dynamic psychotherapy (Fisher and Greenberg, 1977). As I have tried to show in this book, this trend brings present-day psychoanalytic work closer to its origins in the brief treatment of symptoms. Probably the most famous research on the process and outcome of both these psychoanalytic techniques is the Menninger Project (Kernberg, 1972), which studied the progress of patients assigned to both these treatment modes. It is perhaps on the basis of this study, which was conducted "naturalistically" by psychoanalytically trained researchers, that the differences between psychoanalysis and long-term dynamically based psychotherapy can be said to be minimized.

Although the study was not actually designed to compare psychoanalysis and dynamic psychotherapy, the naturalistic setting involved assigning patients with higher "ego-strength" to classical analysis and those with lesser degrees of ego-strength to psychotherapy. In fact, the way the patients were selected and assigned illustrates the tendency still prevalent for people "better off" in the world to obtain psychoanalysis, while less fortunate people can afford only psychotherapy. One way in which the Menninger Project was affected was that the most suitable candidates for psychoanalysis (members of the professional community in Topeka) were systematically excluded from the research for reasons of confidentiality (Appelbaum, 1977a). There were, however, no "qualitative" differences between the two patient-groups in their overall improvement. Moreover, therapists judged to be more skillful did better than less skillful therapists in both treatment methods. If anything, therapists judged less skillful did better when the treatment mode was psychoanalysis, a finding that can be interpreted as indicating either that psychotherapy requires more skill than psychoanalysis, or that the vagueness of the psychoanalytic enterprise allows the mistakes of less skillful therapists to dissipate, or both. In any case, no clear case for the superiority of psychoanalysis over psychotherapy emerged from the long and arduous Menninger Project. In a later, final account of the findings from the Project, Appelbaum (1977a) specifically pinpoints the fact that "clinical language is typically imprecise" (p. 286). As we saw also in the Bellak and Smith (1956) study, it is Freudian metapsychology that is at least partially responsible for this imprecision, or for clinical jargon, to use a less polite term. Schafer's (1978) recent work demonstrates how psychoanalytical jargon can impede therapeutic communication. Appelbaum's (1977a) finding that psychological tests, including projective tests, were better predictors of the results of treatment than psychiatric clinical descriptions also speaks to the probability that clinical jargon is obfuscating clinical judgment.

Appelbaum reports several sources of data in the Menninger study which show substantial change occurring, even "structural" personality changes in the course of "supportive" psychotherapy. Even more important, however, was the finding that the "rich get richer" — that is, the better endowed patients benefit more from their psychoanalysis or psychotherapy. The findings also suggest that some patients needed more "loosening," that is, more access to their affects, while others needed more "tightening," or control, of their affects. This difference once again reemphasizes the importance of symptom-pictures — especially, the distinction between depression (and the hysterias) versus obsessive and paranoid symptoms.

One recent study (Goldberger, Reuben, and Silberschatz, 1975) of the outcome of psychoanalytically based psychotherapy has directly assessed the question of symptom removal. The authors discuss the dispute between the goals of "symptom removal" versus "personality-problem resolution." They write: "Since symptoms have been traditionally conceptualized as *signs* or *indicators* of emotional difficulty and not the difficulty itself, it is natural that in most psychotherapy outcome studies, change is discussed in terms of psychodynamic criteria and little attention is devoted to change in terms of symptomatic criteria" (p. 514). They argue, therefore, that the case for the effectiveness of psychodynamic psychotherapy ought not to rest on symptom removal as the criterion of change. Nevertheless, they accepted the behaviorists' challenge, and instituted a literature search for all studies of adults in which individual dynamic psychotherapy was the treatment mode and in which an expressed criterion of improvement was symptom removal or relief. The symptoms were: (1) compulsions; (2) sexual dysfunction; (3) phobias; (4) hysteria (conversion and anxiety); and (5) anxiety neurosis. Their search yielded 31 studies in which 7 studies showed below 50% improvement and 24 studies above 50% improvement. Goldberger et al. calculate that they had 803 cases in this sample, and that the improvement rate with symptom removal as criterion was 64.5%. They cite this figure as comparing favorably with the figure reported in Gelder, Marks, and Wolff's (1967) widely quoted study showing behavior therapy to be a better treatment for phobia than psychotherapy.

In the light of the open-endedness of psychotherapy, it is not surprising that "after decades of research, the amount of well-established clinically relevant knowledge about psychotherapeutic outcome remains disappointingly meagre" (Frank, 1979, p. 310). Frank summarizes the reasons for this state of affairs by pointing not only to the looseness of therapeutic-process descriptions but to the "need to produce a publishable result" rather than to pick significant variables (p. 310). Thus, massive amounts of work have been done on variables determining acceptance of therapy and attendance at sessions, and many studies have been done with the tacit assumption that dropping out of therapy indicates a failure, excluding the possibility that brief attenders could have left because they had been helped. Frank reviews four generalizations that outcome studies do allow: (1) All forms of psychotherapy are somewhat more effective than unplanned help. (2) Except for the short-term superiority of behavioral methods for phobias, compulsions, obesity, and sexual problems, "no one therapy has been shown to be overall significantly superior to any other, especially over the long term" (p. 311). (3) Whatever the form of the therapy, those patients who show initial improvement tend to maintain it. (4) More of the determinants of the success of therapy lie in the personal qualities of the patient and therapist and in their interaction than in the therapeutic method used. This last generalization seems to me to reflect the affective nature of the therapeutic enterprise, which therefore flourishes better when patient and therapist are in alliance rather than at war.

One important difficulty in interpreting outcome studies, as Frank points out, is their failure to highlight the *striking* benefits that many patients achieve with different forms of psychotherapy. He suggests that research concentrate on those instances and proposes the hypothesis that what brings a patient to psychotherapy is a "combination of specific symptoms *plus demoralization* [my italics] and that much of the improvement in all forms of psychotherapy results from the improvement in patient's morale brought about by features shared by all forms of psychotherapy" (p. 312). One can assume that these common features are the benign attitudes of empathy and warmth that have been found empirically to be important determinants of therapeutic success.

Frank's hypothesis that demoralization is what brings patients to psychotherapy is actually close to my own formulation (Lewis, 1971, 1978) that psychoanalytic psychotherapy should be focused on patients' evoked superego states of shame and guilt and on the sequences from these undischarged states into symptom formations.

SIGNIFICANT ADVANCES IN PSYCHOANALYTIC PSYCHOTHERAPY

One of the most significant advances in therapeutic technique within the psychoanalytic movement has been the development of the concept of a focused dynamic psychotherapy aimed at relatively brief interventions around the critical events that brought the patient to treatment. These focused interventions rely on a distillation of psychoanalytic fundamentals — the defenses and the transference — and the successful use of these fundamentals in brief psychotherapy is considered a "tribute to psychoanalysis, not an attack upon it" (Malan, 1976b, p. 352). The therapist who employs these focused psychoanalytic interventions must have a thoroughgoing understanding of his own defenses and transferences in order to make the most accurate and economical interventions. By implication, therefore, classical or at least long-term psychoanalysis is a technique for training therapists rather than for treating patients.

Malan (1963, 1976a,b) has documented brief dynamic psychotherapy most fully. Malan (1976b) traces the historical development of the idea of a focus in psychotherapy as an outgrowth of experience both with crisis intervention and with the pragmatic needs created by lengthening waiting lists of clinic patients seeking psychological help. He credits Michael Balint particularly for the introduction of the term "focus," citing the fact that although Balint's work is not known in many centers of psychotherapy, the literature on brief psychotherapy uses the word "focus" almost universally.

Malan generalizes the findings of his studies as indicating that the capacity for genuine recovery in certain neurotic patients is far greater than hitherto believed. He suggests also that patients in brief psychotherapy can partially work through nuclear conflicts in the transference. Most important, he suggests that "the more radical the technique in terms of transference, depth of interpretation and the link to childhood, the more radical are the therapeutic effects" (p. 353). These generalizations go counter to the view that the transference must be either avoided or "kept positive" in psychotherapy. On the contrary, Malan's findings suggest that the prognosis is best when both patient and therapist are willing to become *"deeply involved* and to bear the tension that inevitably ensues" (p. 353). In other words, it is in the patient–therapist interactions that the focused interpretations are emotionally understood and released.

My own formulations, based on a very small sample, suggest that the analysis of shame and guilt in the patient–therapist interaction is extremely helpful therapeutically (Lewis, 1971). Shame and guilt are pinpointed as the noxious affects troubling the "demoralized" patient and creating his or her focal conflict. These formulations, arrived at independently, are in clear agreement with Malan's generalizations. Specific attention to the affects of shame and guilt involves apparently trivial but actually very significant differences in the way things are put to a patient. An example from Malan's copious and instructive case material will serve to illustrate this point. Malan describes an incident early in his work with brief psychotherapy in which an ill-chosen interpretation may have contributed to a worsening of the patient's condition. Here is the incident:

> A man walked into a hospital where I was casualty officer, complaining of the fear that he might kill his wife. Questioning revealed that while he was serving abroad in the army during the war his wife had had an affair with another man and had had a child. Being inexperienced and full of enthusiasm for the power of interpretation, I said to him, 'So you have good reason to want to kill your wife.' He

made no clear response to this and went off. Two days later he came back in an ex-
alted state, demanding of everybody, 'Do you believe in the Lord?' He was clearly
psychotic and had to be admitted as an emergency (p. 252).

Malan's interpretation had sided with and probably increased the patient's
humiliated fury. It did not pick up the patient's own most *proximal* complaint: that he was *afraid* he would kill his wife. The patient was, without being aware of it, in a state of guilt for his furious thoughts. Translating "I am
afraid I will kill my wife" into "You must be feeling very guilty for your
furious thoughts" is not only accurate, but it reminds the patient of his own
good judgment. The patient's unrecognized guilt is the source of his fear of
what he might compulsively do: commit a crime and an injustice in the name
of bringing justice to his wife. It clearly rests on the humiliated fury or
shame-rage which the patient has been harboring, and simultaneously
recognizing or registering as "unjust." His psychotic symptoms can be
understood as a condensation of his scorn or ridicule of a therapist who tacitly gives him permission to kill as if he (and the therapist) were the Lord.

This incident illustrates, moreover, that interpretations are very powerful. If they are ill-chosen because they do not accurately reflect the patient's
states of shame and guilt they may do harm; by the same token, if they are
accurate they may be very relieving.

But perhaps the most encouraging trend of all in present-day psychoanalysis is the growing tendency to find links between psychoanalytic and
other therapeutic conceptions (see, for good examples, Wachtel, 1977; Appelbaum, 1979; and Shectman, 1977). Shectman's dialogue between Freud
and contemporary nonanalytic approaches is particularly noteworthy for its
acknowledgment of the unspoken competition between Freudian
psychotherapy and the newer methods and its acknowledgment that conventional psychotherapists are often quick to label the competition as
quacks (just as Freud was labeled a quack). The substantive issues included
in Shectman's dialogue include the issue of "reason" versus "emotion," with
psychoanalysis characterized as having a "long-standing love-affair with
reason" (p. 198). This characterization of psychoanalysis does, of course, fit
the trend away from the pursuit of affects that characterized Freud's later
work. It is cheering to note, however, that Shectman is willing to grant that
this emphasis may have been overdone, leaving out a great deal of the direct
experience of affect. By implication, Shectman also accepts the value of
Alexander and French's concept of the "corrective emotional experience,"
although two generations of psychoanalysts have by now been taught that
this is not a goal of psychoanalysis but only of the lesser-order therapies.
Shectman also acknowledges the value of certain forms of action as well as
insight in producing change, agreeing with Schafer (1978) that psychoanalysis is in need of a new, nonmetapsychological "action-language."

My own focus on symptom formation as the product of undischarged shame and guilt can be seen to be congruent with many of the newer, nonanalytic therapies, as well as with the development of brief, psychoanalytic therapies. As one example, both Rogers' client-centered therapy and his more recent espousal of encounter groups is based on the premise that the neurotic's self-acceptance must be fostered. Rogers (1962) described the process by which patients improved in their self-regard, as measured by the discrepancies between the self and the ideal image. He proposed the view that therapeutic progress takes place along a continuum of experiencing the self and communicating about the self, with the healthy self being able to communicate freely with others about the self. It does not seem to do much violence to Rogers' thought if we suppose that he is referring to a continuum in which guilt and shame play little or no part. The atmosphere of therapy, described as one in which the person "feels himself to be empathetically understood, accepted and received *as he is"* (p. 97) might also be described as an atmosphere which is free of shaming and blaming. The extirpation of shame and guilt, however, appears to be the goal of Rogers' continuum into health. This is, in my view, not only an impossible goal, but an undesirable one. What patients need to understand, as I view it, is the operation of their own states of shame and guilt when these are evoked, and the sequence from these undischarged states into symptom formation.

The concept of a psychiatric patient as someone who is demoralized or suffering from a sickness of the soul is very different on the surface from the concept of a patient as someone whose psychiatric symptoms were learned as a result of some faulty concatenation of contingencies and reinforcements. Neither version precludes the therapist's sympathy for the patient's distress. It was Freud who counseled "opaqueness" and "emotional coldness" in the hope that the patient would come to see how he or she demolishes the self under the influence of the sense of guilt. It is behavior therapists who supplement their learning programs with such necessary "relaxation" techniques as hypnosis or muscle relaxation — those covert invitations to Nirvana that Freud perhaps too quickly abandoned.

My own version of the psychotherapeutic process rests on basic assumptions that neither Freud nor behavior therapists accept: that human beings are social by biological nature and that shame and guilt are "givens" whose function it is to maintain the basic affectional bonds. When these bonds are threatened, shame and guilt work overtime to preserve them through the formation of primary-process neurotic symptoms at the expense of the self. It was this process of symptom formation that was first described by Freud, who offered acceptance and catharsis of specific sources of shame and guilt as the main lines of therapeutic intervention. Within these main lines there is much to be learned of exactly how ideational transformations work, and just what actual discharge of feeling is necessary for symptom relief, and to what extent the affectional bonds are silently controlling the entire process. These unsolved problems are made more difficult by the premature formation of complicated theoretical systems. These are perhaps no more than ways of expressing our professional shame that very illuminating case accounts still sound, as Freud said, more like short stories than like "scientific" documents.

Psychoanalysis, in short, has informed psychiatry beyond measure, but precisely in the parts of its documentary record that describe the affective states out of which symptoms form. One of its major functions, in my view, is as a means of training therapists — sensitizing them to the exquisite tortures that symptoms can involve, and to the myriad ways in which patients evoke their therapists' affects. Classical psychoanalysis, however, has not fulfilled its therapeutic promise. This is partly because its energies have not been directed toward the unraveling of symptoms but to other issues in psychology. These issues form the subject of Volume 2.

Bibliography

Abraham, K. (1960). Notes on the psychoanalytic investigation and treatment of manic-depressive insanity and allied conditions. In *Selected Papers on Psychoanalysis*. New York: Basic Books.

Abramson, L., and Sackeim, H. (1977). A paradox in depression: Uncontrollability and self-blame. *Psychological Bulletin, 84*, 838–857.

Abse, W. (1974). Hysterical conversions and dissociative syndromes and the hysterical character. In S. Arieti (Ed.), *American Handbook of Psychiatry* (2nd ed.). New York: Basic Books.

Ackerman, S., Hofer, M., and Weiner, H. (1978). Early maternal separation increases gastric ulcer risk by producing a latent thermoregulatory disturbance. *Science, 201*, 373–376.

Adler, A. (1931). *What Life Should Mean to You*. New York: Grosset and Dunlap.

Agras, W., Sylvester, D., and Oliveau, D. (1969). The epidemiology of common fears and phobias. *Comprehensive Psychiatry, 10*, 151–156.

Ainsworth, M. (1969). Object relations, dependency and attachment: A theoretical review of the mother–infant relationship. *Child Development, 40*, 969–1025.

Ainsworth, M. (1979). Mother–infant attachment. *American Psychologist, 34*, 932–937.

Alexander, F. (1950). *Psychosomatic Medicine*. New York: Norton.

Alexander, F., and French, T. (1946). *Psychoanalytic Therapy*. New York: Ronald.

American Psychiatric Association. (1980). *Diagnostic and Statistical Manual of Mental Disorders*, Third edition.

Andrews, J. (1966). Psychotherapy of phobias. *Psychological Bulletin, 66*, 455–480.

Appelbaum, S. (1977a). *The Anatomy of Change*. New York: Plenum Press.

Appelbaum, S. (1977b). Factors in psychoanalytic change. Paper read to meeting of *Psychologists Interested in Psychoanalysis*, San Francisco, California.

Appelbaum, S. (1979). *Out in Inner Space: A Psychoanalyst Explores the New Therapies*. New York: Anchor Press.

Arnold, M. (1960). *Emotion and Personality*, Vols. 1 and 2. New York: Columbia University Press.

Aronson, H., and Weintraub, W. (1968). Social background of the patient in classical psychoanalysis. *Journal of Nervous and Mental Disease, 146*, 91–97.

Aronson, H., and Weintraub, W. (1969). Certain initial variables as predictors of change with classical psychoanalysis. *Journal of Abnormal Psychology, 74*, 490–497.

Bach, S., and Schwartz, L. (1972). A dream of the Marquis De Sade: Psychoanalytic reflections on narcissistic trauma, decompensation and the reconstitution of a delusional self. *Journal of the American Psychoanalytic Association, 20*, 451–457.

Bandura, A. (1977). Self-efficacy: Toward a unifying theory of behavioral change. *Psychological Review, 84*, 191–215.

Bandura, A., Blanchard, E., and Ritter, B. (1969). The relative efficacy of desensitization and modelling approaches for inducing behavioral affective and attitudinal changes. *Journal of Personality and Social Psychology, 13*, 173–199.

Barchas, J., Akil, H., and Elliott, G. (1978). Behavioral neurochemistry: Neuroregulators and behavioral states. *Science, 200*, 964–973.

Bart, P. (1968). Social structure and vocabularies of discomfort. *Journal of Health and Social Behavior, 9*, 188–193.

Bart, P. (1971). Depression in middle-aged women. In V. Gornick and B. Moran (Eds.), *Woman in Sexist Society*. New York: New American Library.

Baumeyer, F. (1956). The Schreber case. *International Journal of Psychoanalysis, 37*, 61–74.

Beach, F. (Ed.) (1965). *Sex and Behavior*. New York: Wiley.

Beck, A. (1976). *Depression: Clinical, Experimental and Theoretical Aspects*. New York: Harper and Row.

Beech, H., and Perigault, J. (1974). Toward a theory of obsessional disorder. In H. Beech (Ed.), *Obsessional States*. London: Methuen.

Bellak, L., and Smith, M. (1956). An experimental investigation of the psychoanalytic process. *Psychoanalytic Quarterly, 25*, 385–415.

Benedek, T. (1938). Adaptation to reality in early infancy. *Psychoanalytic Quarterly, 7*, 200–215.

Bergin, A. (1971). The evaluation of therapeutic outcomes. In A. Bergin and S. Garfield (Eds.), *Handbook of Psychotherapy and Behavior Change*, New York: Wiley.

Berlin, I. (1956). *The Age of Enlightenment*. New York: New American Library.

Bertini, M., Lewis, H., and Witkin, H. (1964). Some preliminary observations with an experimental procedure for the study of hypnagogic and related phenomena. *Archivio di Psychologica, Neurologica e Psychiatria, 6*, 493–534.

Bibring, E. (1953). The mechanism of depression. In P. Greenacre (Ed.), *Affective Disorders: Psychoanalytic Contributions to Their Study*. New York: International Universities Press.

Bieber, I., Dain, H., Dince, P., Drellich, M., Grand, H., Gundlach, R., Kramer, M., Rifkin, A., Wilbur, C., and Bieber, T. (1962). *Homosexuality: A Psychoanalytic Study of Male Homosexuals*. New York: Basic Books.

Binswanger, L. (1958). The case of Ellen West. In R. May, E. Angel, and H. Ellenberger (Eds.), *Existence: A New Dimension in Psychiatry and Psychology*, New York: Basic Books.

Black, A. (1974). The natural history of obsessional neurosis. In H. Beech (Ed.), *Obsessional States*. London: Methuen.

Blatt, S. (1974). Levels of object representation in anaclitic and introjective depression. *Psychoanalytic Study of the Child, 29*, 107–157.

Blatt, S., D'Afflitti, J., and Quinlan, D. (1976). Experiences of depression in normal young adults. *Journal of Abnormal Psychology, 85*, 383–389.

Blum, J. (1978). On changing psychiatric diagnosis over time. *American Psychologist, 33*, 1017–1031.

Bornstein, B. (1935). Phobia in a two-and-a-half year old child. *Psychoanalytic Quarterly, 4*, 93–119.

Bornstein, B. (1949). The analysis of a phobic child. *Psychoanalytic Study of the Child, 3/4*, 181–226.

Bowlby, J. (1960). Grief and mourning in infancy and early childhood. *Psychoanalytic Study of the Child, 15,* 9-22.

Bowlby, J. (1963). Pathological mourning and childhood mourning. *Journal of the American Psychological Association, 11,* 500-542.

Bowlby, J. (1969). *Attachment and Loss,* Vol. I. New York: Basic Books.

Bowlby, J. (1973). *Attachment and Loss,* Vol. II. New York: Basic Books.

Bradford, J. (1968). Sex differences in anxiety. *Dissertation Abstracts, 29,* 1167.

Brantigan, C. (1979). Quoted in *The New York Times,* November 20, 1979.

Brenman, M., and Gill, M. (1947). *Hypnotherapy.* New York: Wiley.

Breuer, J., and Freud, S. (1893-1895). Studies on hysteria. In J. Strachey (Ed.), *Standard Edition of the Complete Psychological Works of Sigmund Freud,* Vol. 2. London: Hogarth Press.

Burnham, J. (1967). *Psychoanalysis and American Medicine, 1894-1918. Psychological Issues, 5,* Monograph 20.

Cannon, W. (1932). *The Wisdom of the Body.* New York: Norton.

Cannon, W. (1942). Voodoo death. *American Anthropologist, 44,* 168-181.

Chassaguet-Smirgel, J. (1979). Transsexuality, paranoia and the repudiation of femininity. In M. Nelson and J. Ikenberry (Eds.), *Psychosexual Imperatives.* New York: Human Sciences Press.

Chesler, P. (1972). *Women and Madness.* New York: Doubleday.

Chevron, E., Quinlan, D., and Blatt, S. (1978). Sex roles and gender difference in the experience of depression. *Journal of Abnormal Psychology, 87,* 680-683.

Cohen, M., Baker, G., Cohen, R., Fromm-Reichmann, F., and Weigert, E. (1954). An intensive study of manic-depressive psychosis. *Psychiatry, 17,* 103-137.

Cohen, Y. (Ed.), (1961). *Social Structure and Personality.* New York: Holt, Rinehart and Winston.

Cohen, Y. (1978). The disappearance of the incest taboo. *Human Nature, 1,* 72-78.

Cohn, N. (1975). *Europe's Inner Demons.* New York: Basic Books.

Colby, K. (1975). *Artificial Paranoia: A Computer Simulation of Paranoid Processes.* New York: Pergamon Press.

Colby, K. (1977). Appraisal of four psychological theories of paranoid phenomena. *Journal of Abnormal Psychology, 86,* 54-59.

Condon, W., and Sander, L. (1974). Neonate movement is synchronized with adult speech. *Science, 183,* 99-101.

Costello, C. (1978). A critical review of experiments on learned helplessness and depression in humans. *Journal of Abnormal Psychology, 87,* 21-32.

Crouppen, G. (1977). Field dependence-independence in depressed and normal males, as an indication of relative proneness to shame or guilt and ego functioning. *Dissertation Abstracts, 37,* 4669.

Crowne, D., and Marlowe, D. (Eds.) (1964). *The Approval Motive.* New York: Wiley.

Dahl, H. (1979). The appetite hypothesis of emotions: A new psychoanalytic model of motivation. In C. Izard (Ed.), *Emotions in Personality and Psychopathology,* New York: Plenum Press.

Darwin, C. (1872). *The Expression of the Emotions in Man and Animals.* London: John Murray.

Deutsch, F. (1975). A footnote to Freud's "Fragment of an analysis of a case of hysteria." *Psychoanalytic Quarterly, 26,* 159-167.

Deutsch, F., and Murphy, W. (1955). *The Clinical Interview,* Vol. 2. New York: International Universities Press.

Dohrenwend, B., and Dohrenwend, B. (1969). *Social Status and Psychological Disorder: A Causal Inquiry.* New York: Wiley.

Dührssen, A. (1951). Zur Frage der Häufigkeit zwangsneurotischer und hysterischer Strukturen bei Männern und Frauen. *Zeitschrift für Medizinische Psychologie, 1,* 247-253.

Dührssen, A., and Jorswieck, E. (1965). Eine empirisch-statistische Untersuchung zur Leistungs-fähigkeit psychoanalytischer Behandlung. *Nervenarzt, 36,* 166–169.

Easser, B., and Lesser, S. (1965). Hysterical personality. *Psychoanalytic Quarterly, 34,* 390–395.

Edel, M., and Edel, A. (1968). *Anthropology and Ethics* (Revised edition). Cleveland: Western Reserve University Press.

Eissler, K. (1963). Notes on the psychoanalytic concept of cure. *Psychoanalytic Study of the Child, 23,* 424–463.

Engel, G. (1961). Is grief a disease? *Psychosomatic Medicine, 28,* 18–22.

Engel, G. (1977). The need for a new medical model: A challenge for biomedicine. *Science, 196,* 129–136.

Eysenck, H. (1952). The effects of psychotherapy: An evaluation. *Journal of Consulting Psychology, 16,* 319–324.

Eysenck, H., and Rachman, S. (1965). *The Causes and Cure of Neurosis.* London: Routledge and Kegan Paul.

Faris, R., and Dunham, H. (1939). *Mental Disorder in Urban Areas.* Chicago: University of Chicago Press.

Fenichel, O. (1945). *The Psychoanalytic Theory of Neurosis.* New York: Norton.

Fiedler, F. (1950). The concept of an ideal therapeutic relationship. *Journal of Consulting Psychology, 14,* 239–245.

Firestein, S. (1978). *Termination in Psychoanalysis.* New York: International Universities Press.

Fisher, S., and Greenberg, R. (1977). *The Scientific Credibility of Freud's Theories and Therapy.* New York: Basic Books.

Fliegel, Z. (1979). Depressive phenomena. In L. Saretsky, G. Goldman, and D. Milman (Eds.), *Integrating Ego Psychology and Object-Relations Theory.* Dubuque, Iowa: Kendall Hunt.

Ford, C., and Beach, F. (1951). *Patterns of Sexual Behavior.* New York: Harper, 1951.

Frank, J. (1979). The present status of outcome studies. *Journal of Consulting and Clinical Psychology, 47,* 310–316.

Freud, A. (1946). *The Ego and the Mechanisms of Defence.* New York: International Universities Press.

Freud, A. (1953). Some remarks on infant observation. *Psychoanalytic Study of the Child, 8,* 9–19.

Freud, A. (1954). The widening scope of indications for psychoanalysis. Discussion. *Journal of the American Psychoanalytic Association, 2,* 607–620.

Freud, S.* (1892). A case of successful treatment by hypnosis. In J. Strachey (Ed.), *Standard Edition of the Complete Psychological Works of Sigmund Freud,* Vol. 1. London: Hogarth Press.

Freud, S. (1893). Charcot. *Standard Edition,* Vol. 3

Freud, S. (1894). The neuro-psychoses of defence. *Standard Edition,* Vol. 3.

Freud, S. (1895). Obsessions and phobias. *Standard Edition,* Vol. 3.

Freud, S. (1896). Further remarks on the neuro-psychoses of defence. *Standard Edition,* Vol. 3.

Freud, S. (1901). The psychopathology of everyday life. *Standard Edition,* Vol. 6.

Freud, S. (1905a). Three essays on the theory of sexuality. *Standard Edition,* Vol. 7.

Freud, S. (1905b). Jokes and their relation to the unconscious. *Standard Edition,* Vol. 8.

Freud, S. (1905c). Fragment of an analysis of a case of hysteria. *Standard Edition,* Vol. 7.

Freud, S. (1909a). Analysis of a phobia in a five-year-old boy. *Standard Edition,* Vol. 10.

Freud, S. (1909b). Notes upon a case of obsessional neurosis. *Standard Edition,* Vol. 10.

Freud, S. (1910). The future prospects of psychoanalytic therapy. *Standard Edition,* Vol. 11.

Freud, S. (1911). Psychoanalytic notes on an autobiographical case of paranoia (dementia paranoides). *Standard Edition,* Vol. 12.

*All Freud 1892–1950 references are to the *Standard Edition,* cited here.

Freud, S. (1911–1915). Papers on technique. *Standard Edition,* Vol. 12.

Freud, S. (1913a). Totem and taboo. *Standard Edition,* Vol. 13.

Freud, S. (1913b). The disposition to obsessional neurosis. *Standard Edition,* Vol. 12.

Freud, S. (1914). On narcissism: An introduction. *Standard Edition,* Vol. 14.

Freud, S. (1915). A case of paranoia running counter to psycho-analytic theory of the disease. *Standard Edition,* Vol. 14.

Freud, S. (1916–1917). Introductory lectures on psychoanalysis. (Part III). *Standard Edition,* Vol. 16.

Freud, S. (1917). Mourning and melancholia. *Standard Edition,* Vol. 14.

Freud, S. (1918). From the history of an infantile neurosis. *Standard Edition,* Vol. 17.

Freud, S. (1919). A child is being beaten. *Standard Edition,* Vol. 17.

Freud, S. (1920a). Beyond the pleasure-principle. *Standard Edition,* Vol. 18.

Freud, S. (1920b). The psychogenesis of a case of homosexuality in a woman. *Standard Edition,* Vol. 18.

Freud, S. (1921). Group psychology and the analysis of the ego. *Standard Edition,* Vol. 18.

Freud, S. (1922). Some neurotic mechanisms in jealousy, paranoia and homosexuality. *Standard Edition,* Vol. 18.

Freud, S. (1923a). The ego and the id. *Standard Edition,* Vol. 19.

Freud, S. (1923b). A seventeenth century demonological neurosis. *Standard Edition,* Vol. 19.

Freud, S. (1925). An autobiographical study. *Standard Edition,* Vol. 20.

Freud, S. (1926a). Inhibitions, symptoms and anxiety. *Standard Edition,* Vol. 20.

Freud, S. (1926b). The question of lay analysis. *Standard Edition,* Vol. 20.

Freud, S. (1937). Analysis terminable and interminable. *Standard Edition,* Vol. 23.

Freud, S. (1940). An outline of psychoanalysis. *Standard Edition,* Vol. 23.

Freud, S. (1950[1895]), Project for a scientific psychology. *Standard Edition,* Vol. 1.

Freud, S. (1954). The origins of psychoanalysis: Letters to Wilhelm Fliess 1887–1902. New York: Basic Books.

Friedman, M., and Rosenman, R. (1974). *Type A Behavior and Your Heart.* New York: Fawcett.

Fromm, E. (1943). Sex and character. *Psychiatry, 6,* 21–31.

Fromm, E. (1947). Psychoanalytic characterology and its application to the understanding of culture. In S. Sargent and M. Smith (Eds.), *Culture and Personality.* New York: Viking Fund.

Fromm, E. (1951). *The Forgotten Language.* New York: Grove Press.

Fromm, E. (1955). *The Sane Society.* New York: Rinehart.

Fromm-Reichmann, F. (1959). *Personality and Psychotherapy.* Selected papers edited by D. M. Bullard. Chicago: University of Chicago Press.

Garai, J. (1970). Sex differences in mental health. *Genetic Psychology Monographs, 81,* 123–143.

Gardiner, M. (1964). The Wolf Man grows older. *Journal of the American Psychoanalytic Association, 12,* 80–93.

Gebhard, P., Gagnon, J., Pomeroy, W., and Christiansen, C. (1965). *Sex Offenders: An Analysis of Types.* New York: Harper.

Gelder, M., Marks, I., and Wolff, H. (1967). Desensitization and psychotherapy in the treatment of phobic states: A controlled inquiry. *British Journal of Psychiatry, 113,* 53–73.

Gibson, R. (1967). On the psychology of depression. *Psychoanalytic Quarterly Supplement,* 99–109.

Gide, A. (1950). *Corydon.* New York: Farrar, Straus and Cudahy.

Gleser, G., and Ihilevich, D. (1969). An objective assessment for measuring defense mechanisms. *Journal of Consulting and Clinical Psychology, 33,* 51–60.

Glover, E. (1939). *Psychoanalysis.* London: Staples Press.

Glover, E. (1958). *The Technique of Psycho-analysis.* New York: International Universities Press.

Goldberger, L., Reuben, R., and Silberschatz, G. (1975). Symptom removal in psychotherapy. In T. Shapiro (Ed.), *Psychoanalysis and Contemporary Science,* Vol. 5, pp. 513–536. New York: International Universities Press.

Grace, W., and Graham, D. (1952). Relationship of specific attitudes and emotions to certain bodily diseases. *Psychosomatic Medicine, 14,* 243–252.

Graham, D., Stern, J., and Winokur, G. (1958). Experimental investigation of the specificity of attitude hypothesis in psychosomatic disease. *Psychosomatic Medicine, 20,* 446–457.

Green, R. (1973). *Sexual Identity Conflict in Children and Adults.* New York: Basic Books.

Greenson, R. (1965). The working alliance and the transference neurosis. *Psychoanalytic Quarterly, 34,* 155–181.

Halpern, J. (1977). Projection: A test of the psychoanalytic hypothesis. *Journal of Abnormal Psychology, 86,* 536–542.

Harlow, H. (1962). The heterosexual affectional system in monkeys. *American Psychologist, 17,* 1–9.

Harlow, H., Harlow, M., and Hansen, E. (1963). The maternal affection system of rhesus monkeys. In H. Rheingold (Ed.), *Maternal Behavior in Mammals.* New York: Wiley.

Harlow, H., and Mears, C. (1979). *The Human Model: Primate Perspectives.* New York: Wiley.

Hartmann, H. (1950). Comments on the psychoanalytic theory of the ego. *Psychoanalytic Study of the Child, 5,* 74–96.

Hartmann, H. (1951). Ego psychology and the problem of adaptation. In D. Rapaport (Ed.), *Organization and Pathology of Thought.* New York: Columbia University Press.

Heider, F. (1958). *The Psychology of Interpersonal Relationships.* New York: Wiley.

Heinecke, C. (1973). Parental deprivation in early childhood. In J. Scott and E. Senay (Eds.), *Separation and Depression,* Washington, D.C.: American Association for the Advancement of Science.

Henry, W. (1971). *The Fifth Profession (Becoming a Psychotherapist).* San Francisco: Jossey-Bass.

Henry, W., Sims, J., and Spray, S. (1968). Mental health professionals in Chicago. In J. Schlien (Ed.), *Research in Psychotherapy,* Vol. 3., Washington, D.C.: American Psychological Association.

Herman, J., and Hirschman, L. (1977). Father–daughter incest. *Signs: Journal of Women in Culture and Society, 2,* 735–756.

Hollingshead, A., and Redlich, F. (1958). *Social Class and Mental Illness.* New York: Wiley.

Holmes, D. (1968). Dimensions of projection. *Psychological Bulletin, 69,* 248–268.

Holt, R. (1972). Freud's mechanistic and humanistic images of man. In R. Holt and E. Peterfreund (Eds.), *Psychoanalysis and Contemporary Science.* New York: Macmillan.

Horney, K. (1926). The flight from womanhood. *International Journal of Psychoanalysis, 7,* 324–329.

Horney, K. (1932). The dread of women. *International Journal of Psychoanalysis, 13,* 348–360.

Izard, C. (1971). *The Face of Emotion.* New York: Appleton, Century, Crofts.

Izard, C. (1972). *Patterns of Emotion: A New Analysis of Anxiety and Depression.* New York: Academic Press.

Izard, C. (1977). *Human Emotions.* New York: Plenum Press.

Jacobson, E. (1938). *Progressive Relaxation.* Chicago: University of Chicago Press.

Jacobson, E. (1954). The self and the object world. *Psychoanalytic Study of the Child, 9,* 75–127.

Jacobson, E. (1971). *Depression: Comparative studies of normal, neurotic and psychotic conditions.* New York: International Universities Press.

Janov, A. (1970). *The Primal Scream.* New York: Putnam.

Johnson, D. (1980). Cognitive organization in paranoid and non-paranoid schizophrenics. Unpublished dissertation, Yale University.

Jones, E. (1954). *The Life and Works of Sigmund Freud.* New York: Basic Books.

Jones, M. (1960). A laboratory study of fear: The case of Peter. In H. Eysenck (Ed.), *Behavior Therapy and the Neuroses*. New York: Pergamon Press.

Joseph, E. (Ed.) (1965). *Beating Fantasies*. Monograph #1, Kris Study Group. New York: International Universities Press.

Jung, C. (1953). *Three Essays on Analytic Psychology*. Princeton, N.J.: Princeton University Press.

Kadushin, C. (1969). *Why People Go to Psychiatrists*. New York: Atherton.

Kamil, L. (1970). Psychodynamic changes through systematic desensitization. *Journal of Abnormal Psychology, 76*, 199–206.

Kardiner, A. (1977). Quoted in *The New York Times*, May 7, 1977.

Kaufman, I. (1973). Mother–infant separation in monkeys: An experimental model. In J. Scott and E. Senay (Eds.), *Separation and Depression*. Washington, D.C.: American Association for the Advancement of Science.

Kelley, H. (1971). *Attribution in Social Interaction*. New York: General Learning Press.

Kernberg, O. (1975). *Borderline Conditions and Pathological Narcissism*. New York: Jason Aronson.

Kernberg, O., Burstein, E., Coyne, L., Appelbaum, S., Horwitz, L., and Voth, H. (1972). Psychotherapy and psychoanalysis: Final report of the Menninger Foundation's psychotherapy research project. *Bulletin of the Menninger Clinic, 36*, 1–278.

Kinsey, A., Pomeroy, W., and Martin, C. (1948). *Sexual Behavior in the Human Male*. Philadelphia: Saunders.

Kinsey, A., Pomeroy, W., Martin, C., and Gebhard, P. (1953). *Sexual Behavior in the Human Female*. Philadelphia: Saunders.

Klaf, F., and Davis, C. (1960). Homosexuality and paranoid schizophrenia: A survey of 150 cases and controls. *American Journal of Psychiatry, 116*, 1070–1075.

Klein, G. (1970). *Perception, Motives and Personality*. New York: Knopf.

Klein, H., and Horwitz, W. (1949). Psychosexual factors in the paranoid phenomena. *American Journal of Psychiatry, 105*, 697–701.

Klein, M. (1957). *Envy and Gratitude*. London: Tavistock Publications.

Kline, P. (1971). *Fact and Fantasy in Freudian Theory*. London: Methuen.

Knapp, P., Levin, S., McCarter, R., Wermer, H., and Zetzel, E. (1960). Suitability for psychoanalysis: A review of 100 supervised analytic cases. *Psychoanalytic Quarterly, 29*, 459–477.

Knight, R. (1940). The relationship of latent homosexuality to the mechanism of paranoid delusions. *Bulletin of the Menninger Clinic, 4*, 149–159.

Knight, R., Roff, J., Barnett, J., and Moss, J. (1979). Concurrent and predictive validity of thought disorder and affectivity: A 22-year follow-up of acute schizophrenics. *Journal of Abnormal Psychology, 88*, 1–13.

Kohlberg, L. (1966). A cognitive–developmental analysis of children's sex-role concepts and attitudes. In E. Maccoby (Ed.), *The Development of Sex Differences*. Stanford: Stanford University Press.

Kohut, H. (1971). *The Analysis of the Self*. New York: International Universities Press.

Kubie, L. (1943). The use of induced hypnagogic reveries in the recovery of repressed amnesic data. *Bulletin of the Menninger Clinic, 1*, 172–182.

La Barre, W. (1954). *The Human Animal*. Chicago: University of Chicago Press.

Lacan, J. (1968). *The Language of the Self*. New York: Delta Books.

Lang, P., and Lazovik, A. (1963). The experimental desensitization of a phobia. *Journal of Abnormal and Social Psychology, 66*, 519–525.

Lang, P., Lazovik, A., and Reynolds, D. (1965). Desensitization, suggestibility and pseudotherapy. *Journal of Abnormal and Social Psychology, 70*, 395–402.

Larson, L., and Knapp, R. (1964). Sex differences in symbolic conceptions of the deity. *Journal of Projective Techniques and Personality Assessment, 28*, 303–306.

Lawlis, G. (1971). Response styles of a patient population on the fear survey schedule. *Behavioral Research and Therapy, 9,* 95–102.

Lazarus, A. (1973). "Hypnosis" as a facilitator in behavior therapy. *International Journal of Clinical and Experimental Hypnosis, 21,* 25–31.

Leeper, R. (1968[1948]). A motivational theory of emotion to replace 'emotion as disorganized response.' In M. Arnold (Ed.), *The Nature of Emotion.* Middlesex, England: Penguin Books.

Levenson, M., and Neuringer, C. (1974). Suicide and field dependency. *Omega, 5,* 181–186.

Levi-Strauss, C. (1968). *The Savage Mind.* Chicago: University of Chicago Press.

Levi-Strauss, C. (1976). *Tristes Tropiques.* New York: Penguin Books.

Levy, R., and Rowitz, R. (1973). *The Ecology of Mental Disorders.* New York: Behavioral Publications.

Lewis, H. (1958). Over-differentiation and under-individuation of the self. *Psychoanalysis and the Psychoanalytic Review, 45,* 3–24.

Lewis, H. (1971). *Shame and Guilt in Neurosis.* New York: International Universities Press.

Lewis, H. (1976). *Psychic War in Men and Women.* New York: New York University Press.

Lewis, H. (1978). Sex differences in superego mode as related to sex differences in psychiatric illness. *Social Science and Medicine, 12,* 1999–205.

Lewis, H. (1979a). Guilt in obsession and paranoia. In C. Izard (Ed.), *Emotions in Psychopathology and Personality.* New York: Plenum Press.

Lewis, H. (1979b). Shame in depression and hysteria. In C. Izard (Ed.), *Emotions in Psychopathology and Personality.* New York: Plenum Press.

Lewis, H. (1980a). "Narcissistic personality" or "shame-prone" superego mode? *Comprehensive Psychotherapy, 1,*59–80.

Lewis, H. (1980b). *Shame and Guilt in Human Nature.* New York: International Universities Press, in press.

Lynn, D. (1962). Sex role and parental identification. *Child Development, 33,* 555–564.

MacAlpine, I., and Hunter, R. (1955). *Daniel Paul Schreber — Memoirs of My Nervous Illness.* Cambridge, Mass.: Robert Bentley.

Maccoby, E. (Ed.) (1966). *The Development of Sex Differences.* Stanford: Stanford University Press.

Maccoby, E., and Jacklin, E. (1974). *The Psychology of Sex Differences.* Stanford: Stanford University Press.

Madison, P. (1961). *Freud's Concept of Repression and Defense.* Minneapolis: University of Minnesota Press.

Mahler, M. (1968). *On Human Symbiosis and the Vicissitudes of Individuation.* New York: International Universities Press.

Malan, D. (1963). *A Study of Brief Psychotherapy.* Springfield, Illinois: C C Thomas. [Reprinted by Plenum Press, New York, 1976.]

Malan, D. (1976a). *Toward the Validation of Dynamic Psychotherapy.* New York: Plenum Press.

Malan, D. (1976b). *The Frontier of Brief Psychotherapy.* New York: Plenum Press.

Malzberg, B. (1940). *Social and Biological Aspects of Mental Disease.* Utica, N.Y.: State Hospital Press.

Mannoni, O. (1971). *Freud.* New York: Pantheon Books.

Marks, I. (1969). *Fears and Phobias.* New York: Academic Press.

Marmor, J. (1953). Orality in the hysterical personality. *Journal of the American Psychoanalytic Association, 1,* 656–671.

McKinney, W., Suomi, S., and Harlow, H. (1973). New models of separation and depression in rhesus monkeys. In J. Scott and E. Senay (Eds.), *Separation and Depression.* Washington, D.C.: American Association for the Advancement of Science.

Mead, M. (1949). *Male and Female*. New York: Morrow.

Meltzoff, A., and Moore, W. (1977). Imitation of facial and non-facial gestures. *Science, 198,* 75–78.

Mendel, J., and Klein, D. (1969). Anxiety attacks with subsequent agoraphobia. *Comprehensive Psychiatry, 10,* 190–195.

Mendelson, M. (1974). *Psychoanalytic Concepts of Depression*. New York: Spectrum.

Meyer, V., Levy, R., and Schnurer, A. (1974). The behavioural treatment of obsessive–compulsive disorders. In H. Beech (Ed.), *Obsessional States*. London: Methuen.

Money, J., and Ehrhardt, A. (1972). *Man and Woman, Boy and Girl*. Baltimore: Johns Hopkins Press.

Morris, D. (1971). *Intimate Behavior*. New York: Random House.

Moss, H. (1974). Early sex differences and the mother–infant interaction. In R. Friedman, R. Reichert, and R. Vande Weile (Eds.), *Sex Differences in Behavior*. New York: Wiley.

Murphy, H. (1978). The advent of guilt feelings as a common depressive symptom: A historical comparison of two continents. *Psychiatry, 41,* 229–242.

Murphy, H., Wittkower, E., and Chance, H. (1964). Cross-cultural inquiry into the symptomatology of depression. *Transcultural Psychiatry Research Review, 1,* 5–18.

Nagera, H. (1976). *Obsessional Neurosis: Developmental Psychopathology*. New York: Jason Aronson.

Niederland, W. (1958). Early auditory experiences, beating fantasies and the primal scene. *Psychoanalytic Study of the Child, 13,* 471–504.

Niederland, W. (1959a). Schreber: Father and son. *Psychoanalytic Quarterly, 28,* 151–170.

Niederland, W. (1959b). The "miracled-up" world of Schreber's childhood. *Psychoanalytic Study of the Child, 14,* 383–413.

Niederland, W. (1960). Schreber's father. *Journal of the American Psychoanalytic Association, 8,* 492–500.

Oberndorf, C., Greenacre, P., and Kubie, L. (1949). Symposium on the evaluation of therapeutic results. *Yearbook of Psychoanalysis, 5,* 9–34.

O'Brien, B. (1958). *Operator and Things*. New York: Ace Books.

O'Connor, J., Daniels, G., Karush, A., Moses, L., Flood, C., and Stern, L. (1964). The effects of psychotherapy on a course of ulcerative colitis: A preliminary report. *American Journal of Psychiatry, 20,* 738–742.

Olsen, P. (Ed.) (1977). *Emotional Flooding*. New York: Penguin Books.

Orgel, S. (1958). Effects of psychoanalysis on the course of peptic ulcer. *Psychosomatic Medicine, 20,* 117–123.

Parsons, T. (1958). Social structure and the development of personality: Freud's contribution to the integration of psychology and sociology. *Psychiatry, 21,* 321–340.

Paul, G. (1966). *Insight versus Desensitization in Psychotherapy*. Stanford: Stanford University Press.

Paulhan, J. (1966). The Marquis de Sade and his accomplice. In R. Seaver and A. Wainhouse (Eds.), *The Marquis De Sade*. New York: Grove Press.

Pollock, G. (1973). Bertha Pappenheim: Addenda to her case history. *Journal of the American Psychoanalytic Association, 21,* 328–332.

Pomeroy, W. (1972). *Dr. Kinsey and the Institute for Sex Research*. New York: Harper.

Pope, K., Geller, J., and Wilkinson, L. (1975). Fee assessment and outpatient psychotherapy. *Journal of Consulting and Clinical Psychology, 43,* 835–841.

Puner, H. (1947). *Freud: His Life and Mind*. New York: Howell, Soskin. [Reprinted by Charter Books, 1978.]

Rachman, S. (1967). Systematic desensitization. *Psychological Bulletin, 67,* 93–104.

Rachman, S. (1978). *Fear and Courage*. San Francisco: Freeman.

Rangell, L. (1954). Similarities and differences between psychoanalysis and dynamic psychotherapy. *Journal of the American Psychoanalytic Association, 2,* 734–744.

Rapaport, D. (1967[1959]). Edward Bibring's theory of depression. In M. Gill (Ed.), *The Collected Papers of David Rapaport.* New York: Basic Books.

Rapaport, D. (1968). The psychoanalytic theory of emotions. In M. Arnold (Ed.), *The Nature of Emotion.* London: Penguin Books.

Raskin, N. (1965). The psychotherapy research project of the American Academy of Psychotherapists. *Proceedings of the 73rd Annual Convention of the American Psychological Association,* 253–254.

Rheingold, H. (1969). The social and socializing infant. In D. Goslin (Ed.), *Handbook of Socialization Theory and Research.* Chicago: Rand McNally.

Ricoeur, P. (1970). *Freud and Philosophy.* New Haven: Yale University Press.

Rizley, R. (1978). Depression and distortion in the attribution of causality. *Journal of Abnormal Psychology, 87,* 32–48.

Roazen, P. (1974). *Freud and His Followers.* New York: New American Library.

Robson, K. (1967). The role of eye-to-eye contact in maternal–infant attachment. *Journal of Child Psychiatry and Psychology, 8,* 13–25.

Rogers, C. (1962). A tentative scale for the measurement of process in psychotherapy. In L. Rubinstein and M. Parloff (Eds.), *Research in Psychotherapy,* Vol. 1. Washington, D.C.: American Psychological Association.

Rosenblatt, P., Walsh, P., and Jackson, D. (1976). *Grief and Mourning in Cross-Cultural Perspective.* New Haven: Human Relations Area Files Press.

Rosenblum, L. (1971). Infant attachment in monkeys. In H. R. Schaffer (Ed.), *The Origins of Human Social Relations.* New York: Academic Press.

Sackeim, H., Nordlie, J., and Gur, R. (1979). A model of hysterical and hypnotic blindness: Cognition, motivation and awareness. *Journal of Abnormal Psychology, 88,* 474–489.

Sade, Marquis de. (1966). *The Complete Writings of the Marquis de Sade.* Compiled and edited by R. Seaver and A. Wainhouse. New York: Grove Press.

Salzman, L. (1965). Obsessions and phobias. *Contemporary Psychoanalysis,* Fall 1965, 1–25.

Sandler, J., and Hazari, A. (1960). The "Obsessional": On the psychological classification of obsessional traits and symptoms. *British Journal of Medical Psychology, 33,* 113–122.

Sandler, J., and Joffe, W. (1965). Notes on childhood depression. *International Journal of Psychoanalysis, 46,* 88–96.

Schafer, R. (1978). *Language and Insight.* New Haven: Yale University Press.

Schatzman, M. (1973). *L'esprit assasine.* Paris: Stock.

Schildkraut, J. (1965). The catecholamine hypothesis of affective disorders: A review of supporting evidence. *American Journal of Psychiatry, 122,* 509–522.

Schjelderup, H. (1955). Lasting effects of psychoanalytic treatment. *Psychiatry, 18,* 103–133.

Schnurmann, A. (1949). Observation of a phobia. *Psychoanalytic Study of the Child, 3/4,* 253–270.

Schulte, H. (1938). An approach to a gestalt theory of paranoiac phenomena. In W. Ellis (Ed.), *A Source Book of Gestalt Psychology.* New York: Harcourt Brace.

Sears, R., Rau, L., and Alpert, R. (1965). *Identification and Child Rearing.* Stanford: Stanford University Press.

Seif, M., and Atkins, A. (1979). Some defensive and cognitive aspects of phobia. *Journal of Abnormal Psychology, 88,* 42–51.

Seligman, M. (1975). *Helplessness: On Depression, Development and Death.* San Francisco: Freeman.

Seligman, M., and Hager, J. (Eds.) (1972). *The Biological Boundaries of Learning.* New York: Appleton, Century, Crofts.

Shakow, D., and Rapaport, D. (1964). The influence of Freud on American psychology. *Psychological Issues, 4,* Monograph 13.

Shectman, F. (1977). Conventional and contemporary approaches to psychotherapy. *American Psychologist, 32,* 197–204.

Sifneos, P. (1966). Psychoanalytically oriented short-term dynamic or anxiety-provoking therapy for mild obsessional neuroses. *Psychiatric Quarterly, 40,* 271–282.

Silverman, C. (1968). *The Epidemiology of Depression.* Baltimore: Johns Hopkins Press.

Simner, M. (1971). Newborn response to the cry of another infant. *Developmental Psychology, 5,* 136–150.

Slade, P. (1974). Psychometric studies of obsessional illness and obsessional personality. In H. Beech (Ed.), *Obsessional States.* London: Methuen.

Sloane, R., Staples, F., Whipple, K., and Cristol, A. (1977). Patients' attitudes toward behavior therapy and psychotherapy. *American Journal of Psychiatry, 134,* 134–137.

Smith, R. (1972). Relative proneness to shame or guilt as an indicator of defensive style. Unpublished doctoral dissertation. Northwestern University.

Socarides, C. (1974). Homosexuality. In S. Arieti (Ed.), *American Handbook of Psychiatry,* 2nd ed. New York: Basic Books.

Sperling, M. (1952). Analysis of a phobia in a two year old child. *Psychoanalytic Study of the Child, 7,* 115–125.

Spitz, R. (1965). *The First Year of Life.* New York: International Universities Press.

Spitz, R., and Wolf, K. (1949). Autoerotism. *Psychoanalytic Study of the Child, 3/4,* 85–120.

Sroufe, A. (1979). The coherence of individual development: Early care, attachment and subsequent developmental issues. *American Psychologist, 34,* 834–841.

Stampfl, T. (1970). Implosive therapy. In D. Lewis (Ed.), *Learning Approaches to Therapeutic Behavior Change.* Chicago: Aldine Press.

Stoller, R. (1968). *Sex and Gender.* New York: Jason Aronson.

Stoller, R. (1973). Facts and fancies: An examination of Freud's concept of bisexuality. In J. Strouse (Ed.), *Women and Analysis.* New York: Grossman.

Strupp, H. (1962). The therapists' contribution to the treatment process. In H. Strupp and L. Luborsky (Eds.), *Research in Psychotherapy,* Vol. 3. Washington, D.C.: American Psychological Association.

Tomkins, S. (1962, 1963). *Affect, Imagery and Consciousness,* Vols. 1 and 2. New York: Springer.

Wachtel, P. (1977). *Psychoanalysis and Behavior Modification.* New York: Basic Books.

Weintraub, W., and Aronson, H. (1968). A survey of patients in classical psychoanalysis: Some vital statistics. *Journal of Nervous and Mental Disease, 146,* 98–102.

Weiss, J. (1977). Psychological and behavioral influences on gastrointestinal lesions in animal models. In J. Maser and M. Seligman (Eds.), *Psychopathology: Experimental Models.* San Francisco: Freeman.

Weissman, M., and Paykel, E. (1974). *The Depressed Woman.* Chicago: University of Chicago Press.

White, R. (1961). The mother-conflict in Schreber's psychosis. *International Journal of Psychoanalysis, 42,* 55–73.

Winokur, G. (1973). Genetic aspects of depression. In J. Scott and E. Senay (Eds.), *Separation and Depression.* Washington, D.C.: American Association for the Advancement of Science.

Witkin, H. (1965). Psychological differentiation and forms of pathology. *Journal of Abnormal Psychology, 70,* 317–336.

Witkin, H., Lewis, H., Hertzman, M., Machover, K., Meissner, P., and Wapner, S. (1954). *Personality through Perception.* New York: Harper.

Witkin, H., Dyk, R., Faterson, H., Goodenough, D., and Karp, S. (1962). *Psychological Differentiation.* New York: Wiley.

Witkin, H., Lewis, H., and Weil, E. (1968). Affective reactions and patient–therapist interactions among more and less differentiated patients early in therapy. *Journal of Nervous and Mental Disease, 146,* 193–208.

Wolf Man. (1958). How I came into treatment with Freud. *Journal of the American Psychoanalytic Association, 6,* 348–352.

Wolpe, J. (1958). *Psychotherapy by Reciprocal Inhibition.* Stanford: Stanford University Press.

Wolpe, J., and Rachman, S. (1960). Psychoanalytic evidence: A critique based on Freud's case of Little Hans. *Journal of Nervous and Mental Disease, 131,* 135–145.

Woolf, P. (1960). The developmental psychologies of Jean Piaget and psychoanalysis. *Psychological Issues, 2,* Monograph 5.

Woolf, P. (1969). The natural history of crying and other vocalizations in early infancy. In B. Foss (Ed.), *Determinants of Infant Behavior.* London: Methuen.

Wyss, D. (1973). *Psychoanalytic Schools from the Beginning to the Present.* New York: Jason Aronson.

Zajonc, R. (1980). Feeling and thinking. *American Psychologist, 35,* 151–175.

Zamansky, H. (1958). An investigation of the psychoanalytic theory of paranoid delusions. *Journal of Personality, 26,* 410–425.

Index